ACPL ITEM
DISCARDED

BUS

D1616490

ADVENTURES OF AN ECONOMIST

by Franco Modigliani

"Franco Modigliani has been my brilliant, warm-hearted, and lively friend and colleague for almost 40 years. His memoirs are just like him. Any reader will get to know a delightful person, and learn some economics besides."

—*Robert M. Solow, Institute Professor Emeritus, MIT*

"It is a fun read not only for those with a professional interest in the life-cycle hypothesis for saving or Modigliani-Miller theorem of corporate finance, but for anyone interested in the economic history of the last half of the twentieth century. Franco Modigliani is an exuberant, direct, intelligent, warm and compassionate man, and all those attributes come through in this remarkable tale."

—*Alicia H. Munnell, Peter F. Drucker Professor*
of Management Sciences Director,
Center for Retirement Research, Boston College

"This is a book as much about relationships as it is about ideas. You can't help feeling Franco's passion for ideas and his warmth for those he worked with and taught. I heartily recommend it for its broad overview of the evolution of macroeconomic ideas served up with an incredibly warm story of the career and life of a remarkable teacher, scholar, friend, husband, father, and grandfather."

—*Laurence H. Meyer*

"Franco Modigliani skillfully weaves together lucid summaries of his economic thought with delightful portraits of the thinkers and actors who shaped the postwar economies of the United States and Italy. The result is the fascinating life story of one of the most influential economists of our time."

—*Richard N. Gardner, Professor of Law and*
International Organizations, Columbia University,
Former U.S. Ambassador to Italy

"The topics covered in Franco Modigliani's *Adventures of an Economist* are reminiscent of the wisdom he parlayed to me and my fellow classmates at MIT. In my view, the government officials from Argentina, Brazil, the Czech Republic, Hungary, Poland, Russia, and Turkey would especially benefit from reading his book. They face the challenge of solving unemployment and/or meeting that repayment which may necessitate the printing of money.

"Sections of the manuscript in which Modigliani shares some of his personal experiences as a child and highlights of his academic provide insight as to how he has developed his views. Many of us consider Dr. Modigliani to be the grandpa of modern day economists."

—*Josephine Jiminez, Senior Portfolio Manager*
of the Montgomery Emerging Markets
Fund, Montgomery Asset Management

ADVENTURES
OF AN
ECONOMIST

ADVENTURES OF AN ECONOMIST

Franco Modigliani

TEXERE

New York • London

Copyright © 2001 by Franco Modigliani. All rights reserved.

Published by

TEXERE LLC
55 East 52nd Street
New York, NY 10055

Tel: +1 (212) 317 5106
Fax: +1 (212) 317 5178
www.etexere.com

UK subsidiary office

TEXERE Publishing Limited
71–77 Leadenhall Street
London EC3A 3DE
www.etexere.co.uk

Tel: +44 (0)20 7204 3644
Fax: +44 (0)20 7208 6701

Reproduction or translation of any part of this work beyond that permitted by Section 107
or 108 of the 1976 United States Copyright Act without the permission of the copyright
owner is unlawful. Requests for permission or further information should be addressed to
the Permissions Department, TEXERE LLC, 55 East 52nd Street, New York, NY 10055.

This publication is designed to provide accurate and authoritative information in regard
to the subject matter covered. It is sold with the understanding that the publisher is not
engaged in rendering legal, accounting, or other professional services. If legal advice
or other expert assistance is required, the services or a competent professional person
should be sought.

Designed by The Book Design Group

Library of Congress Cataloging-in-Publication Data has been applied for.

ISBN 1-58799-007-5

Printed in the United States of America

This book is printed on acid-free paper.

CONTENTS

ADVENTURES
OF AN
ECONOMIST

I

MY STORY IN AMERICA

1   *"Here begins the adventure . . ."*

I was born in Rome in 1918 and spent my early years there under fascism. My family consisted of my father, Enrico, a well-known Roman pediatrician; my mother, Olga Flaschel, who devoted herself to volunteering as a social worker; and my elder brother. I had a happy childhood, nurtured by the love of my family, though it seems I was a very obstinate fellow. My memories of my father are incomplete, with a lot of gaps, for he died when I was only fourteen years old, this loss being the only real tragedy of my childhood. A very affectionate man, my father delighted in talking and playing with me. Even now, when I awake in the morning, there runs through my head a Roman jingle that Papa used to hum every so often when we went for drives in the car:

> *Tiritilla, Tiritalla,*
> *morirai senz'assaggialla*
> *la pizza cor zibibbo*
> *calla calla*

which in English would be:

> *Oh me, oh my,*
> *I bet you'll die*
> *Without ever tasting*
> *Hot raisin pizza pie.*

Actually, I almost didn't make it because only in the year 2000 did a kind Italian friend bake one for me, and it was wonderful!

My father called me *ragno conforto* ("comfort spider"), perhaps because when I was a young boy I was very thin, bony, and fidgety, and maybe also because I was wiry like a spider. It seems I was also so obstinate that I soon became the terror of our housekeepers.

As was the custom in those days, my father often visited his sick patients at home. During my early childhood, he used to drive a horse and buggy that he had use of for a certain period of the day, pulled by a marvelous white pony named Pallino. As the years went on, Papa graduated to a more modern means of transportation, and poor Pallino was replaced by a beautiful Fiat 503, usually driven by the chauffeur, Giusti.

With deep nostalgia I recall the delightful summer holidays that we all went on, my father included. The first I can distinctly remember was in 1922, when I was four, at Graun, a little Alpine village near the Passo di Resia. My two cousins, Laura and Maria, were also invited; they were the daughters of Papa's brother, Uncle Guido, and they had the specific duty of helping my parents keep me occupied, for, as I said, I was the real terror of the household. Later, Laura and Maria told me I threw the most awful tantrums and kicked out wildly with my heavy mountain boots.

Two episodes of that holiday have engraved themselves indelibly on my memory. The first was when we decided to take a boating trip on a little lake. Just as Maria was stepping into the boat, it moved and she fell into the water fully dressed, to the amusement of us all, though not Maria! The second episode is redolent of the atmosphere that prevailed after World War I. The hotel fare was scanty, so Papa composed a brief song of indignation that wound up with this verse:

> *Ma perdinci adesso basta*
> *vogliam pane e vogliam pasta*
> *Con bombe a mano*
> *farem venire I Fasci da Milano!*

> *But by golly*
> *That's enough.*
> *We want bread*
> *And we want stuff!*

> *We'll call in*
> *With hand grenades*
> *All the fascist*
> *Black Brigades.*

Did I not say the holiday took place in 1922, a few months before the March on Rome?

Later on, during my father's last years, our holidays were spent at Viareggio, where we had gathered together lots of close friends, our own and our parents'. I also have a delightful recollection of a trip in Italy and France that was later to be much talked about in the family. We traveled in our Fiat 503, driven by my father, in company with the family of Doctor Del Vecchio, who drove an OM car—OM standing for *Officine Meccaniche*. I still have a wonderful photo album of that holiday, which my father adorned with captions in rhyme. From time to time I leaf through the album, with affectionate memories.

The Modigliani family moved to Rome many centuries previously, probably after the Jews had been expelled from Spain. My father, the third of four siblings, had been the first to go to the university, instead of following the family tradition in trade; in this he was aided by his two elder brothers, since his father had died when still quite young.

My maternal grandfather, Emilio Flaschel, was born in Kraków, Poland. He met my grandmother, Ernestina Cagli, in Florence, where she and her family had moved from their hometown of Ancona. Emilio made frequent trips in Italy for his trade, which essentially involved *"arbitrage"* between the dealers in pearls and coral in Poland and Italy respectively. For he had noted that the price of coral relative to that of pearls was lower in southern Italy, where it was produced, than in Poland. Hence, in rural Poland he bartered—often directly with the peasants—coral against baroque pearls (that is, very imperfect ones), which in those parts were quite widely worn as ornaments; while in southern Italy he bartered the baroque pearls against Italian coral, thus realizing a handsome profit. Little by little, he expanded his trade in pearls till he became a great expert, with plenty of commissions in Paris, which at that time was a leading center for the pearl business. After World War I, he opened an elegant shop, *"Gioielleria Flaschel,"* in Rome's Piazza di Spagna. Grandmother Ernestina worked upstairs threading perfect real pearls, at which she had become an expert. I used to call on them now and then, but all those jewels overwhelmed me, and I remember how, upon entering the shop, I was always afraid of causing some disaster. After my grandfather's death, the business remained in the family and was managed by my mother until the beginning of the 1930s. But with the discovery of cultured pearls, commerce in real pearls went downhill and the shop was sold.

My mother, Olga Flaschel, had attended secondary school in France and in Florence. She sported the title, rare in those days, of *"dottoressa,"* because she had attended the University of Rome, where she took a degree with a thesis based on her volunteer social work. She spoke fluent French and

German, and afterward, English, since during the war she had moved to
Israel for some years. She had three sisters, who produced six of my cousins.
My father's three brothers combined had four boys and three girls. We saw a
lot of one another. Ours was a happy and very affectionate family.

My mother was very insistent that her children learn different lan-
guages well. To this end, when I was about four, the celebrated Fräulein
Pabst was brought from Germany to live with us for some years. But at
some point she left and I had no further news of her . . . until, a couple of
months after I had been awarded the Nobel Prize, a touching letter arrived
at Cambridge. Fräulein Pabst, who was then over eighty, had read of my
Nobel award in a German newspaper, and had at once identified the economics professor with her little Francolino, who had been such a source
of tribulation to her more than sixty years before. The members of her
family with whom she was living did not believe her and accused her of
boasting, and they refused to write to me on her behalf. So she had been
determined to write herself, in German, which at the time of her leaving
us I spoke fluently, only thereafter to forget it when it was edged out by
English. Fräulein Pabst also sent me some photos of myself as a child.

My parents were intimately linked in one important aspect: Together,
they devoted much time to a charitable activity, which later assumed my
father's name, Enrico Modigliani, and was dedicated to encouraging
unmarried mothers to keep their babies at least until they were weaned, in
order to avoid the veritable massacre of foundlings that took place in the
orphanages in those days. My parents tried to explain to these poor girls
that to hand their babies over immediately to such institutions was tantamount to condemning them to death, and they paid for the major neces-
sities in those first months of nursing. As a pediatrician, my father held a
view that fifty years later came to be commonly accepted—namely, that
the very high death rate of foundlings in the orphanages was due to lack
of maternal love in the first weeks of life. Enrico Modigliani strongly
favored breast-feeding by the mother and had written a manual to instruct
midwives in their work, including persuading mothers to nurse their
babies in order to bring them security by holding them close and to transmit immune factors through the colostrum and maternal milk.

2   *The Republic of Cacciariserva*

At the end of one summer—maybe in 1934—during the season of Yom
Kippur, my cousins on my mother's side, Maurizio and Mario Mendes,

invited me, my brother, and our cousin on our father's side, Piero Modigliani, to their seaside house at Santa Marinella, which was still a holiday village a few kilometers from Civitavecchia. The villa was situated at a spot called Cacciariserva. We bathed and went for walks. Sometimes we played cards, and although I don't remember why, we got the idea to use sweets in place of the usual chips. The main unit was the *caramella* (hard candy), but we also used smaller units such as gum drops, worth a third of a *caramella*, and peanuts, worth one quarter of a gum drop. Here was a new monetary system whose currency was the *caramella*, which was worth three gum drops and twelve peanuts. Thus, the first player could put a *caramella* into the pool, and the next one could raise it by three peanuts. Having established a currency, what was more natural than to found a state upon it! It was unanimously decided that our state should be called the Republic of Cacciariserva. Of course, the republic had a president, who was Piero, the senior cousin, while Maurizio, the next in age and well known for his contrariness, chose to be leader of the opposition. My brother Giorgio became minister of war and cousin Mario was minister of peace. I, the smallest, was made minister of the Treasury, with the main responsibility of updating the exchange rates if the market prices happened to vary. Since, as I have subsequently learnt, our currency was real and not a token one, the possibility of *arbitrage* had to be prevented.

We also had a national anthem. This was inspired by a figure in a terracotta relief that adorned the dining room, a reproduction of a picture from the Florentine Cinquecento showing a beautiful blond young noblewoman whom my cousins had chosen to call "Sora (Lady) Carletta." The anthem—all of which I have been able to recollect with the aid of my sister-in-law Marcella Modigliani Misani—went like this:

> *Oh thou, Lady Carletta,*
> *Divine, omnipotent,*
> *With your blond tresses*
> *And your skin opalescent,*
>
> *Protect our glorious shores*
> *And our audacious brains,*
> *And see that the Republic*
> *Is never changed to a Reign.*

We had such fun with our republic that we decided to go on with the game after returning to Rome, and we invited our Roman friends and our acquaintances from Santa Marinella to join in. Meetings were held once a month in Viale Mazzini, where Marcella, my brother Giorgio's fiancée, lived. Marcella and her sisters prepared the refreshments, and the other participants also brought something with them. The group soon swelled to quite a size. Most of them became "cabinet members." Maurizio managed to obtain the support of a fine young woman, Miss Alberti, sister of one of his schoolmates, who made up seditious rhymes that we sang to the tunes of popular songs of the time. I recall only a few fragments:

> *Who's that President*
> *who eats and idles?*
> *He is Piero, he is Piero*
> *He is the President*
> *and he doesn't accomplish a thing.*

Another little ditty ran:

> *The ministers are on the razzle*
> *Only the People knows how to speak!*

The "People" were Piero's father, Uncle Silvio, who from time to time took the floor to direct the government in his capacity of *vox populi*.

But right in the middle of our fun the Republic of Cacciariserva came to an end in a way that was as sticky as it was unexpected, for . . . we were at the high tide of the Fascist regime. The police chief of the Prati district summoned Piero and told him that our meetings stank of "subversion." He ordered us to cease talking of a republic with a democratic government and, especially, not to dare to continue singing that seditious anthem, *Let not the Republic Become a Kingdom!* I wonder how he came to hear of our innocent game?

Of all those citizens of the republic of sixty years ago, I believe only two survive: a sister of my sister-in-law Marcella, and myself.

3   The Teachers at the Visconti

Aside from these memories of my childhood, I fancy that my early career held nothing further of any significance. As a schoolboy, I achieved no special distinction until the *liceo* (upper secondary school); indeed, I experienced some difficulties in the first form, the year when my father died. I attended the Regio Ginnasio Umberto I, where I came up against a teacher who loathed me for my lack of discipline. For this reason, he gave me very bad marks. I shall always remember an Italian composition that he returned to me, with the written comment: "They that sow the wind shall reap the storm."

In the second form I made one of the most important and happiest decisions of my life: to transfer to the Liceo Ennio Quirino Visconti, which stood near the Collegio Romano. The Visconti was one of the best schools in Rome, and had turned out several future popes, bishops, cardinals, statesmen like Guido Carli (for many years, governor of the Bank of Italy), and politicians like Giorgio Amendola (son of a martyr of Fascism who became a Communist but was highly respected for his wisdom and intellectual honesty). And, to be sure, the atmosphere in its classrooms was redolent of those great figures. At the time, we were living in Via Torino, next to the Teatro dell'Opera. So the walk from our house to the Liceo Visconti was a long and pleasant one. This morning exertion was at once amply repaid by the excellent teaching I received there. There were two teachers in particular whom I shall never forget. Carlo Graber taught literature and had written a highly esteemed commentary on Dante's *Divine Comedy*. He was a short, very refined man, always elegantly attired in well-tailored suits. Graber treated his pupils very politely but with a shade of coolness. But, when he read the Italian poems he loved, he did so with a wisdom and passion that swept us off our feet. His readings from the *Divine Comedy* were fantastic, unforgettable.

The other teacher I shall always remember was a priest, Don Vannutelli, who taught Latin and Greek with an enthusiasm he managed to instill in me and a humanity that warmed the heart. During the race persecutions, Don Vannutelli helped a large number of Jews who had been his pupils, saving them from arrest or deportation. What a great man he was! He never lost his good humor and wit. And he always joked with us. He would summon the pupils to his desk, addressing them in rhymes: no mumbling, Zoccolotti-Modigliani, come today, come not tomorrow (the rhymes are of course lost in translation). After my schooldays, I never saw him again, but I have always thought of him with gratitude and affection. In those days, Vannutelli was very keen on Sanskrit, and I recall how, while we were busy with our classwork, he would walk up and down with a book of Sanskrit open, pronouncing some mysterious word and chuckling to himself.

Graber and Vannutelli infected me with the love of classical studies. At that time I realized, to my surprise, that I was actually up to learning Greek and Latin—in the very teeth of what my teacher at the Ginnasio Umberto I had said.

8   ADVENTURES OF AN ECONOMIST

*4   How It Came about That I Decided to
Skate over the Third Year of Liceo*

I was in Section A, which was then held to be the best, and my classmates were very clever. I made friends with several of them, but with rare
exceptions, for various reasons, I was unable to develop these friendships
into anything more. The main reason was that, while being exceptionally
happy at the Visconti, I made a decision that even now I can hardly understand—and yet, looking back, it seems like one of those strokes of luck that
we cannot account for. I made up my mind to skip the third year of liceo,
at a time when graduating from school was very tough indeed. To skip the
third year was sheer folly—few tried it, for the final exam encompassed the
full three-year program and the third year was essential if you were to
reach the level required. Perhaps that was why it was ill-advised. In my
own case, moreover, I had already skipped the fifth grade of primary school
and was already a year ahead in the program. And so it came about that I
managed to enroll at the university in the academic year 1935–36, at age
seventeen. I was at the Visconti from 1934–35, and I recall how the major
topic of discussion at the time was the war in Ethiopia.

Looking back on it, I think the real reason behind such madness (wanting
to skip the third year of liceo at all costs) must have been the challenge it provided. It was an act of pigheadedness. My classmate Emilio Rampolla also
decided to skip his third year. I had fraternized with him quite a bit, as we
were the only two pupils who left the classroom during the religion lesson—
which was understandable in my case, as I was Jewish, but much odder for
Rampolla, who was no less than the nephew of Cardinal Rampolla, the Vati-
can secretary of state and the Pope's prime minister. I fancy the reason lay in
the influence of his mother, who was British and a Protestant. At that time,
the Fascist Concordat was in force, and the law exempted non-Catholics from
religious instruction. So it was that Rampolla and I left the classroom; and
while we chatted in the corridors of the Collegio Romano, we conceived the
idea of skipping the third year.

We slaved like mules. I helped him in the literary and scientific subjects
and he helped me with mathematics. Both of us succeeded in passing the
exam, he by a whisker and I by not much more, with a mark of around 7.
Only sometime later did I realize that those two years gained in advance
had been of fundamental importance, for they had enabled me to take my
degree in 1939—before departing for the United States. The fact that I
already possessed a degree was indeed a great advantage: It enabled me to
win a scholarship at the New School for Social Research, which changed
my whole life.

Forty years later, the Liceo Visconti decided to honor me by "tiling" me. During the Ceremony of the Tile a person selected by the alumni association receives a tile from the old paving of the main hall; these beautiful antique handmade tiles were preserved when the floor was replaced. Guido Carli and Giorgio Amendola were also awarded the tile. I was overjoyed to be so honored and had the time of my life at the ceremony. Among other things that took place, a slightly mischievous television program chose to show my school report, along with my graduation marks. Some days later, a friend told me that his son had voiced great disappointment upon hearing my marks, having done better himself! He could not know how tough the classical graduation exam was in those times of education reform for Gentiles—not to mention my having skipped the third year. The beautiful tile from the Visconti Liceo is much admired by people who come to visit me in my study.

5   *The Littoriali, and How I Became an Antifascist*

I graduated from the liceo in 1935, two years early, but I still had no idea what I wanted to do. I took a trip to England for two months, which helped me to improve my English and to appreciate the strongly critical attitude that prevailed in Britain toward the war in Abyssinia. But it was of no help to me in making a decision about my career, which was now imminent. For a while, my family thought I ought to study medicine. Since my father had been a pediatrician, my mother felt it would be natural for me to follow in his footsteps. So I went to the university offices to enroll, but just prior to signing up I realized the mere thought of blood bothered me and I would therefore do better to stay away from medicine. Since I had no other special interests, I did what was customary at that time: I enrolled in law school, which in those days opened the way to a variety of careers.

The law program turned out to be pretty easy and left me plenty of time at my disposal. No great commitment was expected of one, except at exam times. I did not attend the lectures, for they immediately struck me as dreadfully tedious. In this way, searching for something to do, I happened on an activity that had an immediate connection to economics. My mother and Fräulein Pabst had taught me a little German, and I was asked to translate some articles from German into Italian by the Traders' Federation. In this way I made acquaintance with the economic problems dealt with in German publications: At that time, price control was the fashionable topic.

In Italy at the time, interuniversity written competitive examinations—

the *Littoriali della Cultura*—were under way. These competitions comprised a variety of scientific, literary, and artistic subjects—including economics, which was actually somewhat neglected in the universities. Though the competitions were organized by the regime, the cream of antifascist youth took part in them and scored very highly. That year's economic subject was the price controls that had been imposed in Italy in 1935 in order to face the war in Ethiopia. After translating at least a score or so of articles on the matter, I felt sufficiently expert to enter the competition, if not too hopefully. In writing my contribution, I was greatly assisted by my older cousin, Piero Modigliani, son of my father's eldest brother. Piero had lived with us for a few years in Rome and represented a food company, following a very ancient tradition of the Modigliani family. Piero was a highly cultivated, very deep-thinking person. We discussed the upsetting effects of price controls on trade. But, much more important, he led me to read the works of Benedetto Croce, risky enough at the time, and I can still call to mind entire pages of the *History of Europe in the Nineteenth Century* read aloud. During those politically suspect readings Piero confessed to me his doubts about fascism.

To my astonishment, my essay scored the highest. The examiners intimated that I evidently had a certain bent toward economics. And I said to myself: Why not? From that moment, I began to think of myself as a potential economist. All this took place in 1936, when economics was one of the subjects taught in the faculty of law. In actual fact, what was taught was the theory and institutions of the so-called "Corporative State," which had nothing to do with modern economic theory. Nonetheless, on the advice of Riccardo Bachi, who taught economic sciences in the faculty of Economics and Business, I began to study economic literature. I studied Marshall and other classics, but I was precluded from Keynes, for, although the *General Theory* had already been published, I ransacked all Rome for a copy in vain.

Taking part in the *Littoriali* was also important for my political training. For it was during my first years at the university that I began to discover a certain antipathy toward fascism. My father was staunchly antifascist; and I vividly remember, though only a child at the time, how he returned home after voting in the 1929 plebiscite and said: "I voted 'no.'" His premature death, however, prevented me from learning all of his political opinions. My mother, on the other hand, somewhat favored the regime, since at that time it had passed laws of a kind she and my father had hoped for to protect unmarried mothers. I was on the fence then, with no definite opinion. My other relatives were divided on the matter, some decid-

3 1833 04063 0177

edly in favor, others firmly against. Thus, there was no one in the family to give me firm guidance. I recall, however, that my aversion to fascism began with the war in Ethiopia, which struck me as unjust, without reason, and morally shabby. But the real turning point, when my eyes were really opened, came with the Spanish Civil War. Right from the start, I hated Franco's intervention to crush democratic freedom; then I was scandalized by the impudent intrusion by fascism, which set me dead against the regime. This awareness came at the same time as I was working for the Littoriali competitions. I was awarded the *Diploma di Littore at Palazzo* Venezia by Mussolini in person, who shook my hand and presented me with the little gold badge with "M" for Mussolini that I still preserve (out of historical significance, not love).

The competition entailed, immediately afterward, a trip to Palermo, where the winners were to meet, they being *ex officio* the secretaries of the commission for the following year. The ferry departed from Naples harbor. On deck, I met various *"littori"* like myself, but there were also Bruno Zevi, Mario Alicata, Gerardo Zampaglione, and others who were already engaged in the antifascist opposition, and there was Pietro, the youngest of the Amendola brothers. When I disembarked at Palermo my antifascism was no longer in doubt.

Later, this feeling was strengthened by my future father-in-law, Giulio Calabi, founder and managing director of *Messaggerie Italiane*. He was an old acquaintance of Mussolini's. Beginning in 1914 he regularly brought from Paris a secret French subsidy for Mussolini's newspaper, *Il Popolo d'Italia*, founded when he left the Socialist Party because he favored Italy's entrance on the side of the Allies in World War I. The French government wished to fund Mussolini's campaign, and the task fell to my father-in-law. *Messaggerie Italiane* had a contract with the publisher Hachette, which evidently had contacts with the French government, to distribute the French paper in Italy.

Initially, Giulio had felt some approval toward fascism, but he became its deadliest enemy after the fascists murdered Matteotti, the socialist member of parliament, at Macchia della Quartarella, where his corpse was eventually found. In disgust, Giulio Calabi began transferring his savings to Switzerland in 1925, in preparation for his possible exile, for he had divined that fascism had turned into dictatorship and could only get worse. In 1938, as soon as the race laws were promulgated, he sold *Messaggerie Italiane* to his good friend, and well-known publisher Arnoldo Mondadori, to get ready to leave Italy.

6   *My Fate with Serena and Exile*

It was in the winter of 1937–38 that Serena Calabi, who was then living in Bologna, came to Rome for a few days' visit. As I have recounted to my friends over and over again, my friendship with Serena had had its beginning in Florence in the second half of the nineteenth century . . . through our great-grandmothers on our mothers' side. For Serena's great-grandmother, Virginia Paggi Bemporad—sister of Felice Paggi, who published the first edition of *Pinocchio*—lived in Florence, in a three-floor villa that still stands at No. 24 Via Pier Capponi, where Elena, a second cousin of Serena, still lives. My great-grandmother, Clementina Cagli, also took up residence in Via Pier Capponi, when her family moved from Ancona to Florence, in a house right across the street. These very close neighbors struck up a deep friendship that lasted until their deaths. Thus, their firstborn daughters, Matilde Bemporad and Ernestina Cagli—our grandmothers—were born and grew up together in Florence and became inseparable friends; their friendship lasted even after Matilde's marriage to a Bolognese lawyer, Giulio Vita.

A republican and an ardent admirer of Garibaldi, Vita (who was known in the family as the "grandad lawyer") was an intimate friend of Giovanni Pascoli and was nicknamed by his friends *Bottarino* ("frog" in Bolognese dialect, because of his green eyes); this drew a poem (*Nozze*) from Pascoli on the occasion of his marriage that began: "Mother frog gave a wife to her son in marriage." As for grandmother Ernestina, she married Emilio Flaschel and moved to Rome. A tradition says that Matilde and Ernestina wrote regularly to each other three times a week, which was perfectly feasible with the postal services as they were in those days. Each of them bore four daughters, the two eldest being Dina, Serena's mother, and Olga, my mother.

Serena and I had met very seldom, save on one occasion of which we retain a happy memory. We were about thirteen years old. Serena had come to Rome with her father, who was on a business trip, and was given into the care of my mother's sister. Being of the same age, I was naturally invited to meet her. I persuaded her to play "catch as catch can" and as I dragged her along pell-mell I made her fall, tearing her first pair of silk stockings. It was hate at first sight. A hate that faded only very gradually, through our correspondence. It was not until much later, in the winter of 1937–38, when we were twenty, that a relationship bloomed in a matter of a few days that we did not hesitate to call by the name of love. Our love was kindled by long talks about what we thought of life, such that when it was time for her to leave we could not but realize that our ideas and values matched perfectly. Over the following months, our feelings grew stronger through an ardent correspondence and occasional meetings.

Her family had no objection to me, but they felt we were much too young to turn our relationship into anything formal. However, I was invited to spend some weeks in the summer at the villa Serena's family owned at Cortina d'Ampezzo, called by my father-in-law *Il Pisolino* ("the Nap"). And there it was that we were surprised by the publication of the race laws that were to degrade the life of any Italian Jew who wished to remain in Italy. It was no longer possible for Jews to attend public schools or to hold public office, including university teaching, and, what probably affected the Italian Jewish middle class more than anything else, it was forbidden to employ non-Jewish domestics.

I remember that day at Cortina when my father-in-law told us we must leave at once and not waste a single week. For some time Giulio Calabi had been having problems with the regime, since, as mentioned above, the Messaggerie imported French newspapers and magazines and he had refused to bow to the pressures on him, which had started with the war in Ethiopia, to reduce his imports.

Tension with the Regime had reached the point where his passport had been confiscated—only to be returned to him thanks to the intervention of Curzio Malaparte, a man of independent mind, notwithstanding his support for fascism. In view of all this, my father-in-law feared that if he did not leave Italy at once, the Fascists might make more trouble for him by confiscating his passport again. Giulio had long been expecting some such unpleasantness, which was why, after the murder of Matteotti and at great risk—for the export of capital was punishable by death—he had gradually transferred a large part of his savings to Switzerland. He then told his family that they could live abroad, at least for a while, and they all decided to emigrate.

At this point, I was generously invited to join them, reckoning that my situation could be dealt with in a short time. We separated. I returned to Rome to fetch my passport, which was about to expire, and from there went to England to get it renewed at the consulate in London. This route was chosen in order not to arouse suspicion, for going to France would clearly have looked like flight for political reasons, whereas London was a much less politicized destination. And there my passport was duly renewed with no problems.

In accordance with our plan, we met again in Geneva, from which we moved to Lausanne. And it was there that, terrified, we heard the news of the meeting at Munich. Disgusted by the general surrender to Hitler and Mussolini, we realized that there was no point in staying in Europe any longer. So we decided to go at once to France, where it would be easier to obtain a visa for the United States, with the added advantage that my father-in-law had funds at his disposal for getting the necessary affidavits. For, having represented the great publishing house of Hachette, Giulio had very many acquaintances in France.

We spent a pleasant, if not very conclusive, year in Paris. At that time I had yet to take my degree, so during the initial months I went to the Sorbonne to attend the lectures of France's only economist of renown at that time, but French universities struck me as even worse than Italian ones. The students went to lectures in crowds, but, as far as I could make out, with the sole intention of creating confusion, laughing, and joking— doing it so successfully that I couldn't hear the lecture. Just why they attended the lectures, I have never been able to understand. For this reason, I went to study in the Ste. Geneviève library and there went ahead with my study of economics classics. Once again Keynes was not to be found, but I made up for that by studying the theory of fixed costs by John Bates Clark and the classic text of Alfred Marshall, the great master of the age, the Samuelson of the first decades of the century.

In May 1939 our families agreed that, since we were compelled to live together, Serena and I might as well get married, and this gave us great pleasure. We were wedded at the Italian consulate, with the consul ostentatiously giving the Roman salute, from which we and our families and the witnesses refrained, saying merely "Good morning." I did not place the ring on Serena's finger then. I did this after the ceremony, once we were outside the consulate. I told Serena: "I didn't want to give you the ring in the presence of that lout." Our witnesses were Giuseppe Calabi and the famous physicist Bruno Pontecorvo, who was a young friend of ours.

The decision to marry Serena has undoubtedly been the happiest of my life for, as I wrote in the preface to my *Collected Papers*, published in 1980: "Throughout the forty years of our marriage she has always encouraged me to reach for the stars, even while doing her best to keep my feet firmly on the ground." After sixty-two years together, she remains my best critic and friend.

After our wedding, I returned to Italy to present my thesis and take my degree, just in time for our departure for the United States, which took place in August 1939. My father-in-law was not at all easy while Serena and I were in Italy; and for this reason we had worked out a secret code to use in telegrams in the event that in France he should get wind of the Italian frontier's being closed. If we received a telegram that Uncle Ben was very sick, we should be ready to flee; if Uncle Ben died, we should leave thesis and all and immediately head for the border.

7   *The Refugees in Paris*

In Paris Serena and I had an apartment all to ourselves in rue Chauchat. There we were able to entertain lots of friends, some of whom later became famous. Salvatore Luria, for instance, future Nobel Prize winner in medicine—who then called himself Salvatore, not Salvador E. Luria. He told us that his father wanted to call him Salvador, his mother Salvatore, and his mother had the better of it. But when he emigrated to the United States they asked him whether he wouldn't care to change his name, whereupon he said he would and altered his name to Salvador, confirming his father's original choice: "And then I didn't know what to do with that 'E' that stuck, so I kept it as a middle initial."

Among our other Paris friends, I recall Tullia Zevi née Calabi, who at that time played the harp, and the physicist Sergio Debenedetti, who became professor and my colleague at the Carnegie Institute of Technology in Pittsburgh. During those months I also learned to distrust the writer Pitigrilli (Dino Segre), who was a well-known Fascist spy and was ultimately responsible for the deaths of several of our friends, such as the heroic Curiel, a brave man of action, who traveled between Italy and France, well aware that he was risking his life. With deep emotion I recall the last time we saw him off at the station in Paris on his way to Italy: We both felt a lump in our throats, and indeed we were never to see him again. He was shot by the Fascists.

Another person who came to our apartment was Bruno Pontecorvo, whom I had met in Paris the previous summer on the recommendation of a mutual friend. I was immediately struck by his charm, goodness, and intelligence. To be sure, in Paris Pontecorvo made no secret of his extreme left opinions and spoke continually of the reasons underlying them in an attempt to convince us of their rightness. His fundamental reading of the historical events of that time was as follows: The dearest wish of the treacherous French and British capitalists was that Soviet Russia might be overwhelmed and, sooner or later, they would inevitably team up with Hitler and Mussolini to crush her. He took us to a demonstration on behalf of the Spanish Republic, where we heard a speech by the legendary Pasionaria, a famous Spanish communist who was traveling around Europe to collect funds and weapons for the republican army. We, too, supported the Spanish Republic since, among other things, it involved the Italian contingent, the Garibaldi Brigade of the Rosselli brothers and Pacciardi, but we have never been lured by communism because we hated dictatorships of the right or of the left. I remember how news of the Ribbentrop-Molotov Pact between Germany and Russia reached us on the eve of our departure for the United States: The Communist friends we met that day told us they were certain the news was false. We left without seeing Bruno again, curious to know what he thought about it. He was so intelligent, so honest, that we felt it impossible that he should not be disgusted.

Next day, at dawn, we departed for Le Havre to embark on the *Normandie*, and there was no further opportunity to see any of the group. However, we read in the morning papers that the news was confirmed by official sources. Only after landing in America did we learn the official party line, that is, that the agreement testified to Stalin's amazing Machiavellian cunning: Having no doubt that sooner or later France, Britain, and the United States would make common cause with Hitler to destroy the fatherland of communism, he had stolen a march on them by being the first to seal a pact with Hitler that preserved Russia from an attack by Germany and encouraged the latter to orient her expansion westward.

With hindsight, the reasoning ascribed to Stalin certainly hit the mark on this last point, but it was full of holes. In particular, it was a real blunder to believe that the pact would keep German aggression at bay. If Stalin had not made this mistake, he would not have enabled Hitler to destroy France and so, later, to attack the Soviet Union. If the USSR ultimately won out, it was because Stalin erred in his conviction that the West would be ready to ally itself with Hitler in order to destroy communism.

Only once more did I meet Pontecorvo, a few years later in New York when he had already emigrated from France and seemed to have left off his infatuation with communism. This was why I would never have expected his defection to Russia. It astonished us. But evidently, according to his point of view, the USSR, which he saw as "the future paradise of the workers," was the most important objective.

8   We Arrive in the United States and Our First Child Is Born

So we embarked on the *Normandie*, a few days before the outbreak of war, while Poland was about to be invaded. The crossing was made with lights out for fear of German submarines, and all the passengers' radios were confiscated lest panic be aroused by the official announcement of war.

We landed in the United States on August 28, 1939, in New York. Four days later the war broke out in Europe. This was why, when all the family disembarked, we immediately understood that we were to be here for a long time. One might as well lose no time in looking for a job. My brother-in-law, Paolo Calabi, with his degree in industrial chemistry, found a position in a chemical firm in New York. Sometime later, my father-in-law and brother-in-law moved inland, purchasing a farm in Dutchess County, New York State, with three hundred acres of apple orchards. My father-in-law assisted me to start up in business, and of course he chose the book trade, in which he had much experience. I began my American life dealing wholesale in Italian and Spanish books at the Book Center near Fifth Avenue. In the months between 1939 and 1940, before Italy entered the war, we succeeded in importing a sizable stock of Italian books that we sold to the bookshops in the Italian districts: Brooklyn and Little Italy. In those days, the taste of the Italian migrants ran unmistakably toward escapist literature: For every hundred copies of Carolina Invernizio, we sold only one of Dante and Manzoni's *Promessi Sposi*.

Meanwhile, our first child, Andrea, had been conceived; for, during the crossing, Serena had suffered from nausea, which we innocently put down to seasickness. On May 21, 1940, while Serena was in the hospital ready to give birth, the German divisions broke through the Maginot Line, which we (like all France) had been sure must withstand any shock. We therefore took care not to let Serena know and forced ourselves to look cheerful.

As parents we were very inexpert, but I was at least fortified by the teachings and the battles of my father and my mother, and we fought valiantly against the stupid "hygienism" that was then becoming widespread in America. In those days, to nurse one's own children was looked upon as fit only for cave dwellers, whereas it was later discovered to be of vital importance. I recall an epic clash between the head nurse of the maternity ward and Serena. The authoritative nurse had been summoned, after vain attempts by others of her colleagues to prevent Serena from nursing Andrea. Masterful in her starched uniform, the nurse strode into Serena's room and said severely: "Now look here, what makes you think your milk is fit for this child?" Countered Serena: "Because I think even you can see this isn't a calf!"

During the first weeks of Andrea's life, we were assisted by another Jewish exile, Professor Roberto Funaro from Leghorn, former pediatrician to the Italian Royal Family in the periods when they resided by the sea at San Rossore, and a pupil of my father. Likewise, Dr. Kautsky—son of the great socialist, who was the father-in-law of my brother-in-law Paolo and Serena's gynecologist with our second child, Sergio—would not accept mothers who refused to nurse their children: "I am not a psychiatrist and if a woman tells me she does not wish to nurse her child, there is something wrong with her psychologically and I am not in the right specialization to be able to help her." For my part, I was blissfully happy to be a father so young. When I took the perambulator to Central Park, I used to reach a little knoll, my favorite spot, push the perambulator up, and then wait for it to run back down by itself—to the unfailing consternation and disapproval of the old ladies walking in the park.

We spoke to our children in Italian because we didn't want them to pick up our dreadful English accent. Except when Americans were present, we always spoke Italian. Andrea must have been about five when he once asked us why, and Serena replied: "So that when you're grown up you will be able to read Dante in Italian." "And who's Dante?" "Dante is a great poet, and the poor Americans have to read him in English." "OK," answered Andrea, who had realized that this was a privilege. At age sixteen, when he was at Westtown School and his teacher of comparative literature asked him to read a canto of Dante in Italian so that his schoolmates could hear how it sounded, he told us all about it in a letter: "You had your wish."

Meanwhile I was looking for some means of pursuing my studies in economics. Once again I was lucky and obtained a scholarship at the New School for Social Research thanks to the help of a famous refugee, Italian scholar, and professor of political sciences, Max Ascoli—who had left Italy after refusing to swear loyalty to the Fascist regime—and an assistant and dear friend of his, Paolo Contini. I worked by day and studied by night.

9   University in Exile, Eleanor Roosevelt, and Jacob Marschak

The New School had been created in the 1920s for adult university education, but in the 1930s it had become the "university in exile" and had added a graduate school—that is, a postgraduate institute whose aim was to take in the great academics who had suffered persecution under the dictatorial regimes of Russia, Italy, Germany, and Spain. Its founder, Alvin Johnson, was very intelligent and skillful in obtaining funds from the wealthiest men of the time and using them for good ends. The institute's full name was "The Graduate School for Economic and Social Research," and its stars included the renowned psychologist Max Wertheimer, founder of the Gestalt school, and various economists, among them my teacher Jacob Marschak.

Max Ascoli later left the New School and married a Rosenwald (of the family who founded Sears Roebuck). The patrimony of his wife, a pleasant and very clever woman, enabled him for years to finance a well-known and very pro-Roosevelt liberal periodical, *The Reporter.* A great spiritual godmother and patron of the New School was Eleanor Roosevelt, whom Serena and I at once came to admire for her great intelligence and for her commitment to the cause of European refugees and disadvantaged people in general. One of the most exciting moments of my life was in 1944, when following my article on liquidity preference in Keynes—which immediately afterward I turned into my doctoral thesis—there was the ceremony to award the Doctorate in Social Sciences, D.S.S., which I received from the hands of Eleanor Roosevelt.

The crucial figure for me at the New School was Jacob Marschak, who had just emigrated from Britain. Marschak was at once a great economist, a supreme teacher, and an exceptionally humane person. He had led an adventurous life. Born in Russia, he had been expelled by the Bolsheviks and gone to Germany, where he taught for a long time. When the threat of Hitler loomed, Marschak left for Britain. He was a connoisseur of economic theory with a certain bent for mathematical economics and econometrics. Affable, very understanding, and not at all standoffish, Marschak at once took a liking to me and, first, gave me to understand that if I wanted to get ahead as an economist I should study more mathematics. That was a field in which I had no grounding—indeed, ever since secondary school I had felt some aversion to it. But now Marschak persuaded me to apply myself seriously. Fairly painlessly, I mugged up books of math and statistics, subjects I hadn't managed to digest in Italy because, I fancy, they were poorly taught. All of which was tremendously useful to me when I tried to develop my articles. This was 1939–40, when Keynes's General Theory was the central topic of discussion, together with Schumpeter's work on economic cycles. These subjects were not very well known in Europe, but at the New School I was able to attend most interesting seminars.

At that time, the United States was emerging from the depression. Keynes gave us hope that the mysterious disease that had caused the terrible recession of 1929 might be understood, in order to prevent its return. We were set on fire by these studies. We realized that we had reached a frontier and that, by trying to understand Keynes, we were venturing into new fields, fighting an important battle for the future.

Those months were decisive in my life. Marschak invited me to take part in a seminar organized in New York by Oskar Lange, the noted Polish economist at that time. As well as Lange and Marschak, the participants included leading economists like Tjalling Koopmans, who was to win the Nobel, and the renowned statistician Abraham Wald.

In New York Serena and I had settled in the West Side, at the far edge where the city was expanding. From where we lived, near the Hudson, we could see Washington Bridge. After a year's attendance at the New School, I decided to invite Marschak and his wife to dinner at our house. The appointment was for eight P.M. fairly late for American habits, but we had to perform the typical parental duties of giving Andrea his supper and putting him to bed. However, what with the excitement of inviting my teacher, I must have caused some confusion, for Marschak and his wife turned up *after dinner* and were thus not prepared to eat the sumptuous repast Serena had gotten ready, based on a gorgeous mixture of Russian and Italian dishes. But however hard we tried to dissuade him, Marschak was adamant and, in order not to disappoint us, insisted on gracing our table by eating a fine bowl of borscht that had been cooked in his honor.

10   The Great Keynesian Revolution—A Basic Lesson

INTRODUCTION

My purpose in this section is to try to explain Keynes's great contribution to the understanding and cure of mass unemployment, the most serious shortcoming of a market economy. My ambition is to do so in a way that is understandable to a reader with little economics background, provided he is prepared to do a little hard work. I hope to achieve this result by using a novel approach that stresses the commonality between pre-Keynesian models—"the classics"—and that of Keynes. They basically share the formulation of the demand and supply of money, the only real difference being in modeling the labor market—the response of nominal wages to unemployment. The classical model turns out to be a special case of the Keynesian general model, in which wages are assumed (counterfactually) to decline promptly in the face of unemployment. But the difference between rigidity and perfect flexibility turns out to make an enormous difference in the "monetary mechanism"—the mechanism that ensures the clearing of the money market—and the role of unemployment.

As I shall try to demonstrate in the following pages, Keynes's great contribution can be summarized as follows: Before his work, mass unemployment (in developed countries) was considered a random and transitory aberration of the system. Like catching a cold—sometimes it's light, sometimes it's a serious problem, but there is no certain remedy, though if you are patient, "It will go away." Instead, Keynes in the *General Theory* develops a radically different interpretation of unemployment by:

1. Offering a systematic explanation of this illness, proving that it is not a random accident but a physiological response to certain disturbances and, in particular, an insufficient *real* money supply. This explanation, I hold, applies to Europe's mammoth unemployment (though Europe's opinion leaders refuse to understand it, blaming other fictitious causes).

2. Teaching how this illness could be cured (a teaching that EMS countries still refuse to learn).

3. Proving that, if one fails to understand and apply the appropriate cures, this illness could last for a long time (as EMS countries are learning).

It is my ambition that anyone who accepts the validity of the classical theory of money—the so-called "quantity theory"—will, at the end of this essay, accept the notion of Keynesian unemployment and come to admire with me the greatness and originality of his contribution.

I　　THE CONCEPT OF EQUILIBRIUM AND THE MONEY MARKET

I.1　　*The classical model of market equilibrium and the role of price flexibility*

Economists model the whole economic system as composed by a series of markets in each of which the quantity exchanged and its price tend to an equilibrium or sustainable value. If the market is competitive (that is, there are no impediments to the entry and exit of buyers and sellers), the market mechanism generating the equilibrium can be described by the well-known "law" of demand and supply. The demand is described by a schedule indicating the quantity that would be bought at different prices. It can be represented graphically by a curve like DD in Figure 1, in which the quantity (q) is measured along the vertical axis and the price (p) along the horizontal axis. It normally falls from left to right, since we expect the quantity bought to be smaller the higher its price. SS represents the supply curve (function)—a schedule of the quantity offered at different prices—

Fig. 1

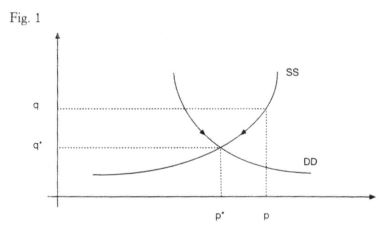

that typically rises as price increases. The equilibrium price and quantity are given by the coordinates of the point of intersection of the demand and supply curves, labeled q* and p* in Figure 1.

This conclusion rests on a fundamental assumption or postulate that may be called the "postulate of price flexibility." It states that, if at any given market price, the supply exceeds the demand, as at p' in the figure, then there will be some suppliers who are unable to sell at least part of what they intended. In an effort to increase their sales they will bid the price down toward the equilibrium value, p*, as shown by the arrow pointing toward the left on the horizontal axis. This movement will persist as long as p exceeds p* and q is below q*. A similar mechanism operates when the price is below p* and the quantity demanded exceeds that supplied: The unsatisfied would-be buyers will bid the price up. Therefore, provided the postulate of price flexibility holds, equilibrium can be described as a situation where the price comes to rest because demand and supply coincide, or where demand and supply coincide because this coincidence implies a maintainable price-quantity pair.

I.2   *Money market equilibrium and the monetary*
                                                            mechanism

In an economy that relies on money (rather than barter) to carry out transactions (as most economies do today), one of the relevant markets—and an exceedingly important one at that—is the so-called "money market." Money is defined as the collection of instruments (one or more) that in a monetary economy are used as "means of payments" for the purchase or sale of goods and services, that is, to execute "cash" transactions. (In the following presentation, in order to simplify it and focus on the critical issue, we will as a rule focus on the behavior of this market in an economy closed to international trade.)

In the money market, as in every other market, there are supply and demand curves. Because the essential function of money is to carry out transactions, it has long been recognized—indeed for centuries—that the demand for money depends on the value of transactions. And this view is accepted by Keynes as well as the classics. In current presentations, the value of transactions is, conveniently, assumed to be proportional to the gross national product expressed in terms of money at an "annual rate" (Y). Thus, the "classical demand for money" can be expressed as:

$$M = kY$$

Here k is a constant that measures the stock of money held, or demanded, by the economy relative to domestic income (1). The value of transactions, Y, can in turn be expressed as the product of the quantity of units sold per year times the price per unit, or

$$Y = PX$$

where P is a price index (for example, the price of a representative basket of goods traded) and X is an index of the quantity (of baskets) traded. The demand for money can therefore be written as

$$(1) \qquad M = kPX$$

This equation can also be rewritten in a form suggested by the well-known American economist Irving Fisher, that is:

$$(1a) \qquad M = PX/V$$

where $V = 1/k$ is again a constant that Fisher labeled the "velocity of circulation," because it is a measure of the value of the transactions executed, on average, during a year, by each unit of currency (2).

The supply for money, M^S is usually considered exogenous from the market system. In particular, in a modern (closed) economy the stock of money is determined by the central bank, or $M^S = M^S$. This money supply, together with the demand equation, gives the equilibrium condition in the money market.

$$(2) \qquad kPX = M^S$$

In what follows we will refer to the *monetary mechanism* as the mechanism that ensures the clearing of the money market, that is, that equation (2) is satisfied. We will show that the mechanism proposed by the classics is profoundly different from the one offered by Keynes.

II THE CLASSICAL MONETARY THEORY

II.1 *The determinants of the price level and the quantity theory of money*

The classical mechanism rests on one fundamental assumption—the postulate of price flexibility, namely, that wages are highly flexible in response to market disequilibrium and, in particular, that in the presence of (above frictional) unemployment they decline promptly until the excess supply has disappeared. Since this assumption ensures that every market (including the labor market) always clears, aggregate output X must be pegged at the "full employment output," say $\overline{X}$, which at any time can be taken as a given. Substituting $\overline{X}$ for X in (2) one can deduce the equilibrium value of P, $\overline{P}$:

$$(3) \qquad \overline{P} = M^S/(k^S) = M^S V/\overline{X}\overline{X}$$

In this equation, at any given point in time, X and V are "real" variables, reflecting the size of population, the state of the arts, payment habits, and so forth: Therefore, *M^S determines P and nothing else*. (Money is neutral with respect to all nonmonetary or "real" variables in the economy); and P is proportional to M^S. This is the essence of the so-called *quantity of money theory of the price level*.

There is an interesting alternative formalization of the classical model that has been suggested more recently. Let us rewrite the equilibrium conditions (3) by dividing both sides of the equation by P.

$$(3a) \qquad k = M_s/P$$

The left side of the equation is the nominal demand divided by the price index, and is usually referred to as "real" demand for money, that is, the quantity of money demanded expressed in terms of goods (3). Similarly, the right-hand side of (3a) is a measure of the "real supply" of money, that is, the existing stock, expressed in terms of number of baskets. The classi-

Fig. 2

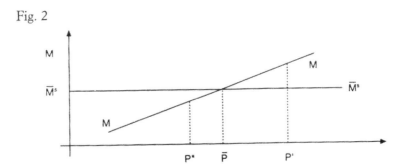

cal money market equilibrium is represented in Figure 2, with the price level P measured on the horizontal axis and the real money supply on the vertical axis. In this formulation the real money demand is a constant, represented by the horizontal line through kX. On the other hand, though the *nominal* supply is fixed at Ms, the *real* money supply is variable, moving inversely to the price level, as shown by the curve M^S. The equilibrium $\bar{P}$ is given by the intersection of the two curves. A higher P, like P', could not be maintained because it would generate excess demand that would cause the price to move toward $\bar{P}$.

II.2   The classical monetary mechanism

In the classical model, if there is an excess demand for the commodity traded in that market, its price must increase to choke off the excess demand. Accordingly, in the money market, if there is an excess demand for money, its *price in terms of commodities* must go up. But what is the price of money in terms of commodities? We know that P is the price of commodities in terms of money (bucks per basket); hence, the price of money in terms of baskets is *baskets per unit of money* (baskets per buck), which is simply the reciprocal of P, and is usually referred to as the *purchasing power of money*. Thus, an excess demand for money must result in a rise in its price, or purchasing power, which means a *fall* in the price level P toward the equilibrium level P*. A similar argument would hold if P were too low, causing an excess supply of money.

But just what is the behavioral mechanism that supposedly ensures that the price level declines promptly in response to an excess demand for money? The answer provided by the classical literature consists of a rather unconvincing paradigm that can be paraphrased as follows: When people find that to transact their business they need more money than they actually have, they strive to increase their endowment of money by promoting the sale of commodities for money through prompt price cuts.

The fundamental, irremediable shortcoming of the classical model consists, as Keynes points out, in the fact that the classical postulate of wage flexibility is manifestly counterfactual (see below). As a result, that model is unable to provide a systematic explanation of unemployment or to give any guidance on how to control it.

III KEYNES: A GENERALIZATION OF THE QUANTITY THEORY TO AN ECONOMY WITH RIGID WAGES—THE THEORY OF UNDEREMPLOYMENT EQUILIBRIUM

III .1   *The rigidity of wages and prices*

The General Theory starts from the realization that the classical postulate that wages and prices are sufficiently flexible in both directions, so that the demand for money quickly adjusts to any given supply, is just a fairy tale. At least in this century, after the enormous decline of the role of agriculture and after the appearance of trade unions, with their power to exclude unemployed people from the bargaining table, the flexibility of nominal wages on the down side does not exist, if it ever did, and the same of course applies to prices, which are very closely tied to wages. The reasons why such a downward rigidity prevails, and why it is not grossly inconsistent with rational behavior, have been analyzed and explained in many papers, which need not be summarized here, especially since the classical postulate is patently refuted by empirical evidence. In fact, it was precisely the failure of wages to decline in England, despite the great and persistent unemployment rate of the 1920s and 1930s and until World War II, that inspired Keynes's *General Theory*. The rigidity has certainly not diminished since then. Suffice it to remember that in the European countries of the EMS area, throughout the postwar period nominal wages have *never* decreased in any country, although the unemployment rates have reached quite high levels; and the same is largely true of prices. The experience in the United States in the postwar period merely confirms that of Europe.

The problem that Keynes confronted in the *General Theory* is to analyze the behavior of an economy in which wages are "downward rigid," that is, will not fall, or at best very slowly, in the presence of excess supply of labor.

III.2　　　　　　　　　　*A generalization of the notion of*
market equilibrium

The recognition that wages do not fall promptly in the presence of an excess supply of labor requires a major redefinition of the notion of "market equilibrium." In the classical model there were two alternative ways of characterizing market equilibrium: (1) when demand equals supply; (2) when price has reached a stable level (at least in the short run). But when price (wage) does not fall, despite the presence of an excess supply, the two definitions are not equivalent. Keynes chooses the second definition of equilibrium, which is applicable regardless of whether prices are rigid or flexible: *A market reaches equilibrium at a point where quantity and price stop adjusting, independently of whether at that point there exists an excess demand or supply.* And the choice is a very appropriate and general one, since it applies equally to the classical model of equilibrium with price flexibility or the Keynesian model of price rigidity: That is, equilibrium can always be operationally inferred from the (at least local) stationarity of price (and, for Keynes, only from that).

III.3　　　*The implications of wage-price rigidity.*
The role of unemployment in
clearing the money market

Since the price level is closely linked to the wage level, the rigidity of the latter induces the rigidity of prices. This can be modeled by replacing in the demand function the variable P with a constant, P^O, the price level that corresponds to the rigid wage W^O:

$$(4)\qquad M/P^O = kX = X/V$$

It is evident from (4) (assuming for the moment that k is a constant, in line with the classical model) that, at a given time, the real quantity demanded depends *only on the level of real income, X, and is proportional to it.* This demand function is reported in Figure 3. The real quantity of money, M, is again measured along the vertical axis and the real income, X, along the horizontal axis. The demand function (4) is represented by the MM line, which passes through the origin and has a slope (1/V). $\overline{X}$ on the vertical axis represents the real income corresponding to "full employment" of the labor force. With rigid wages, the real money supply, M^S/P^O, can again be considered as exogenous, and therefore in Figure 3 is represented as a horizontal line. The equilibrium of the money market is given by the condition that the real demand for money equals the supply, or:

$$(5) \qquad X = (M^S/P^O)V = X^*$$

Graphically, the money market reaches a Keynesian equilibrium at a point (a) where the demand for money equals the supply or existing stock. In the graph the market-clearing value of X, X^*, is lower than the full employment level $\overline{X}$; nevertheless (a) represents an *equilibrium* because, in the money market, the demand for and the supply of money are equal, while in the labor market there is unemployment or excess supply, but because of wage rigidity the wage and hence P are stationary. Thus, X^* can be characterized as a Keynesian underemployment equilibrium.

But to establish that X^* is indeed an "equilibrium," stable and unique, it is not enough to show that at that output the demand and supply of money are equal; one must also show that any value X, other then X^*, such as X' in Figure 3, where the demand differs from the supply, cannot be a stable equilibrium because there is a mechanism that pushes X toward X^*, reducing the excess demand (or supply) until it is eliminated, at X equal to X^*. In particular, $\overline{X}$ cannot be an equilibrium because of the excess demand for money. The above results imply the following crucial conclusion: When the money supply is insufficient to accommodate full employment, unemployment is the variable that clears the money market.

Keynes's masterly contribution consists in describing this mechanism and its working. In order to carry out this demonstration, Keynes had to "invent" and elaborate a series of concepts and interactions that were either new or had been neglected by the pre-Keynesian theories, and in particular by the classical theory. In the process, he gave rise to a new branch of economics, known as macroeconomics, including a subbranch, *international macroeconomics and finance*.

IV   KEYNESIAN EQUILIBRIUM UNEMPLOYMENT—THE MECHANISM

Keynes's construction relies on four basic building blocks:

- Liquidity Preference
- The Investment Function
- The Consumption Function
- The Investment Multiplier

Fig. 3

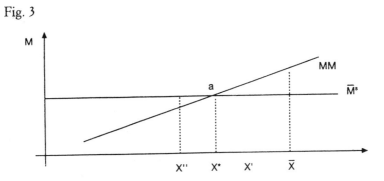

IV.1. Liquidity preference

Liquidity preference is generally identified with the proposition that the demand for money also depends on the interest rate, and is generally regarded as an interesting refinement, but hardly more than that. In reality, it brings to light a very fundamental error or omission in the classical formulation of monetary theory. For that theory—explicitly or implicitly—assumes that money is used exclusively to buy commodities, and hence its price is the so-called purchasing power in terms of commodities (baskets per buck). But it neglects the fact that money is also extensively used (and increasingly so) to acquire *financial assets* whose attractiveness depends on their return. In particular, by selling a buck from current cash holdings one can acquire a buck's worth of (short-term) "bonds" yielding a return measured by the interest rate. This transaction can be thought of as the exchange of a buck now for $1 + r$ bucks in the next period. Similarly, one can acquire a spot buck at the cost of $1 + r$ bucks next period by selling a bond from one's portfolio or by *borrowing at the rate r* (from the market or an intermediary). Thus $1 + r$ is the quantity of money that has to be paid in the next period, per unit of money delivered in the current period, or the price of " money" (now) in terms of money next period. We refer to $1/P$ as the purchasing power or price of money in terms of commodities: $1 + r$ can then be referred to as the purchasing power of money over future money, or also as the *opportunity cost* of (holding) money.

The representative interest rate in terms of which we measure the opportunity cost is usually taken as the return on short-term risk-free debt instrument (or the short-term gain expected from holding long term bonds—which should be equivalent, in a first approximation, except for uncertainty).

Liquidity preference, understood as the recognition of the role of financial assets, far from being an elegant side issue, has a crucial role to play in the transmission mechanism from money to employment.

In order to bring out this role, let us suppose that X exceeds X* like X' in Figure 3, and therefore there is an excess demand for money—that is, the public holds less money in its portfolio of assets that it actually needs or would like to have, at the current interest rate. According to the classical model, the public would engage in a hurried liquidation of goods in their possession, or even promptly reduce consumption, depressing the price of commodities and restoring equilibrium through an increase in the real money supply. Keynes, instead, suggests a much more credible and realistic response: If the private sector happens to possess less money in its portfolio of assets than the desired optimal quantity, at the current interest rate, its response will be to sell some of the liquid assets that it holds in its portfolio, such as short-term bonds, or to borrow (from banks or in the market). This very consideration explains why, typically, the private sector (families and enterprises) keep stocks of liquid assets—short-term risk-free assets (with assured value)—and credit lines that enable them to satisfy unexpected needs for ready cash without having recourse to distress liquidation of goods or to reduced consumption. It should be obvious to anyone familiar with the life cycle model that being short of cash calls for an adjustment of the portfolio and not for abandoning the smoothing of consumption.

What happens when the public tries to sell assets or demands more credit from banks in order to purchase money today for money tomorrow? Evidently the interest rate r, or the price of spot money, will increase. The first impact that the excess demand will have is probably on short-term interest rates on risk-free loans like Treasury bills, which are highly flexible, being traded in near-perfect markets. If the increase of the short-term rate is perceived as sustainable (for example, because it persists), it will spill over to the long-term rates.

Here we encounter the first novelty of the Keynesian structure: An excess demand for money reduces prices and increases the real money supply very slowly (if at all), but will promptly increase the price of money in terms of future money, that is, the interest rate. This increase, in turn, will have two major effects: First, it will tend to reduce the demand for money for a given value of transactions, thereby alleviating the excess demand itself; and second, it will affect investment outlays as described by the second fundamental relation.

IV.2   *The investment function*

The essential characteristic of this function is that when the cost of capital increases, investment declines. For example, when the interest rate on mortgages decreases, the annual carrying cost of a given house decreases. Therefore, more and more people desire homes, or better homes, and construction activity or investment in houses—one of the most important components of the national gross investment—increases. The sensitivity of investment to the interest rate has been long debated. Keynes himself tended to be "interest skeptic," and today in Europe it is fashionable to claim that the cost of money has scant influence on investment. The excuse for not adopting more expansive monetary policies aimed at lowering interest rates is that they would have little effect on unemployment. It is even claimed that a more expansive monetary policy, while having no effect on employment, would have its main impact in increasing inflation.

This view must be regarded as plain "pre-Keynesian nonsense." Money can affect the price level only by increasing output relative to capacity and employment relative to the labor force. A direct effect is conceivable only to the extent that opinion leaders and the public have been brainwashed into believing that an increase in the money supply will cause prices to rise, independently of any effect on the real economy. In this case, of course, firms might respond by immediately raising prices, and workers (or trade unions), by insisting on immediate wage increases. But in this case, the opinion leaders (especially in the banking sector) should take great pains to explain to the public the basis for their irrational beliefs.

Luckily, empirical evidence, at least in the United States, is completely different. The cost of capital, which depends on the interest rate and on other fiscal parameters (and the accompanying availability of credit at banks), is a fundamental variable that explains investment. This result clearly emerges in my work during the last twenty years on econometric models on the United States, Italy, and other countries. It is confirmed by more recent econometric work and by today's vigorous and strong economic growth in the United States, which was set in motion with low interest rates from 1992 to 1996, while Europe lags way behind. Further, the decisive role of the Federal Reserve in stimulating or slowing investment is pretty much unquestioned in the business community.

IV.3   *The consumption-investment*
*   identity: The multiplier*

At the heart of the Keynesian masterpiece stands the "famous" and "powerful" proposition that saving is "identically equal" to investment. It is
famous because nobody had hitherto paid any attention to it, and at the
outset people had a hard time understanding or accepting it, yet it follows
directly from the fact that both saving and investment are defined and
measured as the difference between National Income—the value of goods
produced—and consumption. It is powerful because when the identity is
combined with the saving function, it has the truly novel and stunning
implication that income (and employment) is determined not by the available labor force and its productivity (as held by the traditional view) but by
the investment rate (within the limits of productive capacity and available
labor force). The explanation is provided by the fact that a given level of
investment requires a matching rate of saving, and there will be a unique
level of income that will result in that rate of saving. In particular, a change
in investment will give rise to a change in income such as to produce a
matching increase in saving. The ratio of the rise in income to the rise in
investment is the famous Keynesian "investment multiplier." It is equal to
the reciprocal of the so-called "marginal propensity to save" (mps). Thus,
if the mps is, say, $\frac{1}{4}$ (an additional dollar of income raises saving by
25 cents), the multiplier is 4: A unit increase in investment will result in
an increase in income of 4, for this will increase saving by $\frac{1}{4}$ x 4 = 1.

The "multiplication" derives from the fact that when investment
increases by one, the increase in saving by one is accompanied by an
increase in consumption by three units, and therefore total income rises by
four units. Another way to explain the multiplier is that a new investment
is a direct source of employment and income, and the newly employed will
spend some of it on consumption, thus increasing employment in those
industries that produce the goods they want to consume, and so on. (It is
necessary to clarify that this identity is valid only in a closed economy,
without a government with taxing power, public expenditure, or public
saving; but the identity is easily generalized—see below).

IV.4   *The saving (and consumption) function*

In view of the demonstration in IV.3 that investment determines income
and employment through the saving (or consumption) function, it is evident that this function plays a vital role in Keynes's construction. In

General Theory, he devoted some attention and perceptive remarks to the determinants of saving, but the one point he stressed as essential to his construct is his famous "psychological law," which postulates that the (marginal) propensity to save is positive but less than one. (This is necessary to ensure that the investment multiplier is positive but finite.) But since Keynes, the consumption function has attracted a lot of attention, and considerable progress has been achieved in understanding the basic nature of saving behavior, especially that of National Saving. My extensive work on the subject (and the partly overlapping work of Milton Friedman) reported below (section 21) suggests that, in the long run, aggregate consumption (and hence saving) is proportional to income, with the proportionality factor rising with the growth trend of income. But in the short run, consumption is largely controlled *not by current income but by trend* income (closely related to the *Permanent Income* of Friedman and of my *Life Cycle Hypothesis of Saving*). Therefore, saving, which is income minus consumption, will be an increasing function of the *deviation of current income from permanent income* (Friedman's *transitory income*).

The implications of the above reasoning for understanding the nature of the short-run saving function will be brought out in section IV.5. It will suffice to point out here that the findings reported above imply that consumption is not very sensitive to short-run cyclical variations in income, much less than to permanent changes. Hence the short-run marginal propensity to save will be distinctly higher than the long-run average propensity. This finding in turn suggests that consumption (and saving) behavior tend to exhibit a stabilizing influence on income in the face of cyclical fluctuations in investment, because it implies a small short-run investment multiplier.

IV.5   The underemployment equilibrium—synthesis

Our remaining task is to rely on the four Keynesian building blocks to demonstrate that X* (in Figure 3) is an *underemployment equilibrium, unique and stable*. I will first give an approximate, literary demonstration, and then present a more rigorous proof by graphical methods.

Literary demonstration: The proof consists in showing that any output larger than the Keynesian equilibrium, such as X', is not sustainable. The reason is that, at that output, there is an excess demand for money. From liquidity preference we know that an excess *demand* for money will result in a prompt rise in interest rates. This, by itself, reduces the demand for money by leading people to economize on cash holding. But, in addition, it sets in motion another much more powerful mechanism: It reduces the investment through the investment function, which, through the multiplier, produces a fall in income toward X* and the fall in income *finally* reduces the demand and the excess demand for money. But, as long as X remains greater than X*, there will be an excess demand for money that will move interest rates up and reduce investment and X, causing it to converge toward the stable equilibrium X*. A similar story holds if output is below X*, and there is an excess supply of money.

Graphical demonstration: The graphical apparatus of Figure 4 is basically an extension of one developed in a famous article by the British economist J. R. Hicks and known as the "IS-LM" paradigm. It is designed to demonstrate how output is determined by the real money supply, detailing the role of the four basic building blocks described above.

The analysis involves four variables: real income, X; saving, S; investment, I; and the interest rate. In principle, all of these variables are measured in real terms, but because of the maintained assumption that prices are rigid (in the sense that they do not respond to the remaining variables), real variables are indistinguishable from nominal ones. (This also holds for the interest rate, since fixed prices exclude expectations of inflation or deflation.) Each of these variables is measured along the four semi-axes that extend outward from the origin, as shown in the graph. Thus, X is measured along the vertical axis extending upward from the origin; r is measured along the horizontal axis, extending rightward from the origin; and I and S are likewise measured along the remaining two semi-axes. As a result we end up with four quadrants that on the graph are labeled, counterclockwise, I to IV.

1. We begin our construction with block one, the liquidity preference and its implications for the role of money in limiting output. From equation (5) and remembering that liquidity preference implies that the velocity of circulation depends on the interest rate we have

$$X = (M^S/P^O)V(r)$$

where P^O is the fixed price corresponding to the fixed wage, and X the real output that can be transacted with the given real money supply M^S/P^O. This equation is represented in quadrant I by the rising curve; it is the graph of the velocity of circulation up to a proportionality factor, which is the real money supply: A higher r causes the public to economize cash holdings, increasing velocity.

Fig. 4

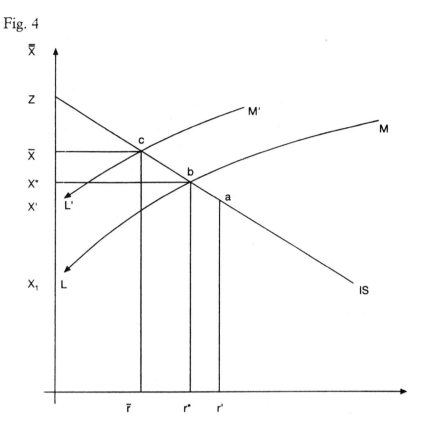

2. The next block, the investment function, is represented in quadrant IV
   by the curve labeled I-r. It shows that the volume of investment
   decreases with the interest rate or the cost of capital. It must be noted
   that the cost of capital is properly not the interest rate but the return
   required by the market. Since the return of an investment is uncertain
   or risky, and investors are known to be risk averse, the required return
   on investments (the so-called capitalization rate for risky outcomes)
   exceeds the interest rate by a so-called risk premium. For present purposes, we can rely on the convenient approximation that the risk premium is either a constant or bears a stable relation to r, so that I can still
   be represented as a function r. It must be understood however that the
   I-r curve may be shifted around by changes in time in a variety of variables, including the risk premium (and taxation). Furthermore, the
   premium also accounts for one important feature of I-r: Although I
   rises as r falls, there is a limit to how far it can be expected to rise. This
   is evidenced in quadrant IV by the finite value of investment I corresponding to a zero interest rate. For even if the market r can be bid

down to zero (which is most unlikely), the required return on investment will still be positive, equaling the risk premium, and one should
expect that the volume of investment returning at least the risk premium should be very finite.

3. We can move next to quadrant II, and the saving function of block 4.
Here we must make a distinction between the long- and the short-run
saving functions. As suggested earlier, *in the long run saving tends to be
proportional to income*, meaning that when income is on trend, saving is
proportional to it. This relation is represented in quadrant II by the
line S'S' through the origin, with slope, say s, determined by the long-
run growth trend: s is also the long-run average and marginal propensity to save. Next, along the X axis mark a height $\overline{X}$, which is equal to
the trend value for the current period. Then to $\overline{X}$ will correspond a
point $\overline{S}$ on the long-run function S'S'; but note that $\overline{S}$ is also a point on
the short-run saving function in the sense that $\overline{S}$ is the saving rate that
would prevail if current income happened to be $\overline{X}$. We can now readily establish that the short-run saving function must be given by a
curve like S-X in the graph, going through $\overline{S}$ but with an appreciably
greater slope. Indeed, consider an income lower than $\overline{X}$ like X* in the
figure. Clearly, because X*-$\overline{X}$ represents a negative transient deviation
from trend we can expect that a relatively small portion of that
decline will result in a decline in consumption, while most of it will be
absorbed by a decline in saving. In short, SY will tend to be markedly
steeper than S'S' because its slope is the "marginal propensity to save
out of transitory income," which may be quite high relative to the
long-run propensity which is the slope of S'S'. Note that if income is
well below trend, saving may fall to zero or even become negative,
but this can only be a transient phenomenon.

The fact that the short-run saving function is steep has an important stabilizing effect on the economy. This can be readily understood
by remembering that the multiplier is the reciprocal of the marginal
propensity to save; failure to distinguish between the long-run average and the short-run marginal propensity to save led, in the early
Keynesian period, to greatly exaggerating the potential instability of
income in response to cyclical variations in investment. With a consumption income ratio averaging around, say, 90 percent, the long-
run multiplier is 10; but a short-run cyclical decline in income may
reduce consumption a lot less, perhaps by ½, which implies a short-
run multiplier of only 2. This stabilizing effect is markedly increased
by the presence of income taxation (see below).

4. The last building block, the equality of saving and investment, is easily represented graphically in quadrant III by means of a straight line through the origin of slope one. It says that to any rate of investment, say I*, in the figure, there corresponds a saving rate of equal amount S* and to that an income X*, on the vertical axis. But from quadrant IV we know that the investment I* corresponds to an interest r*. Returning to quadrant I, consider the point a* with coordinates (r*, X*). These are values of r and X that clear the market for funds to be invested, and also the commodity market by equating the demand for output, that is, consumption plus investment, with the value of output, which is income and hence consumption plus saving. But $\bar{a}$ does not represent a sustainable equilibrium for the entire economy because the combination (r*, X*) does not clear the money market. Indeed, given the real money supply M^*/P^O embodied in the LM* curve, the money market is cleared only by points falling on it. Now $\bar{a}$ is seen to fall above LM*, which means that at $\bar{a}$, the demand for money exceeds the fixed supply, M^S/P^O. Clearly, money market clearing requires a lower demand for money and hence a higher r and smaller X. The full equilibrium point must lie below and to the right of $\bar{a}$. In addition, it must clear also the commodity market. One can readily verify that a*, (r*, X*) in quadrant I, is the one and only point that simultaneously clears all markets and hence represents the Keynesian equilibrium for the economy. (It is Keynesian because the equilibrium output X* is lower than the full employment output, $\bar{X}$).

The convenient way to locate the overall equilibrium, like a*, is to repeat the procedure that produced the commodity market clearing point $\bar{a}$, for different values of r, on the axis: For each r one finds the corresponding I, S, and X, and notes the point with coordinates (r, X) in the first quadrant. Connecting these points, we obtain a curve like the curve labeled a', $\bar{a}$, a*, which is labeled IS and shows the value of output that clears the commodity market for different values of r. It is necessarily decreasing from left to right because as r rises, I and hence S and Y must fall.

The overall stable equilibrium point is now easily located at the intersection of IS with LM, the only point that, being on both curves, implies clearing of all markets. And it is the only stable equilibrium because at any other point there would exist excess demand or supply in at least one of the two markets, giving rise to a dynamic adjustment toward a*. The stable equilibrium X* falls short of s, *the full employment output* $\bar{X}$ in the graph, and yet there is no mechanism that tends to push it toward $\bar{X}$.

But should there not be at least some tendency for wages to come down, at least when unemployment is large and persistent? The answer is a pretty striking no: As noted earlier, in the last five decades we have never seen a fall in nominal wages despite very high and persistent unemployment. It is for this reason that we can refer to X* as a stable Keynesian underemployment equilibrium.

V   QUALIFICATIONS AND AMPLIFICATIONS

V.1   *Wage rigidity is asymmetric*

The rigidity of prices and wages postulated by Keynes is asymmetric-downward only. In the presence of unemployment and unutilized capacity—demand is lower than supply-wages and prices do not fall, or they do not fall fast enough to reestablish equilibrium. They might decline to reestablish it in what economists call the "long run," but as Keynes wisely warned "in the long run we are all dead." A gradual adjustment is not enough to avoid significant and persistent unemployment.

The situation is different if demand exceeds production capacity. In Figure 4, let us suppose that the intersection of the two curves IS and LM occurs at a' in quadrant I, to which corresponds an X' larger than full employment. Demand exceeds capacity, and firms bid up wages in an effort to attract more workers and will be able to pass the higher wages on to higher prices. There will be inflationary pressures. If the quantity of money remains fixed, M^S/P will fall and the MM curve will shift down until it reaches the equilibrium position at a point where salaries will cease to grow. There will be price increases, but this increase will occur only once. At this point the risk is that the central bank tries to limit the increase of the interest rate needed to stop inflation, by increasing M and keeping M/P constant. In this case, inflation will continue and (possibly) eventually accelerate.

An interesting consequence of the asymmetry is that the price level tends to grow without limits for at least a century. Once it grows because of an excess demand or because of other reasons, it never goes back.

V.2   *Keynes unemployment—Wage rigidity or insufficient money supply?*

Keynes's interpretation (as well as Hick's) has emphasized the fact that unemployment is the result of an insufficient real supply of money. But what is the cause of this insufficiency? The classical point of view, echoed by Keynes's critics, is that if wages fell promptly in the presence of unemployment as they should, this would produce an endogenous mechanism increasing the real supply of money until it reached the full employment level. The rigidity produces a market failure for which labor (in particular, unions) deserves the blame and which it should correct. This interpretation is logically correct, but it does not offer a useful guide for how to maintain full employment, because there is no way to force wage flexibility—and there are good reasons for justifying wage rigidity.

But fortunately there are two ways to change M/P. One is inapplicable—to adjust W. Indeed, as Keynes has pointed out, to claim that full employment be maintained through wage flexibility that accommodates the money supply would be asking labor to become the central bank. The other way is extremely applicable as long as nominal wages are rigid, and it consists in adjusting the money supply to accommodate the wage level. As long as the nominal wage W is rigid in practice, unemployment is curable by keeping the money supply at the right level. In other words, unemployment is caused by a lack of money. And since money is determined by the central bank, this is caused by an improper monetary policy. In my opinion, this conclusion, although based on an extremely simplistic model, contains the key (though not the only one) for an explanation of the inexcusably high level of unemployment that Europe is suffering today.

V.3   *Money supply versus interest rates*

Up to this point, we have stressed the fact that, with rigid nominal wages, employment can be controlled by monetary policy. But in reality, the central bank has an alternative tool for exercising its control, namely the interest rate—though on condition it gives up control of M. It is clear from Figure 4 that if the bank were to impose a given value of r, like r* in quadrant I, this would result in investment I*, hence income Y*, and point a* on the IS curve of quadrant I.

But how can the central bank control r? Essentially by being prepared to buy or sell some specified kind of assets (e.g., Treasury Bills or other short-term loans) at a specified yield r*: That yield then becomes the "market rate." It can make that offer operational because it has "money" to buy whatever may be offered, by virtue of the fact that it can pay with its IOU, which is money (or the source of money) for the economy. Similarly, if the public wants to buy, it will tender the IOU that will be canceled. But it is clear that by selling assets the public will increase the money supply, and by buying them it will reduce it. Hence by fixing interest rates, the bank loses control over the nominal money supply, handing over to the public the decision of what quantity it wants. That quantity will of course be the money demand corresponding to the point a* generated by the chosen r*. The money demanded and supplied will be an amount M* such that

$$M^*/P^O = X^* \, V^*$$

where V* is the velocity corresponding to r*. Graphically, it is the money supply that results in an LM curve that goes through a*. There is only one interest rate $\bar{r}$, which is consistent with full employment, investment, and income $\bar{X}$, and requires a money supply $\bar{M}/P^O = X\text{-}V\text{-}'$. This is the interest rate that the bank should choose if it decides to use r as the instrument for policy, and it should result in the money supply $\bar{M}$.

There have been long debates on whether it is more efficient for the central bank to fix short-run targets for the interest rate or the quantity of money, or to use some rules combining the two. This is not the place to enter into the details, but it should be emphasized that an analysis requires that uncertainty be taken into account: In other words a bank that fixes M cannot predict with certainty which level of interest rate and X will be generated, and similarly if it fixes r, cannot be sure about the quantity of investments and income that will result.

Note that this debate would make no sense in the context of the classical model. For high-wage flexibility would ensure that, whatever the money supply, the real supply is always at full employment level, and so is r. Money supply policy still has a role to play in stabilizing prices, but interest policy has no role; there is no need for it, and any attempt at fixing r away from $\bar{r}$ must end either in unemployment or inflation!

This view has been associated in recent times with extreme "monetarism."

V. 4   *The liquidity trap*

In addition to demonstrating how wage rigidity can cause unemployment, Keynes can boast another result of great theoretical value, whatever its empirical relevance: A market economy using money as a store of value may be unable to avoid involuntary unemployment.

This conclusion is readily established with the help of Figure 4. It rests on one basic proposition: While, in general, an expansion of the money supply will reduce the price of money now in terms of money later—that is, r—there is a limit to the extent to which r can be bid down. Without engaging in a lengthy argument as to what that limit might be, we can assert with confidence that it cannot be less than zero. Indeed, in a world in which money is essentially costless to store, who would ever want to exchange money now for less money tomorrow?

Back to Figure 4: Suppose that, at zero r, the rate of investment, I(o), *is smaller than the full employment rate of saving*. As noted earlier, this is perfectly possible, especially recalling the existence of a risk premium. Then output X must be smaller than full employment output, $\overline{X}$! No monetary or feasible interest policy can get the system back to full employment, since as a rule it cannot create a negative interest rate; nor, for that matter, could classical perfect wage flexibility.

From a practical point of view the important question is the empirical relevance of the liquidity trap. Some hold that it has never occurred, while others hold that it played an important role in the 1929 crisis, and perhaps in the recent Japanese crisis. But it must be acknowledged that there are several possible remedies to a liquidity trap, though they are outside the market system. One possibility is fiscal policy, including public investment (see below); another is to bring about a negative real rate through steady deflation.

V.5   *Fiscal policy*

So far in our analysis we have ignored the role of public expenditure and taxes, because we have not allowed for the existence of a public sector. Once we take into account the government, private saving is no longer equal to private investment but to investment *plus public deficit*. This generalization can be readily accommodated by our Figure 4 by simply replacing the 45-degree line of quadrant III with another, which is above it by the deficit amount. If the deficit is a constant independent of any other variable (a case convenient for exposition, though not very realistic), the new curve will be parallel to the old one. Consequently, to any given r and corresponding I there will correspond a higher saving and hence income. But this means that the deficit will have the effect of shifting up the IS curve by an amount equal to the deficit times the multiplier.

This result is important in that it implies that fiscal policy offers *an alternative tool to control employment*. To illustrate, suppose the economy finds itself in the underemployment equilibrium, a*. Then, by creating an appropriate deficit through increased expenditure or lower taxes, IS can be shifted up until it intersects LM at the height $\overline{X}$. This possibility could be exploited, for example, to counter a liquidity trap.

The Keynesian recognition of the possible employment effects of fiscal policy has given origin to a widely held view that the essence of Keynes is the advocacy of fiscal deficits. While this association might have had some basis in the early years of the General Theory in the immediate aftermath of the Great Depression, it is totally false at present. In particular my view, which I believe would be broadly acceptable to those who understand the fundamental Keynesian message, is that employment stabilization should be primarily the responsibility of monetary policies, while the main effect of budget deficits should be recognized as that of redistributing resources between generations.

V.6   *Nominal versus real rigidity*

Our analysis has relied on the Keynesian assumption of asymmetric nominal wage rigidity. At the time this hypothesis became widely accepted it was at first a source of alarm, with respect to the success in maintaining a stable economy, for it meant that one could not rely on the classical wage flexibility mechanism to offset the many shocks that could destabilize the system, employment in particular. But by the 1950s and '60s, nominal rigidity became a source of optimism.

This is because unemployment was regarded as being principally of the Keynesian type (that is, given by an insufficient level of aggregate demand). It was therefore easily controlled by varying the supply of real money. But in the presence of *nominal wage rigidity*, the supply of real money is the same as the supply of nominal money, which the central bank, adaptable to the demand for money, was ready to control by varying the nominal stock of money M. The monetary authorities (it was believed) held in their hands the decisive instrument to prevent sustained unemployment, though they could still err on the high side, fearing unemployment more than inflation. And this is broadly consistent with what happened throughout most of the 1950s and '60s, both in Europe (unemployment below 3 percent and some inflation) and in the United States up to the Vietnam War.

What, then, explains the enormous rise of unemployment in the European Union, up to some 12 percent in the late 1990s (and of inflation) and the change from optimism to dark pessimism about the ability to find a quick solution? The answer on which I worked for many years will be found in chapter II, section 10 and following. But not to keep the reader in suspense, let me specify here the three main culprits: (1) the transition from nominal wage rigidity to aggressive real wage targets, reinforced by (2) the two great oil crises, and (3) the many large errors in monetary policy in the form of an inadequate money supply after the oil crisis, on the part of the Bundesbank, the *de facto* central bank of the Union since the mid-1980s, and then by its successor, the European Central Bank (ECB). The United States was mostly affected only by item (2), and accordingly unemployment was fairly high only through the two oil crises, but then abated as it rose in Europe, and is at present less than half the European rate, while it was half as high in the 1950s and '60s.

But looking at the future I believe that, especially in Europe, there is reason to expect an improvement over the existing situation, as all major parties have learned from their mistakes and hopefully will avoid a repetition; but there is of course always room for new, unexpected sources of trouble!

V.7.   *The open economy*

The one major issue that has been bypassed in this survey is the analysis of the open economy. Unfortunately, openness introduces numerous complications that could not be accommodated here. It will suffice to say that the new international macroeconomics and finance owe a great deal to Keynes; and that the distinction between nominal and real wage rigidity remains crucial and interacts with the two principle exchange regimes, fixed or floating.

11   Abba Lerner, the Agent of Revelation

My views on Keynes, on both the elementary model and liquidity preference, were worked out between 1942 and 1943 and published in 1944, though in a form that I think much less clear and comprehensible than the way I have presented them here.

I remember that the inspiration and stimulus for this article stemmed from an argument with Abba Lerner, Marschak's successor, possessed of a sharp mind, full of imagination. Lerner wished to launch a new doctrine that he himself had named "Functional Finance" but which his colleagues sarcastically dubbed "Fictional Finance." Lerner was led to invent this paradigm by the conviction that he must radically alter the traditional views on the function of public expenditure and taxes. The function of expenditure must not be the traditional one of providing the necessary public services, and that of taxes must not be to pay for the public services but, rather, to stabilize employment by increasing or diminishing disposable private income and aggregate demand.

I rejected this formulation because it presupposed that the so-called limit case of Keynes was the prevailing situation in the market economies. In that case alone, as we have already seen, is fiscal policy the only one that can maintain full employment. But this is in actual fact a very rare case, if it ever existed. Otherwise, the main instrument to sustain full employment is monetary policy, not fiscal.

12   The Ladies of New Jersey and That Brown Shoe; Bard College

The reflections that follow were developed over a period of several years, but the fundamental insights became clearer when I began working on the 1944 article. At that time I was given my first teaching post at the New Jersey College for Women (now Douglas College), which belonged to Rutgers University, New Brunswick, in New Jersey, a few miles south of New York. Marschak found me the job and suggested I give up dealing in books. For a few days I couldn't make up my mind, for the book trade earned us a living. Then I sought advice from my father-in-law, and he, perceiving my interest in economics, encouraged me to abandon the trade and start teaching. "What makes you happier," he asked, "selling books or studying economics?" "Economics, of course," I replied. "So, go for it!"

In this way, I embarked on a commuter existence. Another reason this post was offered to me was that, in the meantime, the attack on Pearl Harbor had taken place and many teachers were leaving their colleges to move to Washington. As a result, a post became vacant for one term. Nowadays, it amuses me to tell my younger colleagues about my workload: four courses per semester, two in economics, one in statistics, and one in economic history. I also retained a course I was very keen on at the New School for Social Research in New York. These days young teachers at the beginning of their careers feel themselves exploited if they have to teach more than two courses per semester.

One morning Serena awoke when I had already left to catch the train and found two odd shoes on my side of the bed, one brown, one black. Fearing the worst, she rang me at school: I looked down at my feet and, alas, had to confirm that I had donned shoes of different colors. During the afternoon lesson I tried desperately to hide my feet beneath the desk—not an easy thing in front of thirty girls.

When I had finished my duties at the New Jersey College for Women, I went on to Bard College, at that time part of Columbia University. Bard was my first encounter with a real American campus—and it was decisive in my life. It occupied a magnificent position north of New York, on the bank of the Hudson. At that time it was a male college with a progressive teaching method, for it followed a highly advanced doctrine of education: Grades had been abolished; assessments of students had to be argued and discussed. This was an absolute novelty for me. I taught a course in economics and a specialized course in mathematical economics. There were some very capable students, mostly on scholarships, whereas the paying students ranged between good and bad. Several of them were the same age as me, some of them older. They called me "Doc" and made fun of my fluttering tie.

I was impressed by the fact that the American campus covers a vast area with buildings for teaching, for offices, and for teacher and student residences. (The word "campus" is used everywhere except at Harvard, where it is traditionally called "The Yard," and to say "campus" means you aren't one of the élite!) The classes were very small, never more than ten students, and this encouraged personal relationships. It was immediately clear to me how that system was more humane and more efficient than the intolerable impersonality of Italian universities, which involved a few barons teaching crowds of anonymous students, surrounded by little coveys of petulant, knee-bending assistants. The comradeship and friendliness that often spring up between teachers and students are a characteristic of higher education in the United States and one of the reasons for its undoubted success. Some of the students at Bard College helped me to improve my English, which in 1942 was still a bit weak, and assisted me in preparing my article on liquidity preference for publication. In the period when I worked alone at Bard I had enormous fun. We often went riding together, and on one occasion some students who had a house on campus invited me, in my capacity as expert, to an Italian dinner—to which I was supposed to contribute spaghetti. I cooked it to perfection, *al dente*, but when I had to strain it I was terrified to find there was no colander. I tried to make do without one, but through my lack of experience all the pasta ended up in the sink, and since this wasn't very clean I had to start again from scratch. So I was demoted from expert to mere consumer.

From the summer of 1942 I continued commuting for a few months. I went to Bard on the train and stopped there for two or three days. But in 1943 we settled on the campus with all the family. And there I managed to finish my article on liquidity preference, helped by Serena, who corrected and typed it, and began to expand it into my doctoral thesis for the New School.

At Bard I also taught a course for military personnel. I taught mathematics to a group of Air Force pilots, who had to learn spherical trigonometry. The course was part of the Army Special Training Program (ASTP). By a strange chance, I found myself at the head of the department of mathematics, with, under me, a colleague who was to become a very well-known mathematician—whereas I spent my evenings cramming for the classes I had to teach next morning! When Serena and the rest of the family joined me, we took a delightful apartment. Our neighbors were the family of Werner Wolff, a psychology professor of genius and an innovator, and his wife, Kate, who taught music and played the piano. We became great friends. Wolff invited Serena to attend his classes and to contribute to them with her experience in bringing up Andrea—who ended up in his book as an "interesting" case.

13   The Relationship Between Demand and Employment: The Beveridge Curve

In the simplified model we argued as though an increase in demand by X percent generates an equal increase in employment, at least while in the presence of unemployment. Actually, the relation between demand and employment is more complex and is explained by a very ingenious model, called the Beveridge curve, in honor of Lord Beveridge[4], who developed it. I give here very much a summarized account in order to help the reader understand the nature of unemployment and its relation to the aggregate demand of Keynes.

The starting point is that in a dynamic economy unemployment and employment are not made up of people who work steadily and others who never work. Suppose there is 10 percent unemployment; this does not mean that 90 percent of the workforce is in steady jobs and the remaining 10 percent permanently idle. On the contrary, there is a continual flow of persons who lose their jobs and become temporarily unemployed, and persons who find jobs and move from the ranks of the unemployed to those of the employed. In this way, more or less all the unemployed, at some time or other, will enter employment.

In this economy of fluxes it can easily be seen that the stock of unemployed is the product of the flux of those who lose their jobs multiplied by the length of time needed, on average, by a newly unemployed person to find work. By way of example, if the flux of those who lose their jobs is one million per month and, on average, they take three months to find new jobs, we have three million unemployed. The flux may be taken as a stable parameter of the economy that reflects the dynamic of the system (for example, the rapidity with which firms are born and die) and also the size of the economy. For both reasons, this flux is much wider in the United States than in Germany—not to mention Italy, where dismissal is practically taboo.

But what determines the length of time necessary, on average, for persons who have lost their job to find a new one? That depends on the availability of jobs, and this availability can be measured by the number of personnel firms wishing to hire but are unable to hire, since they cannot find suitable workers. This measure is known as *vacancies*, or the number of "vacant" jobs. Obviously, the more jobs there are to fill, the shorter, on average, will be the time needed to find a job. Hence, for a given flow of persons leaving their jobs, unemployment and vacancies move in opposite directions.

This inverse ratio between the two variables is called the Beveridge curve. It is illustrated in Figure 5. The variable U, measured along the vertical axis, is the rate of unemployment—the number of unemployed (U) expressed as a percentage of the work force—and the variable V, measured along the horizontal axis, is the *rate* of vacancies. At point a, the vacancies are many, the average search time is short, and unemployment is therefore low, as is presently the case in the United States. At point c, on the other hand, there are few vacancies or jobs to fill, search time may become very long, and unemployment is very high, as is currently the case in Europe.

To understand the relation between aggregate demand and unemployment, one must bear in mind the budget constraint that links the unemployment variable (U), vacancies (V), and the total demand for workers (D), which we may consider to be proportional to aggregate demand. By definition, V is the difference between demand and the number of jobs filled, which is the same thing as employment. Recalling that unemployment is, in turn, the difference between the workforce and employment, we can establish the following relationship between the variables with which we are concerned:

$$U = 100 - D + V$$

where the small letters denote the capital ones expressed as a percentage of the workforce. For a given value of demand D, the equation represents a relation between the two variables U and V, which can be shown graphically in Figure 5 by curve cc. This is a straight line with slope one, and an intercepted line on the vertical axis equal to 100–D.

Suppose, for instance, that D is 98 (that is, the number of workers

Fig. 5

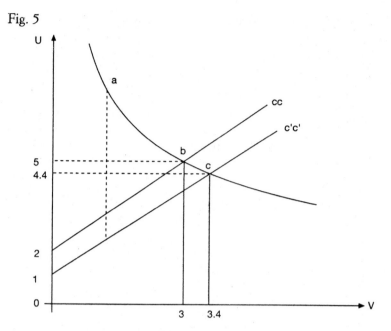

required by firms is equal to 98 percent of the workforce); then the intercept would be 2. Equilibrium in the labor market corresponds to intersection point b in the figure. Here, the vacancies are 3 percent and the unemployment 2 + 3, or 5 percent.

Let us see what happens when aggregate demand grows: D increases, the curve ccshifts downward parallel to itself, as indicated by c'c', and the equilibrium point moves to c. As is easily foreseen, a rise in the overall demand reduces unemployment and increases employment. Likewise, a reduction in aggregate demand causes c to shift upward and unemployment to increase. But an increase in demand, say by 1 percent, reduces unemployment by less than half of one percentage point, for, while one part of the additional demand leads to an increase in employment, another translates merely into an increase in vacant jobs.

The Beveridge curve offers another "bridge" for Keynes's model. Suppose we start from a point like b and aggregate demand falls and unemployment rises; then, following the insight of Keynes, we can expect that wages will not fall and therefore prices will remain constant, and this continues to hold good even if demand increases, pressing toward point b. But if demand continues to rise, there will come a point where the jobs vacant will be so numerous (unsatisfied demand so high and unemployment so low) that firms will try to compete to obtain workers by offering higher wages. At the same time, workers will find plenty of job opportunities elsewhere and will threaten to leave just when the entrepreneur has most need of them, unless their wages are raised. The increase in the cost of labor plus the existence of demand that the firm is unable to satisfy lead to a rise in prices, and this sparks off the inflation process, which can end only if the aggregate demand (in real terms) is brought back to below the critical level. Note that the critical level of unemployment will be reached well before it descends to zero. What is the critical level, then? This difficult question is much in fashion in the United States today, since experience from the end of World War II until the 1990s suggested that it lay between 5.5 and 6 percent. To everyone's surprise, just before the turn of the twenty-first century, unemployment in America fell below 5 percent without there being any evidence of an episode of inflation.

Personally, I think the critical level is drawing near, if it has not yet been reached, and so I agree with the current policies of the Federal Reserve as it seeks to contain income growth within the bounds of the workforce and productive capacities.

14   How and Why We Chose the United States

Serena and I spent some really fruitful years in the United States. But until the Second World War ended, we did not face the question as to whether we would definitely settle there, for we continued to think we should sooner or later return to Italy. Both of us were immediately impressed by the efficiency of American life, whose rhythm delighted us when compared with that of Italy: a good breakfast, a quick, light meal at midday, taken near one's place of work, no postprandial siesta. Back to work at once, with one's head clear till five o'clock, then home, with supper at six or seven. That gives you time to spend with your children before their early bedtime, around eight when they are little. Afterward, there is time to read, talk, go to the cinema or the theater, or do a bit more work.

We were also impressed by how warmly we were accepted—even though after Pearl Harbor we were technically "enemies." I was invited to register for the draft for the U.S. Army, to which I of course had no objection, for America's war was also mine. However, I ended up not doing military service, thanks to the generosity of the U.S. Army's recruiting system. For one of its essential principles was to try to exclude the fathers of small children, provided the children had been conceived before the start of the war, and my son Andrea exactly fulfilled this requirement, having been born in 1940. Just as I was due to leave, the draft commission informed me that they had managed to recruit others who were not fathers, and so I was exempted.

Not long after, I was offered the chance to return to the New School. There I had two functions: One was as a researcher at the Institute of World Affairs, which had just been set up by the New School; the other as a teacher of economics, in particular of econometrics, at the school itself. My research project at the institute was to construct, together with Hans Neisser, an econometric model on a vast (for those times) scale of the world economy that would evidence the relations between the various countries. I took part first as a researcher, then as codirector until 1948. It should be borne in mind that the most powerful instrument available at that time was an electric calculating machine, and the project was pretty ambitious. But in the end we succeeded in devising a structure that was subsequently used as a guide and source of ideas for other similar projects. The model was published in 1953 and thereafter was frequently imitated. In it, for the first time, the world economy was seen as the result of the interaction between the behaviors of individual economies, which, through international trade, were deeply influenced by the trend of the international economy. The overall philosophy of the model was that of a simultaneous system. It was the first example of a model in which the behavior functions of the individual variables and individual countries were formalized with econometric methods. To be sure, the methods of estimate were a little naive, not at all sophisticated. Since it was a closed system of simultaneous equations, the estimates should have been performed with appropriate methods, but the latter, alas, had not yet been invented, nor would be for some years to come. The decisive contribution in this direction came from the Cowles Commission, thanks also to the tireless work of my teacher Jacob Marschak.

At that time, Serena and I took scant interest in American domestic politics. We were of course great admirers of Franklin Delano Roosevelt and his wife, Eleanor, but otherwise we took little notice because until 1946 we expected to return to Italy. We rejoiced in every success of the partisans in Italy as the news came in, and we shared in the sense of political renewal that came immediately after April 25, 1945. Disappointment set in with the fall of the government headed by Ferruccio Parri—sarcastically and unjustly called "Fessuccio Parmi" (in a play on words that translates as "stupid, it seems to me"), but above all with the great success scored by the "Common Man" movement (the Italian equivalent of "Know Nothings" founded on indifference and mistrust toward politics). The resurgence of Fascist "qualunquismo" disturbed us greatly, and we began to have second thoughts. After all, we had already been living for a while in the United States of America and we liked it. In 1946 our second son, Sergio, was to be born, so we were about to be the parents of two American children. The news coming from Italy told of a swift return to old practices, the bad habits of the past. The situation in the universities had in no way improved: There were few vacancies, and these were carved up as usual by the typical "big shots." We therefore decided to stay put and request American nationality, which was duly granted in 1946. Serena was in her ninth month of pregnancy when, on August 28, she entered the courtroom to receive citizenship, and her "impressive" size caused havoc among the ushers, who followed her everywhere with a chair, saying: "If it's born now, we shall end up on the front page of tomorrow's *Times!*" Sergio was born on September 1, 1946.

15   *How the National Saving Rate Is Determined: The First Skirmish*

It was in 1946 that I began to take a serious interest in saving, a subject I have continued to reflect on ever since. My studies had started because it was held that national saving underpins the availability of capital, which, in turn, contributes to increasing the productivity of the system. And hence, saving (thrift) was regarded with approval as a cardinal virtue. There was then a very widespread conviction that for families the amount of saved income grows with income, so for a nation it grows with the increase of *per capita* income. In addition, there was a general fear, inspired by certain passages of the *General Theory*, that people might save too much; if this occurred, it was said, a serious depression might ensue. For saving entails the reduction of a component of aggregate demand, consumption, without necessarily leading to an expansion of investments that will compensate for the fall in consumption. This might therefore bring about an inadequate level of demand, and hence a level of production and employment lower than the productive capacities of the economic system.

Now, I had never really been convinced by the idea that the amount of savng would rise with income. I thought it was merely one of the fashions of the moment, and I set to work on the problem, pursuing the idea that the amount of saving might have variations, but not a rising trend.

This last conception ran counter to two very widespread views. The first was the celebrated "fundamental psychological law" of Keynes, according to which an increase in income involves a variation of consumption, but smaller than that of income, and thus involves an increase in saving. The second theory entailed treating saving as one of the several goods on which income can be spent: considered as a luxury good for which the expenditure grows more rapidly than the income. The richer one is, the larger the amount of income spent to "purchase" wealth, as might be the case with jewels and antique furniture. According to this theory, it was well understood that the expenditure on saving may diminish to the point of becoming negative, which was what had happened at the blackest point of the Great Depression. The fundamental question, however, remained: Why save? What causes individuals to delay consumption?

The answer given by the theory then current was highly unsatisfactory: It was thought that an important motive that made saving a "luxury" article was the fact that it served to accumulate a "patrimony" for the rich, who intended to flood their heirs with inherited goods—a motive defined by Keynes himself as "pride." This explanation gave birth to another consequence, which was to be revealed as profoundly erroneous—namely, that the main source of the existing capital stock in a firm is the process of hereditary transmission of fortunes accumulated by the previous generation. This explanation satisfied me not a jot.

My idea from the late 1940s was a different one—that is, that the variable to observe was not absolute income but, rather, the ratio between current income and the normal income that a person could expect. Large (or small) savings are effected not by one who is rich (or poor) but by one who is transitorily rich (or poor). All unknown to me, a very similar hypothesis was being worked out at this time by James Duesenberry at Harvard[5]. As a matter of fact, both our studies where further developments of two pioneering research studies, one by Kuznets in 1946[6], the other by Brady and Friedman in 1947[7]. The latter, by analyzing the behavior of a sample of family units, were able to show that the consumption function (the ratio of consumption to income) shifted upward over time as average income rose, so that the amount saved depended not on absolute income but on the ratio of the family income to the year's average income. In a classic paper, Kuznets succeeded in reconstructing a picture of national accounts dating back to the mid-nineteenth century. On the basis of these data, he showed that the amount of income saved had had some fluctuations, but no growth, until 1930, and had subsequently fallen drastically during the Great Depression, despite the fact that *per capita* income had increased tenfold.

The model we arrived at, which was soon to become known as the Duesenberry-Modigliani hypothesis, sought to reconcile the cyclical variations in the saving rate with the surprising stability that emerged from the long-term data. Our function hypothesized that current consumption was determined not only by current income but also by the maximum point, the peak attained by current income in the past, which, in an economy with an upward trend, could be taken as an indication of the level toward which one tends to return.

With a steadily growing economy, in my view, this determined a continual upward shift of the consumption function, with a ratchet effect that, together with the increase in income, implied a constant saving/income ratio, despite the increased income. But if the income shrank, growing at a rate below the trend, the consumption function remained steady (because the maximum income remained constant) and therefore the consumption/income ratio rose and the saving/income ratio fell. Thus, the amount saved depended not on current income but on the difference between the latter and the previous maximum income, called "transitory income."

Our models were published in 1949 and made a strong impression, challenging for the first time the uncritically accepted opinion that the richer you are, the more you save. But the solution of Kuznets's enigma was, at bottom, altogether *ad hoc*, lacking analytic foundations. These were to be supplied later on by my *Life Cycle Hypothesis of Saving* (LCH).

16   *My Missed Engagement . . . with Harvard*

At about that time I received, as a bolt out of the blue, a formal invitation from Harvard. Since Harvard had then by far the best economics department in the country, I could hardly let the opportunity slip. So there I went, with a mixture of curiosity and expectation. A field day awaited me. First, I was received, as by prepared script, by the head of the economics department, whom I discovered on that occasion to be a well-known reactionary, backward-looking, anti-Semitic, and opposed to anything that had even a faintly European flavor. The faculty who appreciated my work had insisted he offer me a job. Unable to refuse, he greeted me by saying, "Look, Modigliani, if you have any common sense you won't accept this job we are offering you, because you know . . . we have people here of the caliber of James Duesenberry, Sidney Alexander, Richard Goodwin, and many others. . . . You'll never make it. Why don't you go back to the New School where you'll be a big fish in a little pond? Don't try being a big fish in this pond where there are plenty enough big fish already. . . ." I felt very flustered as I left the room. Such aggressiveness spurred me on to accept the challenge, but the offer they made me also implied a drop in salary— and why should I have to deal with such a boorish and antiquated department head and leave my pleasant colleagues at the New School? After a moment's thought, I returned to give him my reply. I said, "I think you're right," and refused the offer.

This took place early in the morning. Knowing that I was to have an

interview that day and curious about me, Joseph Schumpeter and Gott-
fried Haberler, whom at that time I knew only slightly, had invited me to
lunch. When I arrived, they immediately asked me how it had gone. I told
them everything and explained how I had refused. They reproved me, saying I had committed folly: "You shouldn't have listened to a person like
Professor Burbank. You should have accepted." But by then I had come to
think that if the Department of Economics at Harvard was headed by a type
like this, then Harvard wasn't good enough for me. So back I went to the
New School. And I have never regretted my decision.

17   *Reproach from Milton Friedman, or, When*
I Thought of an Alternative to Price Control

The following year, I was offered the fellowship in political economy at the
University of Chicago, which I accepted with pleasure. And here I must tell
of an episode that explains certain aspects of my relationship—never of
friendship, but of real professional respect—with Milton Friedman, with
whom I had some famous clashes during the polemic with the monetarists
in the 1960s and 1970s. It should be said that my article on liquidity preference had been interpreted in many academic quarters as a refutation of
Keynes in favor of the classicists. That was how Schumpeter, too, had seen
it. This fact had undoubtedly led Friedman to recommend me for the fellowship I received at Chicago. The grant was quite a prestigious one, not
to say generous—some $3,000 a year, a considerable salary in those days
and one sufficient to maintain a family like ours.

Economic journalism was just then keenly focused on the topics of price
and rent controls, which were still very fashionable in Britain and the
United States in the years immediately after the war but were theorized to
some extent everywhere as a device to prevent ruinous inflation, or to
avoid massive income redistribution from consumers to producers through
an increase in retail prices. But laissez-faire conservatives had for long
opposed this solution, on the grounds that it led to an inefficient utilization
of a scarce resource-living space-allowing useless waste to a lucky few, who
would occupy more space than they would have in a free market, while
others were compelled to occupy less space than they would have liked,
and so to live in overcrowded conditions or pay exorbitant rents "under
the counter." Also, bear in mind, for example, the position of a scrupulous
landlord who finds himself unable to offer lodging even to his own son or
his own parents. This situation also deterred the building of new houses,

indefinitely prolonging the shortage from which price control stemmed. Bad utilization of resources and waste are caused by the artificially low price, which conceals the true social value of the good that is lacking and fails to create an incentive to economize its use or to increase its provision. Now, this criticism is perfectly justified, as all Italians know from living their whole lives in a regime of rents frozen below the market price—known by the euphemism *equo canone* (fair rent)[8].

Shortly before going to Chicago I wrote a letter to the *New York Times*, partly inspired by a talk with a brilliant young French economist, Marcel Allais (forty years later, he was to receive the Nobel Prize), suggesting that, by using fiscal policy, it was possible to safeguard the principle invoked by each of the two camps: distributive equity and efficient allocation. This fascinating possibility can be illustrated with an example. Assume that in normal conditions the available quantity of a good is Q (per month) and the corresponding price is P (say $1). Now suppose that for some unforeseen and unpredictable reason the quantity reduces to q (for instance, owing to a disastrous harvest or the cessation of imports) and that, in the absence of countermeasures, the price rises from P to p (say $1.3), or 30 percent, making consumers poorer and producers richer. In order to prevent this, the government authorities establish a "fair" maximum price that producers may ask. The fair price might be the historic price P ($1). At price P there will be an unsatisfied demand, Q–q, on the hypothesis, adopted in our example, that the quantity available does not increase as the price rises, for at least a certain period of time. To prevent this situation from causing black market phenomena, favoritism, corruption, and riots, it becomes necessary to restrict the demand within Q through rationing. If, for instance, the rationing is rigorously fair, each of N citizens will be given one coupon per month, which confers the right to purchase one ration, Q/N, of the rationed good.

It would be highly desirable, as the exponents of laissez-faire preach, to eliminate this system as inefficient and unfair. But if we eliminate price control and rationing, the following system is generated: The price immediately surges to the equilibrium level, p. Consumers become poorer, as they are forced to spend pQ instead of PQ to obtain the same quantity Q, thus having (p–P)Q less to spend to purchase all other goods. At the same time, producers would increase their earnings and their spending capacity by the same amount, with a percentage increase in their earnings of 100 (p–P)/P (30 percent) and, by an even greater amount, in their profits. This is the unfair and capricious effect that the exponents of rationing complain of.

My proposal aimed to resolve the dilemma. It entailed: (a) eliminating the price control and rationing; (b) that at the same time the government should compel producers to pay a specific tax of p–P per unit of output, or 30 cents–or, equivalently, an ad valorem tax of (p–P/p) x 100, or 23 percent; the income from this tax will clearly be (p–P)Q; and (c) that the yield from this tax should be used to pay each consumer an "indemnity" for the increase of prices equal to (p–P) x Q/N (per month), which represents precisely the increase of the cost of the rationing (Q/N) due to the price increase. (Note that the total cost of this indemnity exactly coincides with the tax yield.)

What are the effects of this alternative approach? The key point is the prediction, based on a study of the economy, that producers will not be able to transfer the proposed tax to consumers. The reason is simple: To transfer the tax, they would have to increase the price. But since at price p the market absorbs the available quantity Q, if they raised the price the quantity sold would fall below Q—that is, there would be an excess of supply. This would drive the price back to p. In other words, p is the only market equilibrium price, given that the supply is Q, whatever the tax imposed (within certain limits), and the whole tax is inevitably absorbed by the producers.

The results are: (a) the producers' income net of the tax returns to PQ, exactly as if the price control had continued; (b) no consumer can be harmed by the plan, since each one remains able, if so desiring, to consume a quantity equal to the old ration, Q/N, and to have the same purchasing power for all other goods; this is because the ration now costs (p–P) x Q/N more, but this is precisely the additional income the consumer receives through the indemnity. On the whole, however, consumers will be better off because they will have the possibility, according to their income and preferences, to consumer more or less Q/N. The "fanatics" for Q will consume more, increasing their expenditure by more than their subsidy, and thus renouncing a share of other goods in favor of those who are induced by the high price of Q to consume less than their ration.

In conclusion, the plan frees price to perform its function of inducing consumers to economize voluntarily on the scarce good as much as is necessary to limit the demand to Q, as the school of laissez-faire recommends, but at the same time it prevents the abolition of the price control from causing a large income redistribution between consumers and producers. I must confess that although my plan was much appreciated by economists, it was never put into practice. Only during the first stage of the 1973 oil shock was there a moment when the U.S. administration took it seriously into consideration. But that was all.

No sooner had I arrived at Chicago than I received an invitation to meet

Milton Friedman. I found him indignant: "Your suggestion in the *New York Times* is immoral, shame on you! It's a trick to make fun of the rules of the market. The rules of price formation must be allowed to work freely without any manipulation." As I have often had occasion to say since then, the attitude of laissez-faire conservatives, including the monetarists, stems essentially from a political, perhaps ideological, conviction: The monetarists do not wish to give government discretionary power because they think government is incapable of doing better than the "invisible hand," owing to its stupidity and its personal interests, while they have scant concern for the problems of income distribution. Thus, as later happened, they will argue that it is inopportune to entrust the central bank with any decision-making power, for it is sure to behave foolishly or in line with its own interests.

18   *The University of Illinois*

A few months after my arrival at Chicago I was contacted by Howard Bowen, who had just been appointed dean of the College of Commerce of the University of Illinois. Bowen asked me to come and work at his university on a project titled "Economic Expectations and Fluctuations." The conditions offered were excellent, and the university was prestigious, full of brilliant young economists. I accepted. At the University of Illinois my career went much faster than it could have done at Harvard, for I became full professor at the age of thirty-two. Moreover, I had the opportunity to move away from the East Coast and get to know the Midwest—which was most important for an American born in Europe, for the Midwest is big country and very different.

The "Economic Expectations and Fluctuations" project aimed at explaining the role of expectations in the formulation of economic programs in order to answer the question: Can expectations per se be a source of instability for an economy? In the course of the project I developed some basic ideas that were to play a decisive part in my subsequent studies. The first was the idea that planning a firm's production process is largely connected with the convenience of reducing fluctuations in production, as against seasonal sales fluctuations. If production proceeds at a constant pace, costs, especially labor costs, are smaller than when there are wide fluctuations. If workers are hired, only later to be dismissed, or if they are kept idle at first and thereafter made to work overtime, costs are greater than if a steady production rhythm is the rule, but then production does not depend on the sales of the period. Rather it depends on expectations for the entire seasonal production cycle.

Second, I realized that this approach to corporate production planning has interesting implications for the nature of the forecasts needed for decision making. The conclusion that emerged was that, when sales have a seasonal trend, barring rare exceptions, the only information useful for production-planning purposes is the information that runs up to the next seasonal peak, whereas within certain limits what will happen after that can be ignored. After the seasonal peak sales will fall, but the amount is irrelevant, since the firm has to produce a sufficient quantity between now and the peak in order to surmount it. Thus was born the concept of irrelevant expectations—that is, expectations that have no importance for current behavior.

The third idea I developed in my research stemmed from my study of economic forecasts: The inability to take account of seasonal factors may lead to serious errors in forecasting. Nonetheless, many entrepreneurs, like the press, seem not fully to understand seasonal adjustments and fall back on the quite inadequate reliance on the variation during the same quarter of the previous year. Only recently has the Italian press begun to make use of nonseasonal monthly variations.

While I was still at the University of Illinois, I was invited to become a member of the Cowles Commission, an organization then based in Chicago and connected with the Econometric Society. In this way I was enabled to link up once more with Jacob Marschak and Tjalling Koopmans, and to come into contact with another group of important economists, including Kenneth Arrow and Carl Christ, and statisticians like Herman Chernoff, Howard Raiffa, and Herbert Simon, who was to play a very important part in my life.

19   Richard Brumberg—Enlightenment Between Minneapolis and Urbana

My fundamental experience at the University of Illinois was the friendship (and academic collaboration) I embarked on with a brilliant and pleasant young man, Richard Brumberg, a first-year graduate student, who soon became a good friend of the whole family. At the start of our acquaintance, he attracted us with a gesture as delightful as it was unexpected. Serena had gone to Florida to see her parents, so I had the task of preparing supper for our family. Dick invited himself, saying he would see to it, and arrived with a brace of wonderful lobsters sent by his parents, who also lived in Florida.

At that time, Kenneth Kurihara had asked me to write an article on saving for a book to be titled *Post-Keynesian Economics*. Ever since publishing my article on the Modigliani-Duesenberry hypothesis, I had neglected the problem, and now I had no clear idea of what I could write. Impressed by Brumberg's intelligence and imagination, I had the lucky inspiration to invite him to collaborate with me on the article. Immediately after we agreed on this, I was invited, quite by chance, to take part in a conference on saving organized by the University of Minnesota, and I asked Dick to go with me. The conference turned out to be deadly dull. Speaker after speaker repeated ad nauseam the idea that saving increases with income, that the richer you are the more you save, and that this holds good not only for individuals but also for firms.

I had never swallowed the theory that saving was the privilege of the rich and that the poor were destined to consume more than their income. Dick and I found these ideas hard to credit. On the car trip back from Minnesota we talked at length, trying to pinpoint just where our colleagues went wrong. By dint of talking we were rewarded with a ray of light: Far from acquiring wealth as an end in itself, the role of saving was to accumulate resources to spend later on, to put them aside during periods of fat cows in order to transfer and consume them during periods of lean cows, with the aim of maintaining a stable average consumption over the course of one's life: periods of fat cows, like the middle part of a person's life; periods of lean cows, like the years following retirement when earning capacity is greatly diminished. In order to understand saving, much more attention must be paid to a subject almost ignored—namely, the life cycle of income and saving, in particular during the period of retirement, and the fundamental role of negative saving.

During our trip we tried to establish the micro- and macroeconomic implications of this formulation, according to which the fundamental accumulation function was that of financing future consumption in excess of income; that is to say, the aim of saving today is to be able to afford, at a future time, to spend more than one's income. To that end, we began by hypothesizing a temporal profile of income and consumption, stylized and as simple as possible. We assumed that the "representative" individual lived L years, and in the first N years worked earning a constant income, Y per year; that in the remaining M years he ceased to work, earning O, and that throughout his life he opted to consume at a constant rate C, equal to the mean income in the course of his life, that

Fig. 6   *Income, Consumption, Saving, and Wealth as function of age.*

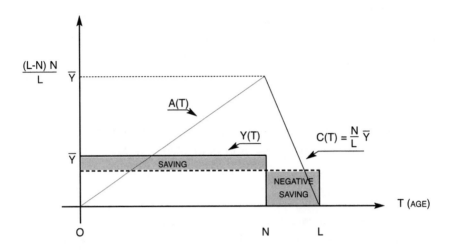

is, NY/L. Consequently, this individual saves Y–C = (M/L)Y in each year of his active life, and thus accumulates capital that reaches its peak at the end of the nth year. From then on, saving becomes negative, or an amount equal to consumption in all the other periods, or (N/L)Y, and his wealth gradually diminishes until it returns to zero, which is the initial wealth (by hypothesis). Therefore, during his life accumulated saving is equal to zero, and consumption is equal to income. All this is shown graphically in Figure 6, which was published for the first time in an article in 1966[9] and has since become the "trademark" of the LCH model.

Back home, we shut ourselves up in the university to formulate the simulations of the model, and two days' frenzied work left us amazed and fascinated. Despite the extreme simplification of the model, we realized, without any shadow of a doubt, that our new paradigm for the first time made it possible to explain, on the basis of the "classic" hypothesis of rational behavior, a set of phenomena that until then had not been accounted for (or had found merely *ad hoc* explanations), and also enabled us to predict other important regularities that were not observed till years later.

To account for our euphoria, I have decided to reproduce two tables that appear in one of the two fundamental articles on LCH, "Utility Analysis and Aggregate Consumption Functions"[10], which report the main simulations of those two days of feverish and "glorious" toil. The model was much later to be dubbed "overlapping generation."

Table 1
Saving in a Stationary Economy with Stable and Falling Prices*

Generation of decade		Stationary economy			Growing economy		
		Constant prices	Prices fall 50% in decade T		Constant Prices	Prices fall 50% in decade T	
		Decade T	Decade T	Decade T+1	Decade T	Decade T	Decade T+1
		(1)	(2)	(3)	(4)	(5)	(6)
	Income	0	0		0	0	
	Consumption	16	32		97 2/3	195 1/3	
T–4	Saving	- 16	- 32		- 97 2/3	- 195 1/3	
	Initial Assets	16	32		97 2/3	195 1/3	
	Income	20	20	0	320	320	0
	Consumption	16	22	22	195 1/3	230 2/3	230 2/3
T–3	Saving	4	- 2	- 22	124 2/3	89 1/3	- 230 2/3
	Initial Assets	12	24	22	70 2/3	141 1/3	230 2/3
	Income	20	20	20	320	320	640
	Consumption	16	18 2/3	18 2/3	230 2/3	248	408
T–2	Saving	4	1 1/3	1 1/3	89 1/3	72	232
	Initial Assets	8	16	17 1/3	52	104	176
	Income	20	20	20	320	320	640
	Consumption	16	17	17	248	256	469 1/3
T–1	Saving	4	3	3	72	64	170 2/3
	Initial Assets	8	8	11	32	64	128
	Income	20	20	20	320	320	640
	Consumption	16	16	16	256	256	496
T	Saving	4	4	4	64	64	144
	Initial Assets	4	0	4	0	0	64
	Income	20		20			640
	Consumption	16		16			512
T+1	Saving	4		4			128
	Initial Assets	0		0			0
	Income (per decade)	80	80	80	1280	1280	2560
Aggregate	Consumption (per decade)	80	105 2/3	89 2/3	1027 2/3	1185	2116
	Saving (per decade)	0	- 25 2/3	- 9 2/3	252 1/3	94	444
	Initial Assets	40	80	54 1/3	252 1/3	504 2/3	598 2/3
	Saving ratio	0	- .321	- .121	.197	.073	.173

* All variables are measured in terms of their purchasing power at prices of the year $T-1$.

Table 1 is a picture taken in period T of an economy in which five generations of adults coexist. This is a "stationary" economy, in the sense that each
generation has received in its past, and expects to receive in its future, the
same income during the working stage (in the table, 20 units per decade, or
2 per year). The youngest generation, ages twenty to thirty, entered the
workforce in the period T, and is therefore referred to as the T decade generation. Its essential characteristics are described in the four lines of column 1;
the first line shows its total income in decade T (20), the second its consump-

tion, the third its saving, and the fourth its wealth at the start of the decade.

Since in this stylized simulation we assume that no legacies are left or inherited, initial wealth is zero. Hence, the total income of this generation during its life will be 4 x 20 = 80, and the consumption per decade, as in Table 1, is 80/5, or 16 (line 2); thus, saving is 4 (line 3). The four immediately preceding lines describe the behavior of the generation that began working in the decade T–1 and that in decade T is aged thirty to forty years. Plainly, in the stationary economy income, consumption and saving are identical to those of generation T. But their initial wealth is equal to the saving of the first decade, or 4. Note that the consumption can also be calculated by summing the income expected during the remaining life (60) and the initial wealth (4) and dividing the result by the number of decades remaining in that life, that is, 4(64/4 = 16).

The same story repeats itself, *mutatis mutandis*, for generations T–2 and T –3. But it changes for generation T–4, which, having reached age sixty, is presumed to retire. Here income is zero, but consumption is equal to the patrimony accumulated up until that moment, 16, which enables the same rate of consumption to be maintained as during the working period. As in Table 1, this consumption reduces capital from the peak of 16 to zero.

But the point we found "exciting" in the table was the figures in the last five lines, which report the flow of income, consumption, and national saving in period T, obtained by summing the value of these variables for each of the five generations. Aggregate consumption is equal to income, and therefore national saving is nil! Clearly this result would remain unaltered if each person's income and thus the national income were, say, ten times greater (or smaller): Both income and consumption would increase in proportion, leaving saving at zero. The moral: In a stationary economy the rate of national saving is zero, regardless of *per capita* income.

How, then, to explain the positive saving of so many countries and the very great differences in the share of income saved between one country and another? (Note that these differences were unknown at the start of the 1950s, for only a very few countries had national accounting, and only became clear some ten years later.) A good part of the answer is suggested in Table 2, evidencing the role of economic growth and its variability from country to country. Table 2, indeed, presents the result of our simulation of the effect of economic growth, assuming that the income of a working person is the same for all the generations present, but also that this income—and hence the national income—doubles each decade. This implies a growth rate of the national income of 7 percent per year, which is far higher than any achieved by the industrialized countries after the war, but which helps to illuminate the mechanism activated by income growth.

Table 2
Saving in a Growing Economy

Generation of Decade		T	T-1	T-2	T-3	T-4	T-5	T-6
					Behavior in calendar decade			
T	1) Remaining decades of life	5	4	3	2	1		
	2) Income, y	20	40	80	160	0		
	3) Total expected income	60	80	80	0	0		
	4) Initial assets, a	0	4	13	35 1/3	97		
	5) Total resources				195 1/3	97		
	(2) + (3) + (4)	80	124	173				
	6) Consumption, c	16	31	57 2/3	97 2/3	97		
	7) Saving, s	4	9	22 1/3	62 1/3	-97		
	8) End assets	4	13	35 1/3	97 2/3	0		
T + 1	2) Income		40	80	160	320	0	
	6) Consumption		32	62	115	195	195	
	7) Saving		8	18	44	124	-195	
	4) Assets		0	8	26	70	195	
T + 2	2) Income			80	160	320	640	39
	6) Consumption			64	124	230	390	39
	7) Saving			16	36	89	249	-39
	4) Assets			0	16	52	141	39
T + 3	2) Income				160	320	640	128
	6) Consumption				128	248	461	78
	7) Saving				32	72	178	49
	4) Assets				0	32	104	28
T + 4	2) Income					320	640	128
	6) Consumption					256	496	92
	7) Saving					64	144	35
	4) Assets					0	64	20
T + 5	2) Income						640	128
	6) Consumption						512	992
	7) Saving						128	288
	4) Assets						0	128
T + 6	2) Income							1280
	6) Consumption							1024
	7) Saving							256
	4) Assets							0
A g g r e g a t e	Income					1280	2560	5120
	Consumption					1027	2055	4110
	Saving					252	504	1009
	Initial Assets					252	504	1009
	Saving ration					.197	.197	.197
	Asset/Yearly income ratio					1.97	1.97	1.97

The first eight lines of the table present the time profile of the relevant variables for the generation of year T. In the first column, which refers to the year when generation T entered, the values are the same as those of the stationary economy of Table 1. But in the next generation, T + 1, income doubles, going to 40 units per decade, an income received by anybody working in that decade, regardless of age. Making the simplest hypothesis that the income expected in the remainder of active life corresponds to that currently earned, we see that the total of available resources during the remainder of life is 3 + 40 + 4, which, divided by the number of decades remaining, or 4 (line 1), gives a consumption of 31 (line 6). But consumption (line 7) is higher than in the first decade, because the consumption planned for the retirement period has increased more than the available resources. In the next columns we follow the course of generation T until decade T + 4, when that generation retires, before disappearing in the decade following.

In the second block of four lines we follow the generation of the decade T + 1 through its life, beginning at decade T + 1, until decade T + 5. Likewise, in the subsequent blocks we similarly observe the life of the subsequent generations.

If now we look at column T + 4, we find a picture of a dynamic economy in which five generations coexist—from the oldest, aged sixty to seventy years, which entered the workforce in year T and whose economic status is described in the first seven lines, down to the youngest, which has just started work and is described in the last four lines. If we sum the value of each variable for all five generations, we obtain its value for the whole economy. These aggregate figures are reported at the foot of the table.

The fundamental result is that now national income is well above consumption, and there is consequently plenty of saving, which in this example amounts to nearly 20 percent of national income! Although each member of this economy consumes all its income in the course of life and leaves no legacy, just as in the stationary economy of Table 1, the growth has the effect of generating aggregate saving.

And it is easy to check that the amount saved rises with the rate of growth; for example, with a more "realistic" growth rate, say around 3 percent, the saving rate would be around 12 percent. It is obvious, moreover, that if the income of each generation at any point in time, and hence the national income in decade T + 4, were ten times greater, consumption would also be ten times greater and therefore the amount saved would remain unaltered. Therefore, our "rational" model explained:

1. Why, unlike what was believed by all those at the Minneapolis conference, in a steadily growing economy the amount saved did not

depend on the *per capita* income, as had already been empirically established in my work and that of Duesenberry; and

2. Why that amount, on the contrary, varied with the growth rate of the income, with zero value at zero growth—a really astonishing conclusion, which was not to be proved valid until years later.

The model helped to clarify what the empirical evidence had highlighted, in contrast to another dogma of that time, that is, that only the rich saved, while the poor consumed more than they earned; we suggested, on the contrary, that within certain limits consumption was a stable portion of lifetime (or permanent) income. This was the very basis of our model: During his working years the individual saved, but the amount saved depended mainly on the ratio of working years to retirement years, and there was no reason to think that this ratio varied systematically with life-time income.

In a burst of enthusiasm Brumberg and I agreed to develop our insight in two articles on what was soon to be known as the LCH. According to Kenneth Kurihara, the first examined individual behavior[11], the second aggregate behavior[12].

But before we were able to complete the task, both Dick and I had to leave the University of Illinois owing to a famous episode remembered in American academic history as "Bowen's War" (of which I shall tell here-after), which devastated the ranks of teachers. Richard decided to go to Johns Hopkins at Baltimore, an excellent university (where Kuznets, Machlup, Domar, and Christ were then teaching), while I chose the Carnegie Institute of Technology at Pittsburgh.

So, from summer 1952 onward, we continued our studies mostly sepa-rately, but in a coordinated way, completing the first article, then develop-ing the second, which was much more complex; we often had recourse to the mail (in those primitive times there was neither fax nor e-mail!) and sometimes we worked during Dick's visits to Pittsburgh, where he was always a very welcome guest. The article was finished in mid-1953, at the same time that Dick completed his doctoral thesis based on some tests on the LCH; after which he went to Cambridge, England, and I never saw him again. For Richard, that so intelligent, so brilliant, so promising young man, so joyful and lively, died very young—of a cerebral embolism, I think. The last souvenir I have of him is a photo sent from Venice, standing sur-rounded by pigeons in St. Mark's Square. It arrived with the legend "Visitor in Venice." From birth, Blumberg had had serious circulation problems, having been born a blue baby. I recall that his fingers were often violet colored. Nowadays, he would have been saved by a heart operation, but it was beyond the medicine of that time.

His sudden death came as a terrible blow to me, and afterward I lost all interest in revising the manuscript of our second article, titled "Utility Analysis and Aggregate Consumption Functions: An Attempt at Integration" for eventual publication. I feared, among other things, that it was too long. So the text circulated only within a small group of experts, though I frequently referred to it in subsequent writings that illustrated its content. The fundamental message therefore became fairly well known, but it was not till twenty-five years later, in 1979, when I gathered part of my writings into a first collection of three volumes (with the help of a brilliant student of mine, Andrew Abel), that I decided to include that manuscript, just as it had been left at Richard's death.

20   Senator McCarthy, Bowen's War, and the Black Earth of Illinois

My experience at the University of Illinois ended in a fierce political clash. At the center of the storm was no less than Howard Bowen, that excellent economist and most able young dean hailing from the East Coast, who had been chosen by a decidedly liberal president yet found himself at the head of an extremely aged and conservative economics faculty. To start with, Bowen had summoned new, very capable teachers like Margaret Reid and Dorothy Brady, who had produced fundamental studies on the dynamic of saving, and Leonid Hurwicz, who refereed my article on liquidity preference.

I have always thought that in the United States a liberal is a conservative with a heart and a conservative is a liberal without one. The differences of content are less accentuated than in Europe. Yet in that episode this conviction of mine was severely put to the test. Life soon became very difficult for Bowen because of the elderly faculty members, persons with no profound economic culture, ignorant of mathematics, tied to pre-Keynesian views, but born and bred in the "black earth" of Illinois, rough, backward-looking midwesterners. They felt Bowen had hired too many Europeans, too many people from the East and from California, too many liberals, too many people who did not come from the legendary black earth of Illinois.

At that time Senator McCarthy was at his zenith and the tide of McCarthyism seemed unstoppable. In every European, every intellectual from the East, every liberal, they smelled a "communist." Thus, political cleansing was set in motion in every body, every institution of a public nature. Illinois was a state university, and its board of trustees was therefore elected by the entire population. The McCarthyites wished to dismiss Bowen, together with all those he had hired in the faculty of economics. In actual fact, the witch-hunt for communists provided a comfortable screen behind which vested academic and personal interests were at work. These up-to-date, well-prepared young economists from the East, from the West Coast, from Europe, had to be eliminated, above all because they were a nuiance to the old guard, who felt themselves overpowered, inferior, since they knew neither macroeconomics nor mathematics; and the students were deserting the classes of the older teachers and crowding into those of their younger colleagues.

The old guard arranged a clash that remained famous throughout the American academic world. The "battering ram" of the McCarthyites was a member of the board of trustees, Red Grange, universally known by the nickname "the Galloping Ghost," renowned mainly as a football player and for his ferocity on the field. The Galloping Ghost it was, then, who led the fight against Bowen, who defended himself like a lion before the board of trustees. Unfortunately, elections were being held just then, also involving the members of the boards of the state universities, and the MacCarthyite right won. The new members of the board of trustees managed to discredit Bowen and force him to resign.

The new faculty Bowen had set up dispersed, to a man. I was practically the only one who stayed on, and then only for a year, because I was supposed to complete my research on expectations. I knew that sooner or later the McCarthyites would turn their attack on me, the last remaining survivor of Bowen's group. And I was duly called to account by the new dean. Bowen had been replaced by a person of little consequence whose dearest wish, however, as official representative of the McCarthyites, was to get rid of me, as I had said my say without mincing matters. In the meantime, though, I had already been appointed full professor and had therefore been granted tenure, which meant I could not be dismissed for political or ideological reasons. I was thus fairly easy in the knowledge that they couldn't fire me on the spot. There were only two ways for the dean to send me packing: either by showing there was no course I could teach at that university, or by proving me academically incompetent.

Done as soon as said. One day I was summoned by the dean, who greeted me with the following speech: "Dear Modigliani, in the past you taught two subjects. One was macroeconomics, but you are evidently quite incompetent in that subject. There are plenty of old professors here who can teach it better than you. The other subject you have taught is mathematical economics, and I have to admit you are competent in that subject. But, you know, I'm afraid this subject, for which I personally have great admiration, can no longer be taught because it doesn't agree with the trustees. . . ." This political threat, indirect as it was, reminded me of Fascist times, but I knew perfectly well that its real intention was simply to induce me to resign on my own account, for, legally, the dean could not send me away so easily, despite all his made-up excuses. He wound up with, "You may complete your research, but I can't guarantee you a job in a year's time. . . ."

The confrontation between Bowen and the McCarthyites was followed with the greatest interest in other American universities, being viewed as an example of political interference in the university system. And it was to remembered for a long time to come. Those taking part were dubbed "the veterans of 'Bowen's War.'"

Nonetheless, we retain many happy memories of the time we spent at Illinois. Among other things, we made friends with a neighbor, Soulima, who was the son of Igor Stravinsky and who taught piano at the university. He, too, experienced that grim, mean atmosphere. For when Soulima happened to have need of two grand pianos, Red Grange opposed the purchase. McCarthy's men had the habit of poking their noses into the university's investments, allowing no freedom of action, as they saw themselves as representing the electors, the taxpayers. Soulima's son, Jonathan, soon became bosom buddies with our second son, Sergio. And with Sergio we had occasion to reflect on a mistake we had made. For we had decided to give our sons names that sounded good with "Modigliani." It took us two years to realize that Andrea in English is a female name—which forced our son to use the French "André" as a nom de plume. As for "Sergio," it sounds very odd in American. Stravinsky's grandson once knocked on the door and said, "I'd like to play with Sir John." I remember that, shortly after, Sergio went to the Stravinskys to play with Jonathan, but returned in disgust, saying: "There's only an old fellow there!" When we explained to him that that old fellow was the famous grandfather Igor on a visit, Sergio wasn't a bit impressed.

At that time I was looking around and had already had offers from various universities. I was lucky to choose the Carnegie Institute of Technology, now Carnegie Mellon, where I spent eight very valuable, very creative years from 1952 to 1960. All the works cited in justification of my Nobel Prize were conceived or completed during that period.

When I left Illinois, the local newspaper carried this headline in big letters: MODIGLIANI LEAVES WITH A BLAST, "NOW THERE WILL BE PEACE IN THE DEPARTMENT OF ECONOMICS: THE PEACE OF DEATH!" Not until forty years later did the

University of Illinois decide to show its regret for that dismal event by awarding me an honorary degree. So we lost the battle, but in the end we won the war!

21 The Epic of the Life Cycle Hypothesis of Saving *(LCH)*

ANALYTICAL FOUNDATIONS. As I have already said, the LCH model starts out from the classical theory of the "consumer's choice," except that in the past this model was applied to the choice of a basket of goods to consume, in a given period of time, within the limits of the family income. The choice aimed at maximizing the consumer's utility. We applied it, however, to the choice of how much to consume in each period of life, within the limits set by the total resources available over a person's entire lifespan. This approach had some precedents, found mainly in the work of Irving Fisher[13] and Umberto Ricci[14], but nobody had used it to study the micro- and macroeconomic implications developed in what follows. Many of these surprising implications of the LCH stem from combining this rational formulation with the reasonable hypothesis that,

1. on average, consumers prefer to consume available resources at a fundamentally stable rate, and

2. the preferred distribution of consumption by age does not depend systematically on the amount of lifelong resources.

I soon became aware that in this hypothesis the role of saving was similar to the role of inventories that I had studied in my research on expectations. Inventories had the function of stabilizing production by insulating it against seasonal sales variations; saving had the function of enabling the consumer to maintain a fairly constant rate of consumption in the face of variations of income.

This formulation had implications that were radically different from the model dominant at the time, in that the amount of consumption chosen in each particular period (*age*) of life depended, in the final analysis, on the total resources available during the entire lifespan (*life resources*). By contrast, in the conventional view and in empirical studies, consumption (and saving) in any period was assumed to depend on the income of that period.

Now, since current saving is the difference between income and current consumption, and consumption depends on lifetime income, it follows that the amount of current income saved will be greater the greater the percentage difference between current income and lifetime income. This difference has been called (by Friedman) "transitory income." This gives rise to one of the revolutionary implications of LCH for individual behavior: In the short term the share of income saved does not depend on lifetime income (that is, on whether one is rich or poor, in the traditional sense). It depends instead on being temporarily rich or poor—that is, on having received in the current period an income transitorily greater or smaller than the average one expected in the remainder of life.

THE LCH AND THE PERMANENT INCOME (PI) OF FRIEDMAN.

This conclusion was arrived at independently, and at more or less the same time, by Milton Friedman in the book that did so much to make him famous: *A Theory of the Consumption Function*, published soon after our article in the volume edited by Kurihara. But there was a difference in the starting point between our LCH and the so-called *Permanent Income Hypothesis* (PI) of Friedman, which was to prove crucial as regards their macroeconomic implications. Friedman's formulation relies on the "simplifying" assumption that the life of the representative individual had an infinite duration, that in each year of his life he expected to receive a constant income—the so-called permanent income—except for a transitory component, and that he intended to consume his resources at a stable rate that was not systematically linked with his permanent income. Since Friedman's PI can be considered as perfectly equivalent to the lifetime income of the LCH (expressed as an annual average), it is clear that in the short term the relationship between consumption, current income, and permanent income is substantially the same. This relationship is amply discussed in Friedman, and its results fully apply to the LCH.

The most original implication common to the two models concerns the relationship among current saving, permanent—or lifetime—income, and current income. A fundamental implication of both models is the hypothesis that the share of permanent income consumed—and therefore the proportion saved—is independent of the size of permanent income: Families with a high level of permanent or lifetime income save, on average, a fraction of this income similar to that saved by permanently poor families (a fraction that is zero in the basic LCH model). Now it is well known, and confirmed by several empirical studies, that when families are classified according to their current income, the share of current income saved is found to increase systematically with income, going from negative values for the lower incomes to very positive values for the higher ones. But this empirical evidence proves not to contradict the hypothesis of the two models, however paradoxical that may seem.

8

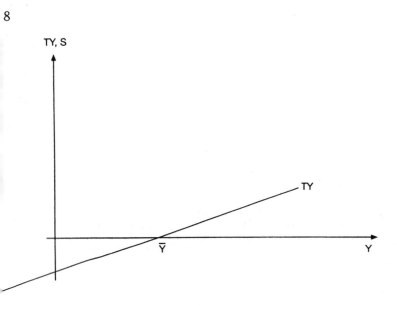

income, Y, and thus has a positive intercept on the vertical axis. It
; that TY-TY has, in contrast, a large negative intercept and increases
atically with current income, zeroing out around the mean income
en rising to another positive high value for the other incomes. But
n being arbitrarily imposed, these characteristics of the graph are, in
   inherent in the nature of the relationships, precisely because, as
en, the mean transitory income must grow with current income.
v, in the basic model where current consumption always coincides
ermanent income, current saving is S = Y-C = Y-PI = YT, that is, *sav-
1cides with transitory income*. Therefore, the curve TY-TY in Figure 8
presents the relationship between saving and current income, and
ɔe denoted S-S. It is this relation that is often indicated as the "fam-
ing" function. Therefore, even if lifelong saving is nil for all, rich or
he share of current income saved increases systematically with cur-
come. It goes from negative values for those currently poor who, on
e, have a notably smaller current income than the permanent one
gure 7) owing to mainly negative temporary shocks (see Figure 8),
kedly positive values for the totality of the currently rich households
ch temporarily rich households predominate.
   how can one prove that the positive relationship observed between
1t saved and current income is not really explained by the old para-
hat only the rich save? There are various ways of demonstrating this,
ɔed both by Friedman and in my sundry writings[15]. One interesting

Fig. 7

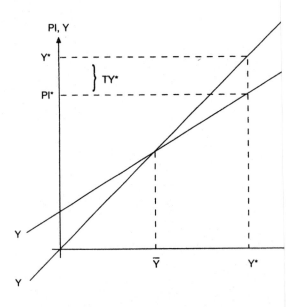

The reconciliation of the hypothesis with the above
relationship among the three concepts of income: pe
and current, the last being the sum of the first two.
must be a positive link between current income and t
tory income received, on average, by the members
The implications of this phenomenon are illustrated
current income, Y, is measured on the horizontal axis
income, PI, and current income are measured on tl
curve Y-P represents the relationship between peri
income, which is the key to the argument. For each
the figure, the height of the curve Y-P, PI* measures the
income of the families whose current income is aroun
on the contrary, is a straight line that goes through t
one; for each value of Y, the height of this curve is also
each value of Y the distance between the straight line
Y-P measures the mean amount of the transitory incor
income class. For example, those with a current incom
mean permanent income PI* and a mean transitory
TY* in the graph. Therefore, from Figure 7 we can de
between TY and Y, reported in Figure 8 as TY-TY (wher
the vertical axis), by subtracting the curve PY-PY from
In the graph, PY-PY has a lesser slope than Y-Y, w
value of Y around the current (and permanent, in a s

way, worthy of mention, is the following: First of all, it is easily understood that the slope of line S-Y, representing the ratio of saving to current income, will be greater in proportion as the variability of transitory income is greater, since this variable increases the correlation between current income and transitory income. Now, the transitory component of the income varies greatly from one job to another: For example, it is smaller for public employees than for self-employed workers or entrepreneurs; it is even greater for farmers, owing to wide accidental fluctuations in both harvest and prices.

The theories that link consumption to permanent income, therefore, predict that the slope of curve S-Y should be low for a sample of state employees, whose current income is close to their permanent one, and high for a sample of, say, farmers. This conclusion was verified with complete success. The fact that the curve was very steep for farmers had already been noted and interpreted, both in the sense that the rich save more than the poor, and in the sense that farming households save more than urban ones. Actually, the steep slope was interpreted, wrongly, as a high "marginal propensity" to save. It was thought, essentially, that farmers had a propensity to save a large amount of each increase of income, whereas that curve actually stemmed from a propensity to save a large share of transitory income, which for farmers is an important part of their income. Moreover, with the dangerous tendency sometimes shown by economists to do bad sociology, a "bucolic" interpretation was put forward—namely, that this difference was due to the virtue of the simple life versus the corrupting influence of the big city! In actual fact, the average saving of farmers as a group has often turned out to be lower than the average of those holding other jobs.

A further interesting implication of the two models—often verified in practice—is that if we compare two samples, A and B, such that sample A comes from a group on average notably richer than sample B, we shall find that the poorer sample apparently saves more than the richer one, in the sense that at any given level of income the saving of sample B will be greater than that of A. This is why, comparing the result of the survey of household balances performed in different years, we find that the share of income saved at a *given* income level dwindles in time, even though the proportion of the average income saved remains stable[16].

OTHER MICROECONOMIC IMPLICATIONS OF THE LCH: THE "HUMPS." While the consequences of the two models just illustrated are common to both, in many respects the models have profoundly different implications.

At the microeconomic level the LCH model implies behavior in saving and wealth as a function of age similar to the one shown in Figure 6, but

Fig. 9. *Income and consumption*

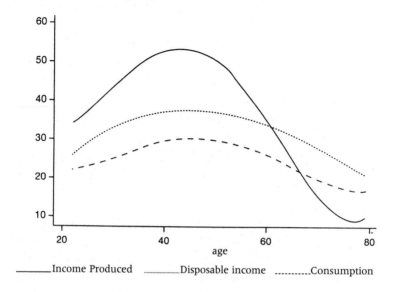

_____Income Produced   ....Disposable income   ....Consumption

with appropriate modifications. In Figure 6 it was assumed that income
was constant during the working stage and suddenly fell to around zero
in the retirement stage. The empirical evidence for many countries confirms this picture but suggests a more gradual trend, which is illustrated
for Italy by the dotted curve in Figure 9, based on a work being published
by Tullio Jappelli. It shows the trend of average income produced by age
of the household head and the effect of seniority at work on pay;
However, around retirement age the income profile of a representative
individual is fairly flat, owing to the different choice of retirement age.
This is illustrated in Figure 9, where three curves are shown: The relevant
curve at the moment is the most humped one one, which shows the trend
of average income produced (net of direct taxes) by age. For Italy—in
recent years—the apex is between ages fifty-five and sixty of the household head. Income subsequently falls rapidly but less steeply than in
Figure 6 because, in reality, exit from the labor market is often gradual.
Again in Figure 9, the dashed curve shows the trend of consumption,
which also is not altogether constant as in the stylized case represented in
Figure 6. Instead it shows a hump that mainly reflects the life cycle of the
numerical composition of the household, with the marriage, birth, and
then exit of the children from the family nucleus, and lastly widowhood
(see Figure 10). But the hump is much flatter than the income one, which
produces a strong hump in the saving profile by age, represented in Figure
11 by the dashed curve: The saving rate rises moderately up to middle age,

Fig. 10. *Life cycle of the number of family members.*

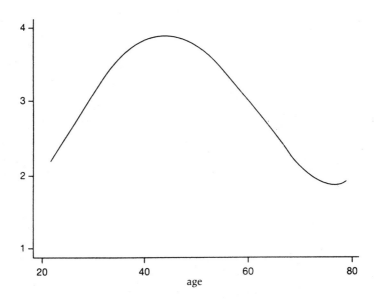

then falls rapidly, becoming negative after age sixty-five.

To understand the saving trend in Figure 11 it must be recalled that for some decades now, in the more advanced economies, an important part of saving in the accumulation stage takes the form of *contributions to pension funds.* By far the most important among these contributions, especially in Italy, are those paid directly to public funds administered by social security authorities. These contributions have two special, unique characteristics: The first is that the accumulation in these funds is compulsory (forced); the second, linked with the first, is that the premiums paid to social security (in the same way as many direct taxes) are materially paid by employers through deductions from the wage produced or earned, and thus do not appear on the pay check. After retirement, the accumulation from social security payments is used to pay pensions, which may be considered as a compulsory reduction of the reserves set aside in the first stage.

Plainly, this program of compulsory accumulation and decumulation, which exists in many countries, represents a mechanism intended to help households behave in the general way that, according to the LCH, they would rationally choose. However, social security, as it currently stands, is but a pallid imitation of the rational behavior of the LCH, precisely because it is compulsory and therefore subject to rigid rules.

In the LCH it is assumed that the family unit will choose when and how much to accumulate or decumulate, in order to stabilize the con-

Fig. 11. *Life cycle of saving*

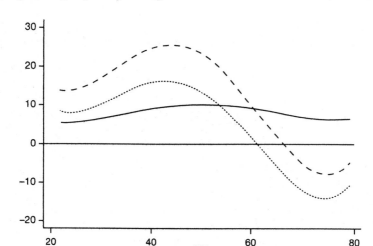

_____ Private saving ....Cumpulsory saving ....Total saving

sumption rate; with social security, instead, individuals are compelled to save a fixed share of their current income prescribed by law, with the risk of having to destabilize their consumption. In addition, that fixed share means that the decision about the distribution of consumption between active life and retirement is imposed by law (with the consent of the labor unions). This implication has very serious consequences for a country like Italy, where pensions may reach over 80 percent of working income, which, with a fairly low pensionable age and considerable longevity, requires an enormous level of contributions (nearly one half of a dependent employee's income compared with 12.5 percent in the United States), such as to leave scant possibilities for private saving to alter those decisions.

Note, *en passant*, that workers in Italy think that a large part of the pension contribution is paid by the employer, because the law says so. But, in reality, one should not confuse the person materially responsible for making the payment and the person who bears the cost—what economists call the problem of the incidence of taxes. In effect, whoever pays the pension contribution, it generally ends up as a burden on the employee (as it should).

These considerations find confirmation in Figure 11, where the dotted curve shows the trend of compulsory saving in Italy by age, according to our estimates. It has a strong hump and becomes negative around age

Fig. 12. *The life cycle of wealth*

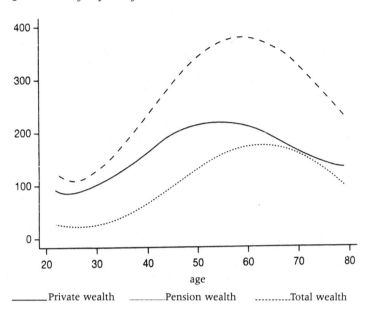

sixty, when the pensions paid out begin to exceed the contributions paid in. Obviously, the size of compulsory saving in Italy is enormous, reaching a peak at around age forty-five, when it represents about one third of the income produced and accounts for about one half of total saving.

The other distinctive implication of the life cycle is that the wealth, too, shows a hump, rising until retirement and falling thereafter.[17] This implication is fully confirmed in Figure 12, again based on an Italian sample. The figure has three curves: The middle one is private wealth (the sum of the financial activities, the value of real property, and personal firms, which results from the accumulation of personal savings); the bottom one is pension wealth, resulting from compulsory saving (the discounted value of the future pension benefits net of welfare contributions); and the top one is the sum of the two, or the overall wealth of the household, represented by the dashed curve. Here the hump predicted by the LCH is considerable. Wealth reaches its peak around ages fifty-five to sixty, when retirements begin, and from then onward it systematically diminishes. This trend clearly represents the crucial proof for the LCH theory.

The conclusions reached above are in flat contrast to those reported in various studies in recent years, which claim to have found no evidence of the hump. For example, in introducing a collection of writings on the subject[18] a well-known expert on saving, James Poterba, concludes that for the countries studied in the collection, households, on average, continue to save at all ages, even the most advanced. Since wealth at any age represents the amount of saving accumulated up to that age, as long as saving is positive wealth must increase, and this rules out the hump. Poterba therefore concludes that the writings in the volume provide very scant support for the life cycle model. But in reality those studies, and sundry others, suffer from a fatal blemish—that is, they err in their interpretation of the concept of income and thence of saving, which underpins the LCH model, according to which the relevant income is the one *produced* and saving is the difference between this and consumption, as we said above. The authors of the studies have misrepresented these concepts, identifying income with what we called above disposable income and saving with our *private saving*. But as was seen, this is tantamount to *subtracting from the income produced and from total saving all the compulsory saving*. Since in the original formulation of the LCH no explicit mention was made of compulsory saving, which was then of small importance, the two measurements of income and saving coincided. But once compulsory saving was introduced, it should have been plain to all that it must be considered as an essential component of saving and therefore of income.

The erroneous concept of income used in the other studies, that is, disposable income, is reported for Italy in Figure 9 by a dotted curve; and the corresponding concept of private saving is reported by the solid curve in Figure 11. As was to be expected, both disposable income and private saving have lost nearly all the hump that characterized the correct measurements, because from these was subtracted the large hump of compulsory saving, understood as ensuring that everybody behaves according to the prescription of the LCH: that is, to save when you are young and strong and to consume that saving (in the form of a pension) when your ability to earn dries up. When the hump levels out, the disposable income trend becomes very similar to that of consumption, and therefore the personal saving is almost constant throughout life. On this mistaken basis so many authors declared the LCH to be dead . . . prematurely!

THE LCH AND BEQUESTS. Although the total income and saving trend is the only concept relevant for testing the LCH, the trend of private saving by age is important to clarify another problem that has worried those involved in empirically verifying the LCH, namely, how transfers by bequest affect saving and wealth.

It is often believed that a crucial element in the LCH model is the absence of conspicuous hereditary transfers by one generation to the next.

This is a serious mistake! To be sure, in our elementary formulation we had neglected hereditary transfers, but this was only a convenient approximation in setting it out (for example, in Figure 6 it enabled us to assume that wealth started from zero and thereafter grew only by saving). In reality, as was demonstrated in many papers, beginning with the second article I wrote with Brumberg, the phenomenon of inheritance is not inconsistent in *principle* with the LCH, and (with appropriate specifications) does not alter the essential implications of the LCH without inheritance (summarized in six points in the subsection below). But in order to distinguish the LCH from the more or less traditional hypothesis that the sole reason for saving is to accumulate an estate for one's heirs, it needs to be shown that, on average, accumulated wealth is also used to stabilize consumption and in particular to finance consumption in the retirement period—that is to say, that wealth is a hump-shaped trend. Plainly, for Italy the LCH passes this crucial test.

To establish the importance of the *inheritance motive* reference must be made to the trend of private wealth by age. This follows from the fact that private wealth is the sole component of total wealth that, if not consumed, is transferable by inheritance. On the contrary, the wealth that consists of a right to a life annuity, like a pension, becomes zero with the pensioner's death. (If the pension partly covers a survivor, the latter can continue to receive a part of the annuity, but once again no capital can be transferred to offspring or third parties.)

Assume now that we find a hump in the total wealth but not in the *private* wealth that continues instead to augment during the retirement period, through positive personal saving (which means that a part of the reduction in pension wealth, which takes place through the pension paid, is used to increase transferable private wealth). But if elderly retired people, on average, continue to accumulate transferable wealth, the most reasonable interpretation is that they do so (mainly) to leave an inheritance. In this case, then, it must be concluded that the evidence is consistent with the LCH but with an "inheritance motive," even if it is impossible to establish at which point in life accumulation began to be influenced by this motive.

But, as can be seen from Figure 12, at least for Italy, private wealth, too, systematically diminishes after age sixty. Can we therefore conclude that the households in our sample do not trouble themselves about leaving an inheritance to their heirs? The answer to this question is no, for a variety of reasons that are too technical to be worth discussing here.

To sum up, the available information suggests that an actual motive for net accumulation for inheritance purposes (which means leaving an inheritance greater than the one received) is relevant only for the very rich (and especially for the *nouveaux riches*).

MACROECONOMIC IMPLICATIONS: SAVING AND INCOME GROWTH. As was said, the difference between the two models becomes much more marked with regard to respective macroeconomic implications. The difference stems from the fact that the LCH model recognizes the existence of a life cycle of income, of consumption, and hence of saving, which reflects the retirement period and the life cycle of the household. Friedman's simplifying postulate that life is infinite does not enable him to take account of the effect of this cycle or to deal with the problems concerning bequests. The result is that Friedman's model has very few macroeconomic implications. The only one he explicitly mentions is that national saving should diminish with the increase in growth rate, since the growth expected increases the income level expected and therefore consumption with respect to current income. As we mentioned, this conclusion is refuted by the empirical evidence, which, on the contrary, discloses a strong positive tie between saving and growth, just as predicted by the LCH.

The fundamental reason why the LCH implies that national saving depends on the rate of income growth (and not on its level) is that, in the presence of stable growth, the aggregate life income of any given generation is smaller than that of all the younger generations. This holds true whether the growth of national income is due to the growth of the population or to the growth of productivity. In the first case, the generation that has reached retirement age comprises fewer households than the preceding ones, and thus receives a lower income. In the second case (the one illustrated in Table 2), the *per capita* lifetime income of the retired generation is smaller than that of the active generations. Now, according to the LCH, the consumption of each generation is more or less proportional to its lifetime income; it follows, then, that at a given moment the active generations will save at a rate that will enable them, once retired, to consume more than those presently in retirement, belonging to a poorer generation. This generates a positive saving rate, greater as the rate of growth is greater.

On the basis of the above results, the main innovations of the LCH with regard to private saving can be summarized in the following six points:

1. The saving rate in a given country is completely independent of the *per capita* income.

2. The national saving rate is not simply the result of the different thrift of its citizens, in the sense that different national saving rates

are consistent with identical individual saving behaviors during the life cycle.

3. If the individuals of different countries behave in the same way, the net saving rate will be higher in proportion as the long-term growth rate of the system is higher; it will be nil if the growth rate is nil.

4. An economic system can accumulate a considerable stock of wealth, relative to income, even in the absence of legacies.

5. The relation between wealth and income is a decreasing function of the rate of growth, reaching its maximum value at a zero growth rate.

6. A key parameter that affects the wealth/income ratio and the saving rate, at parity of growth rate, is the prevalent length of the retirement period.

The implications of the LCH, concerning the relationship between saving and growth of *per capita* income and population have received ample confirmation in several empirical studies from the 1960s onward, when the national accounting data of many countries of widely differing experience became available. The first series of tests is described in my presidential address to the International Econometric Society in 1965, subsequently published in 1970[19]. On the basis of a large sample of thirty-six countries it was shown that the growth rate of income and the demographic structure by age were by far the most important variables for explaining the differences in the private saving rates (which varied from -2 to 21 percent). An amusing feature of this article is the first footnote, which says, among other things, how grateful I was for the advice and assistance of a student, Antonio Fazio, who in the meantime has become the governor of the Bank of Italy.

Later on, in a work written with Tullio Jappelli[20], we took into consideration the very marked reduction in Italian national saving, which from 26 percent at the start of the 1960s (when Italy, along with Japan, had the highest saving among the industrialized countries) had more or less halved by the end of the 1980s. This was due: (a) for more than two thirds to the huge rise in the public deficit, which moved from an impressive surplus (increasing the national saving rate by more than five percentage points) to an enormous deficit that reduced it by three percentage points; (b) for about one third to the fall in private saving by 4.5 percentage points, half of which was attributable to the marked fall in income growth rate and the other half to inflation (through the "inflation illusion").

Fig. 13. *The life cycle of annual increase of wealth*

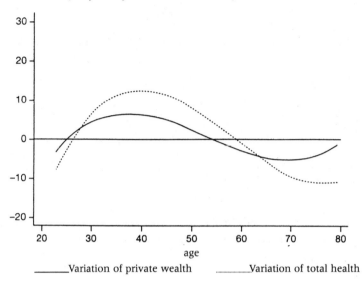

_____Variation of private wealth   ....Variation of total health

A notable example of the importance of the income growth rate comes from China. In an article[21] written in collaboration with a colleague from the Chinese central bank, Shi Cao, the Chinese private saving rate was found to have grown from 4.5 percent in the 1960s through the mid-1970s, to an enormous level, around 25 percent, at the start of the 1990s; and this increase was accompanied by a rise in the income growth rate from 4 to 12 percent in the same period. High government saving is driving national saving up to 35 percent, probably the highest in the world and more than three times its American counterpart, even though China today is still one of the poorest countries in the world.

An article in 1991[22] shows that the widespread phenomenon of a fall in the private saving rate between the 1960s and the 1980s can largely be accounted for by the general fall in the growth rate and by the high rate of inflation (in this connection, see the next subsection).

OTHER MACROECONOMIC IMPLICATIONS. The LCH model supplies further indications on other variables that may affect the saving rate and were previously ignored completely. The basic point is that, for a given rate of growth, the saving rate tends to increase with the wealth/income ratio (since the saving rate is equal to the product of the growth rate multiplied by the wealth/income ratio). In the stylized version of the model that ratio is influenced exclusively by the length of retirement, and therefore by institutional and demographic characteristics. But, in reality, the wealth

/income ratio may be affected by several other institutional factors. A few examples may help to clarify the point.

1. One obvious factor is the existence and diffusion of the social security system, which had been neglected in the original work because in the 1950s this system was relatively underdeveloped. The impact of this factor has been the object of several studies that have shown it to be extremely complex. A growth in pensions and contributions should tend to increase compulsory saving and thus total saving, if, and in proportion as, the economy is growing, but only if private saving remains fixed; actually, it would appear that this should tend to diminish through the increase in the pension to which one is entitled. But, surprisingly, this effect is doubtful because, as has been evidenced by certain authors such as Martin Feldstein[23] and Patricia Munnell[24], an increase in pensions encourages a lengthening of the retirement period, and this lengthening, in turn, tends to increase saving. In effect, in a study performed with a student of mine, Arlie Sterling[25], we found evidence of the two opposite effects and concluded that these effects tend largely to cancel each other out. For Italy a certain negative, though small, effect has been found (Nicola Rossi). Social security also influences saving and *national* wealth, and this is briefly dealt with below, chapter III, section 37.

2. The scarcity of forms of insurance tends to increase the wealth/income ratio, because it induces individuals to accumulate and maintain reserves in the eventuality of uninsurable events. This particularly affects saving by young persons, but also the decumulation of wealth by the elderly, through the availability of life annuities that ensure against the "risk of life."

3. The shortcomings of the credit system, which limit households' access to loans, encourage accumulation of resources before making a purchase, especially of consumer durables (house, car, etc.), and in this way they determine the increase of the wealth/income and saving ratio for any given level of growth rate. This effect has been empirically demonstrated by two of my foremost pupils, Tullio Jappelli and Marco Pagano, and partly accounts for the difference between the low saving in the United States, with a developed and not much regulated credit system, and the high saving in countries like Italy and Japan, where credit for consumption is strictly regulated.

4. In a number of articles I have also shown that the private saving
   rate can be appreciably reduced by a high rate of inflation. This is
   one of the many negative effects produced by inflation owing to a
   phenomenon I have called "inflation illusion"—that is, errors
   induced by inflation. Briefly (as is demonstrated below, chapter III,
   section 30), inflation of, say, X percent tends to increase the interest
   rate by an equal amount, in order to compensate the debtor for the
   loss of purchasing power of his capital. A rational consumer should
   calculate the return from investments in fixed-income securities by
   using the nominal rate corrected for inflation (the so-called "real"
   rate). The evidence suggests that consumers largely fail to make this
   correction; as a result, they overestimate their own income and
   increase their own consumption (and thus reduce saving).

THE SOURCES OF THE WEALTH OF NATIONS. Point 5 in the summary of
the implications of the LCH (see page 81) considers (private) wealth, which
also represents an important contribution to the LCH. In the previous conventional models it was assumed—implicity, at least—that the saving of the
"rich" continued throughout life, ending up as legacies, and these legacies
were thought to be the main source of national private wealth. The amount
of this wealth was largely unknown until Raymond W. Goldsmith's monu-
mental work (*A Study of Saving in the United States*, 1956, *and The National
Wealth of the United States in the Postwar Period*, 1962). Goldsmith found that
wealth was four to five times private income, with a fairly stable ratio over
time. The LCH suggests that the humped wealth due to accumulation for old
age may, by itself, account for a large part of the national wealth. In the stylized model in Figure 6, for example, the wealth/income ratio is equal to half
the years of retirement (L-N in Figure 6). Having assumed a retirement duration of ten years, in the example in the table, the national wealth/national
income ratio is found to be equal to 5 (which, however, diminishes if there is
economic growth; see Table 2).

The similarity of these figures to the subsequent estimates obtained by
Goldsmith was astonishing and suggested that the wealth of a country could
be largely accounted for by the LCH and that the simplifying hypothesis that
inheritance transfers were of scant importance was acceptable. But it must be
acknowledged that the coincidence between the result of our simulation and
Goldsmith's estimates needs to be taken with a grain of salt, recalling that for
the LCH the wealth/income ratio is influenced by a variety of other variables,
such as the growth rate (which reduces it), the length of retirement, the rate
of return on capital, and social security. I was later to return to this interesting subject—the role of accumulation for old age in the wealth of a country—

at the end of the 1980s, following a famous polemic with two young, brilliant economists, Kotlikoff and Summers (see below, section 26). With regard to the effect of social security on saving and personal and national wealth, the topic is dealt with in full in chapter III, section 37.

EPILOGUE. Forty years after the LCH hypothesis was formulated there is ample evidence that much of the accumulation (and decumulation) of wealth is hump-shaped, that is, intended to finance future consumption (especially during the period of retirement from work). The precaution motive, too, is important for young and elderly people, but even this is determined by expectation of future expenditure.

In a modern society, a goodly part of hump saving occurs in compulsory form (social security), yet even this kind of saving reflects the social approval of a system designed to ensure that each individual will accumulate sufficient reserves for old age, according to the prescriptions of the LCH. The humped wealth is able to account for a large slice of private national wealth in a modern economy, but inherited wealth also contributes to a limited but not negligible extent.

Reviewing the forces that control the share of income saved, one realizes why an expert faced with the question of how to increase saving does not find it easy to give a practical answer!

22   Carnegie, Herbert Simon, and American Cheese

It was during the eight years spent at the Carnegie Institute of Technology that I matured as an economist. The dean of the institute was another young man, Lee Bach, a highly capable economist and administrator who had founded a revolutionary school, the Graduate School of Industrial Administration (GSIA), the first of a kind that was to be very successful.

The central figure at Carnegie was Herbert Simon, pioneer, encyclopedic genius, and expert in economics (for which he was awarded the Nobel in 1978), political sciences, administration, and psychology. He was among the first to be fascinated by Artificial Intelligence. In the 1960s his main objective was to reproduce the way the human brain thought and functioned from a cognitive point of view. He made use of large computers, then being developed, to test his theories. He began with a program that was able to prove theorems or, alternatively, to acknowledge the fact that it could not solve them. The machine knew that it didn't know. Socrates himself would have recognized the spark of intelligence here.

A team of high-class scholars surrounded him, like Charles Holt, Merton Miller, William Cooper, Abe Charnes, Richard Cyert, and James March, all exceptional persons. There were excellent students, too, like Jack Muth, who later became a hero of our time for laying the foundations for the so-called hypothesis of rational expectations, which in 1995 was to enable Robert Lucas to win a Nobel Prize. The atmosphere at the Carnegie Institute was one of tremendous ferment and novelty, and, as I said, its driving force was Simon.

The whole group eagerly took part in devising the curriculum for a new business school that, unlike the practice prevailing at the time, was to be based not on common sense and imitation of the "best existing practice" but would have a strong analytical component. It was to be underpinned by disciplines like economics, administrative science, mathematics, statistics, accounting, and the use of computers, and that was targeted on "problem solving." This idea was thereafter gradually accepted by the best American and international business schools.

Simon and I had always enjoyed very friendly relations. But while I was a restless sort of person, always changing my residence and my job, Simon has never stirred from Carnegie. He believed the mountain ought to come to Mahomet. I remember a famous exchange he had with Serena. Herbert claimed that traveling was a pointless waste of time, as he could find out everything about anywhere in the world just sitting in a library. "What can't you find in a library, Serena?" "Smells, Herb, colors!" replied Serena, leaving him dumbstruck. Smells, colors, indeed. So, that year, Simon took a trip around the world.

At times he could be a bit cruel with younger colleagues. I remember one occasion when Simon was surrounded by young, brilliant, newly appointed professors who had converged from universities all over America. He explained to them that, in actual fact, the best they could reasonably hope to aspire to in the future was to prepare themselves to be postmen, delivering the mail. Any other job whatever was destined to be better performed by computers; however, computers might perhaps have some trouble in moving easily over rough ground, a thing postmen could easily manage. And I glimpsed a twinge of dejection in those young faces. Still, despite his obvious intention to be paradoxical, Simon ultimately wasn't entirely off the mark. But he was quite wrong to cite the specific case of mailmen. Not even his imagination could have encompassed the fax or, worse, the success of the Internet and e-mail.

His main criticism of the approach of economists was that they attacked the fundamental problem of predicting public response to any exogenous change by using the criterion of maximization of profit or individual utility. But, in his view, this criterion neglected the cost implicit in calculating the optimal, which might even be very high and thus discourage investigation to discover the maximum obtainable return. According to Simon, it was difficult to quantify the maximum, and he therefore suggested that, on the contrary, to save effort people should normally be content with a satisfactory choice. Simon set the criterion of satisfyzing against the maximizing normally employed by economists. My opinion on this matter was that, in substance, maximization offered a simpler, even if not entirely accurate, solution for predicting economic behavior.

In any case this theoretical debate has contributed to the analysis of how firms behave in an oligopolistic environment. Simon's distinction between the two criteria is, indeed, useful to analyze the importance of the outside world for a firm's activity. Given the cost of a decision, if you find yourself in an environment in which a satisfyzing solution is sufficient to produce profits, you don't go beyond it, for it would be more expensive. If, on the contrary, you find yourself in a very competitive setting, you are compelled not to be content with a satisfyzing solution, and you have to pay the cost of finding a maximizing solution. The difference between the two principles may therefore be fairly useful in distinguishing a monopoly situation from a competitive market: In a monopoly situation a firm is less efficient than in a competitive market. And this is one reason why monopoly situations reduce the general well-being, giving rise to suboptimal solutions.

Simon was such a "fanatic" for all possible systems for saving on the cost of decisions that when we went to lunch, wherever it was, he would invariably order the same sandwich; American cheese on white bread. The reason, he explained, was that, since any restaurant in America will have that, his system saved time spent dithering over what to order, then having to think of something else when you found your first choice wasn't available.

Simon, Charles Holt, Jack Muth, and I worked at a book on production planning[26] which, once again, focused on the problem of short-term decisions about how much to produce, how many workers to hire, and how much stock to keep in the warehouse. In the book, we developed a mathematical model incorporating my concept of reduction of production fluctuations with respect to seasonal sales fluctuations. The philosophy of the model was to minimize the total costs stemming from the warehouse stock, from hiring and firing staff, and from being unable to fulfill customers' orders. The problem could be solved fairly easily by applying the optimal rule: Each variable (production, employment) was programmed by using a "weighted" average of the sales forecast for each future month. The forecasts, in turn, were based on past sales and seasonal coefficients. But the method for obtaining the weighting coefficients was a mathematical one and by no means elementary, being based on the Laplace transforms.

23   Mo-Mi, Mi-Mo

In 1957, Merton Miller and I produced two articles, one signed Modigliani-Miller, the other Miller-Modigliani—hence the nickname "Mo-Mi" and "Mi-Mo"—that were to become classics and to be cited as justification, first for my Nobel Prize, then a little later for Miller's.

Mo-Mi argues that in a perfect capital market the financial structure of the firm—that is, the ratio of indebtedness to equity capital—does not affect the market valuation of the firm as a whole, a thesis that seemed unheard of at that time. Practically all over the world Mo-Mi has become compulsory reading for students of business economics, who, alas, end by detesting us, recalling this article as a nightmare. It is indeed difficult reading, for it was not originally intended for students but was written with the aim of putting our colleagues in business finance in a tight spot, by showing them that what was thought to be the central problem of that subject (which was the optimal distribution of the sources of finance between equity capital and borrowed funds) was really a false problem. In fact, as Mo-Mi demonstrates, with well-functioning markets not distorted by, for example, taxation, the financial structure should not influence the market value of the firm.

The main contribution of this article is not so much in its specific conclusion as to whether the firm does or does not benefit from using borrowed funds instead of share capital, as in having radically altered the approach used until then in dealing with the problems concerning the structure of corporate financing. The traditional approach was to treat this problem in terms of profit maximization; and since the cost of a loan, that is, the interest rate, is usually less than the return on shares, the obvious conclusion was reached that, within ample margins, recourse to borrowing was more advantageous than issuing new shares. But that conclusion is not justified, because, while shareholders divide up the profits or losses, whatever they are, debt must be repaid with interest, even at the risk of bankruptcy and total loss of the equity capital. Hence, replacing share capital with borrowing may indeed increase the expected rate of return on equity capital, but at the cost of increasing risk (for example, the probability of failure). How can it then be argued that an increase in expected profit, in exchange for greater risk, is really advantageous for the shareholders? Above all, bear in mind that: (a) the shareholders might have very different preferences in the matter, and (b) individual shareholders have the possibility of increasing expected return at the cost of increasing risk by augmenting their portfolio of shares through personal borrowing. Only the market can supply an answer, by raising or lowering the value of the share according to whether investors as a whole approve or disapprove of the decision.

Mo-Mi therefore concludes that, in reality, profit maximization is not an operative concept in a context of uncertainty—in which, that is, any decision may have a series of possible alternative results. Maximization of expected profit, too, is a thoroughly unsatisfactory prescription, since it takes no account of risk. The only operative rule for corporate managers is not maximization of profit, according to the old paradigm, but rather maximization of the firm's market value.

Once this principle is accepted it is easy to understand that (in a rational market and in the absence of fiscal provisions that favor one or another form of financing) management cannot count on increasing the total market value of the firm (share value plus debts) by replacing equities with loans at the market rate. This remains true even if it should be less than the expected return on the shares, so that the expected return per remaining share would increase (but at the cost of becoming more risky). This is because in a well-functioning market each shareholder can, if he wishes, increase the expected return on his net investment (and his risk) by the same amount as the firm can, by personally borrowing in order to purchase more shares in proportion to what the firm would do. There is therefore no reason why the market should be prepared to pay a premium because management has performed an operation that anyone can do on their own behalf, if they wish. If the premium existed, the shares would be overvalued and thus an indesirable investment. These are precisely the considerations upon which our proof is based.

Note that if the decisions made by management in maximizing market value are not welcome to any particular shareholder, the latter can simply sell his shares at the maximum price and make new, more desirable investments.

Nowadays, a vast consensus has arisen among teachers of finance that, in perfect and well-functioning markets, the composition of liabilities cannot have much influence on the market value of the firm as a whole; but also that the theorem is not necessarily valid in the presence of distortions, like taxation, that discriminate in favor of debt capital.

The second article dealt with dividend policy. With perfect markets and no taxes, it makes no difference whether high or low dividends are paid: The firm's market value should remain unchanged. This theory, too, opposed conventional views according to which an increase in dividends, within certain limits, would raise the value of the shares. At that time, our colleagues were struggling with the question of whether it was possible to deceive investors (seen rather as outsiders than as the owners of the firm) by offering them the restitution of their own capital in the form of dividend. We showed that, following rational behavior, with neutral taxation, the dividend is irrelevant. Contrary to what was thought, the dividend policy of corporations (the sum deducted from the returns in order to distribute dividends) should have no impact on their valuation, provided, of course, that the amount of the dividend does not alter the choice of the investments to be made, including investments in liquid assets. In this case, the expected flow of the entire firm and thus its market value should not change as a function of the dividend policy. The latter, indeed, determines only how much of the profit takes the form of cash dividends and how much is translated into a capital gain. In these conditions, therefore, rational investor should have no preference for one form or the other.

Innumerable objections were made to our articles. One, in particular, was based on the consideration that stockholders may prefer cash to reinvesting in risky shares. It follows that the price of the shares of a firm with a high rate of retention, that is, sums set aside, should be relatively lower than that of a firm with a high divdend policy. To this objection Merton and I replied on the basis of experience that shareholders normally reinvest dividends from their firm in other firms, thus exposing themselves, in turn, to the same type of risk inherent in reinvesting their dividends in their own firm. For that matter, anyone preferring cash to reinvestment can always obtain it by selling a share of that firm or of others. In general, the tax system rewards reinvestment.

These articles still receive wide recognition because they are regarded as a milestone on the way to the development of modern finance theory. Mo-Mi, in particular, underpins important subsequent developments in the valuation of derivates, like options.

In any case, the overall message of the two articles was accepted by the academic and financial communities: The market value of a firm is determined exclusively by the capitalization of the expected income flow, at a rate reflecting its risk, but does not depend on its liability structure.

24 *Kennedy and the Round Table of Economists*

Carnegie granted me a sabbatical year in 1957–58, during which I was a visiting professor at Harvard, where I stood in for Leontief (who was on leave). And I must say that I had personal experience of the proverbial quality of Harvard students. I have had superlative undergraduate students and exceptional graduate students. At the end of 1959 I was again invited to be a visiting professor, but this time at MIT. I intended to accept, but the administration at the Carnegie Institute was against it. In that period I felt rather annoyed by the university, for I had the impression that the administration did not intend to invest resources in the economics sector. To my dismay, they decided not to replace an excellent economist, Alexander Henderson, who had worked alongside me and died prematurely. I would have liked to have at least one other distinguished colleague on the faculty. But the administration told me that, yes, maybe in the future, they would consider investing in such, but later rather than sooner.

Serena and I therefore decided it was time to move on and accepted MIT's offer and an invitation to occupy a permanent chair at Northwestern University, with the proviso that I be allowed to retain my post of visiting professor at MIT. The year 1960, then, was a crucial one, for I fell in love with MIT. It was a delight to have so many colleagues who were both at the top of the profession and pleasant. The administration aimed only to oil the wheels of the teacher's life, and the students were all of the first quality.

That year also saw the election to the presidency of a man who was to become one of the best-loved in the world: John Fitzgerald Kennedy, born in Massachusetts. One episode remained famous in our circle. Kennedy had already won the election but had not yet taken office. Paul Samuelson was invited by the president-elect to spend a weekend at Cape Cod to discuss the new government's economic policy. At that time, in the year I was visiting professor at MIT, we economists used to have lunch together, and a round table was reserved for us in the university faculty club, just as though we were knights, bound by some ancient code of honor. We all sat together, and our lunches were spent in lively debate. Among the fixed guests were Samuelson, Solow, Kindleberger, Rosenstein-Rodan, Franklyn Fisher, and others. When Samuelson received that fateful invitation, we were all very curious at his return from Cape Cod and gathered round him to learn how it had gone. Was the president intelligent? Did he know something of economics? Samuelson's reply has gone down in history. To the second question, he answered: "Not particularly." But to the question of whether Kennedy was intelligent, he replied: "Like a good undergraduate student at Harvard." Now, that remark could have been interpreted by the majority of people as rather condescending. But it was nothing of the sort—for among us economists, to say that, especially of a politician, was a great and sincere compliment, given that Harvard undergraduates are highly select and uncommonly intelligent.

Kennedy was, in any case, a great president. He knew how to listen intelligently to the best economists. In particular, the Council of Economic Advisors he appointed became the most distinguished ever. It helped him to promote an excellent package of measures that got the economy out of the doldrums in which Eisenhower's restrictive policy had left it. The impulse Kennedy gave the economy was to endure right up to 1969. The year 1959 was the year of recession. In 1960, Kennedy started with a feeble growth rate of 2.2 percent, which then exploded to 5.6 percent in 1963 and remained at that level, under Johnson, until 1968. However, the level at which the growth rate stabilized was too high, since it stood above the growth rates of the workforce and productivity, and thus partly laid the groundwork for the inflation that was to arrive in 1969.

The assassination of Kennedy in 1963 was a national tragedy, felt by us as keenly as all other Americans. We will never forget the figure of Jacqueline Kennedy, when she insisted on continuing to wear her pink wool suit, its skirt stained with her husband's blood, throughout the ceremony when Johnson was sworn in during the return journey to Washington. When she was implored to change her clothes, she refused, saying that Americans had the right to see what had been done to Jack. And afterward, too, during the funeral, it was she who decided that their children should be present at the final farewell to their father, and she who organized everything down to the smallest details with tremendous strength of will and intelligence. In those days, children were screened from the reality of death and kept away from funerals. But Jacqueline taught Americans and the world that they had the right to be helped to understand and to accept the tragedy by taking part at the ceremony and the honors with the rest of the family.

At MIT everyone knew I had the commitment to go to Northwestern and, *noblesse oblige*, no one tried to deter me. The University of Northwestern gave us a grand welcome. We found a large furnished house awaiting us near the campus, and we were taken to various areas in order that we might choose where to buy our home. But we made too many comparisons with MIT and could not make the decision to put down roots. Everyone was too kind, too solicitous, and maybe we had the feeling as of being animals in a zoo, with everybody asking us about Italy. Well, our hearts were still back at MIT. Judge, then, how happy we were when, at Christmas, the dean of the Sloan School at MIT phoned me and asked: "Franco, now you've had a taste of Northwestern . . . what about coming back to us?" We had no hesitation, and in June 1962 Serena returned to Massachusetts alone and bought our house in Belmont, where I joined her as soon as I had finished my classes in Evanston and where we spent 36 happy years.

In 1964, along with the great economic growth, a most important event took place: Serena and I became grandparents to our first grandchild, Leah, daughter of Andrea. What joy, what satisfaction to be a grandfather at age forty-six. I remember how I entered the Faculty Club and made the announcement, inviting anyone to beat my record—but nobody could. Another grandchild, Julia, followed two years after. And, later on, Sergio had a boy, David, and a girl, Amelia. Our life has been immensely enriched by children and grandchildren.

25   The Famous Class of the 1960s

It was during the 1960s that I found myself teaching a class of exceptional students, many of whose members are now the leading economists of the moment, including Robert Hall from Stanford University and Joseph (Joe) Stiglitz, who was chairman of the Council of Economic Advisors under Clinton (interesting to note how Clinton's first council was made up of former MIT students). Stiglitz was later vice-president of the World Bank. There was Peter Diamond (now Institute Professor at MIT) and Bob Gordon, who today teaches at Northwestern and has written important articles on the theory of prices and wages. Richard Sutch, with whom I wrote some papers on interest rates, teaches economic history at Berkeley. And Nordhaus of Yale, who was a member of Kennedy's Council of Economic Advisors and wrote with Tobin a book on how to estimate correctly national income in a more comprehensive way, taking account of activities that bypass the market, such as domestic services, and how to calculate so-called indirect effects like pollution and quality of life.

Among those studying in my course on money was my pupil, afterward colleague and friend, Stanley Fischer; Charles Bischoff, architect of the investment sector of the MPS (MIT Pennsylvania Social Sciences Research Council) econometric model for the Fed; and Allen Blinder, professor at Princeton, who was for some time vice-president of the Fed. Another student of mine was Larry Meyer, who also is now a governor of the Fed, and collaborated with me on the American model together with Dwight Jaffe, professor at Berkeley, with whom I wrote an essay on credit rationing. Let me also mention Lucas Papademos, now governor of the Bank of Greece; Robert Merton (winner of the 1997 Nobel Prize), one of the founders of finance applied to derivative instruments; Albert Ando, now professor at the University of Pennsylvania, who has continued my work on econometric models; and George Ackerloff, later to be celebrated for developing the "lemon theory," in the American meaning of that word: the "swindle" you suffer when you buy a used car that doesn't work. Ackerloff explains, for instance, why secondhand cars are so cheap: presumably because people who go to buy them from dealers specializing in used cars, acting on a rational basis, think those cars must perforce have some defect, since the dealers are experts and would therefore not sell them if they didn't know they had a defect.

26   *Everything You Always Wanted to Know About the Public Debt . . .*

In the 1940s and 1950s I was inclined to share the opinion, prevalent among Keynesians, that deficits might play an important role in sustaining aggregate demand, and I tended to agree with the Keynesians' views, commonly accepted, that these deficits had no adverse effect, direct or indirect, on the health of the economy, rejecting the classical view, according to which a deficit would impoverish future generations, who would thus suffer heavier taxes to pay for the burden of interest accruing on the public debt. In particular, I was prepared to rebut this argument with the counterargument that, after all, the heavier taxes would be accompanied and offset by the greater incomes obtained by the holders of the public debt. I began a thoroughgoing revision of this concept in the late 1950s, when I returned to studying the subject in the light of life cycle saving.

The result was an article that makes demanding reading in the *Economic Journal,* the leading British economics periodical, in which I concluded that in general it was true that the deficit spared the current generation from taxes at the expense of future generations. Since then I have returned several times to the topic, refining and generalizing the analysis. Some twenty years later I summarized the conclusions of my analysis reviewing the history of the replies, often contradictory, given to the question, "What are the consequences of deficit and public debt?"

The first opinion is that of the sensible but not economically expert person, based on the intuitive notion that the debt of a state is, *mutatis mutandis,* like that of a family, in the sense that future generations will have to pay the interest accruing on the debt and the capital itself; this will reduce their future consumption capacity. Moral: Public debt is harmful because "it establishes a mortgage" on the income of future generations.

The second opinion was formulated by the eighteenth-century economists at the court of Versailles and propounded again two centuries later by the early Keynesians. It refutes the first opinion and turns it upside down with subtle arguments. The comparison between family debt and public debt does not hold, for the former is a debt "external" to the family itself; while public debt is "internal" to the country, being a debt that we must somehow pay to ourselves. This is the famous thesis of the Chevalier de Melun, the French economist who two hundred years before the Keynesians asserted that public debt is like a debt owed by the right hand to the left hand that does not weaken the body. To be sure, future generations will have to pay the service on the debt, but they will also receive the interest accruing on it. In other words, what counts is disposable income, or income produced minus taxes paid plus interest received. When taxes increase and interest is paid, these two flows cancel each other out, and disposable income will not be affected by them.

The third point of view is much more sophisticated and harks back, more elegantly, to the initial theory according to which the burden does indeed exist, since the future income level can be influenced through the amount of capital we leave as inheritance for the future. To this end, we must recall a fundamental identity-namely, that national investment equals national saving, which is its source of finance. But national saving, in turn, is the sum of private plus public saving. The latter is defined as excess earning (net of transfers) on current account expenditure (that is, excluding expenditure for public investment). It is therefore equal to the current deficit with inverse sign; or, in other words, the deficit represents negative saving: By reducing national saving, it reduces investment. When the state goes to the market to sell equities to finance the deficit, it reduces the rate of private saving available to finance private investments. But since the investments are productive, reducing the investments and the disposable capital stock from then on reduces the income of future generations. It is in this sense that an expenditure financed with public deficit instead of with taxes favors the current generation, who will pay less tax, at the expense of the future one, who will have less capital and therefore less income.

If this argument is valid, and bearing in mind that, according to the life cycle hypothesis of saving, wealth is proportional to income (with a coefficient of proportionality that once again depends on the rate of income growth—but this time with a negative sign), we should find that the stock of private capital in relation to income is lower in proportion as the public debt is greater with respect to income. I have performed a test of this kind on the United States, considering a time period of about sixty years starting in 1900, in which the growth rate showed a fairly constant trend, and the results fully agree with the forecast of the model: One dollar of public debt edges out about one dollar of private capital because the desire for wealth is satisfied by the debt issued by the government instead of by productive physical capital.

The advantage of this application of the life cycle hypothesis is that it enables us to measure the overall burden of the national debt. Obviously, some subordinate hypotheses must be considered. The burden exists because the deficit edges out the capital, but if public debt is used to finance public capital, then the latter will have a profitability of its own that will offset the edging out of private capital. As a general rule, what counts is not the deficit but the deficit minus the value of the income—producing activities, financial or physical, that the government can hold.

The reason why the Chevalier de Melun's argument is false is therefore that, if there were no public deficit, individuals, having the same wealth, would obtain the same income entirely from capital. But in the presence of deficit, this income is generated not by capital but by taxing people, that is, through a fiscal levy that impoverishes the country. The public debt has a market value, but only because the purchaser is entitled to establish a mortgage on the taxpayers for the amount of the interest and the capital at refund. That mortgage impoverishes taxpayers to the same extent. Thus, the use of saving to purchase state equities adds nothing to the national wealth, whereas if it were used for private investment it would enrich the country, because the investment has the "external" effect of increasing the productivity of labor.

There are exceptions to the foregoing. There is the Keynesian limit case in which saving cannot be invested because there are no more investment opportunities. In that case, plainly, nothing is edged out by the deficit. The burden of the deficit is effectively such only when an economy's resources are fully utilized. If the economic system possesses unused capacities (men and machines), then the public deficit does not necessarily edge out investment (and might even cause it to increase through the multiplier). One must be very cautious on this point, however, and not draw hasty conclusions. Whether the deficit does or does not edge out private investment depends not only on the availability of resources but also on the monetary policies applied by the authorities at that moment. If the resources are not fully utilized, a monetary policy should be adopted leading to full employment, without current public deficit.

A further case is when the economy has unutilized resources, but there is a precise intention not to utilize them. For example, at the beginning of the 1980s, during the tough battle against the inflation caused by the oil shock, underutilization was felt to be necessary in order to curb the rise of prices. In situations like this, where nonutilization of resources is deliberate, the public deficit could edge out investment, despite the unutilized resources. But every time there is undesired unemployment, in the presence of positive real interest rates, this indicates that the real quantity of money is insufficient, and that increasing it could raise aggregate demand and employment, without having recourse to deficit; which is exactly what occurred in the United States after 1991.

Last, we must recall the case where the transfer of resources from the future generation to the current one, through indebtedness, is really desirable, as in the case of war. For, by issuing debt, the generation living through the war makes later generations contribute to the war effort. Hence, the generation that has undergone the war will emerge from the conflict with a certain amount of public debt to sell in order to sustain a higher level of consumption. This will cause a reduction in the net saving of the postwar society, since the saving of the younger generations will be absorbed by the purchase of bonds already in circulation rather than by financing new productive capital. Moral: The choice of how to finance public expenditure, whether with taxes or with debt, enables the distribution of sacrifices between present and future to be controlled.

One final important consideration is whether the debt is internal or external to the "family." Imagine the case of an external debt. In this case, even the most strenuous supporters of the absence of any future burden of the debt must admit that external debt involves an obvious burden, since the interest must be paid outside the country. In my model it is suggested that if the resources are fully utilized, it is quite irrelevant whether the debt is internal or external. Internal indebtedness edges out investment, and the income deriving from it is lost. If we borrow abroad, we continue to be able to fuel investment, but the income so produced has to be paid to the operators who reside outside the system, and thus society loses the same amount as before.

A fourth point of view is the result of a famous article by Robert Barro, who has rejected the third point of view and has rediscovered and revitalized the conclusion that the deficit does not shift the cost of the current generations' public expenditure to future ones and is therefore not a burden. Barro has, however, developed the argument in a much more subtle way. This is the point of view I have called "supersophisticated" and that in the United States was to prosper and be utilized during the Reagan administration. Barro's thesis, christened the "Ricardian neutrality hypothesis," was expounded in a 1974 article, *Are Government Bonds Net Wealth?*[27]. Barro argued that in reality financing public expenditure through deficit increases wealth and private saving to such an extent as to offset the public deficit, while leaving national saving unchanged. The theoretical premises for this paradox are: (1) that human beings are absolutely rational and perfectly able to assess the consequences of the economic decisions that concern them, and (2) that life has infinite duration, or that the consumer has made an immutable decision about the distribution of his income and his wealth between himself and his heirs. At this point the government enters, saying: "We shall reduce your immediate fiscal burden by $100, replacing the lost yield with a loan whose interest will be paid by future generations." If you are rational, you will reply as follows: "Why should I allow the government to decide to improve my position and worsen that of my heirs as compared to what I decided for them, because of the interest they will have to pay? I made that decision and I see no reason to alter it. And so I must take the money made available to me by tax relief and invest it in government bonds to the same amount, in such a way as to transfer it to my heirs, so that when they knock at their door with a demand for tax, increased to pay the interest, they will hand him the returns on those government bonds. And in this way they will find themselves in the same situation as I predicted for them . . ."

If the empirical reality coincided with this logical construction, it would be irrelevant whether government finances itself through taxes or through the issue of debt, for Barro's rational consumer will increase his saving by an amount exactly equal to the deficit, or negative saving, of the government; thus national wealth is unchanged. This conclusion runs counter to my LCH model, where saving is independent of government behavior and so national saving decreases with the deficit.

Barro is wrong. First, because even if the consumer were superrational à la Barro, it by no means follows that the choice between taxes or deficit would be indifferent. Suffice it to imagine a person who has no children and another who has twenty. In this predicament, to choose between levying a tax or increasing the debt may make an enormous difference. A person without children would rather that the taxes be paid by descendants and will therefore prefer that the government finance itself through debt. In contrast, the rational person with twenty children will prefer to pay the taxes at once. In this case it is not true at all that the two hypotheses cancel each other out. But, above all, the idea that a consumer bases his saving on a calculation of fiscal policy and its effects on his heirs is quite unreal. The evidence suggests that very few intend to leave an inheritance and even fewer adjust it to offset fiscal policy. In the course of the polemic with "the two Larrys," Kotlikoff and Summers, I showed that, in the United States at least, during the twentieth century legacies did not account for more than 15 to 20 percent of total wealth, which depends much more on my LCH. Legacies and inheritances are therefore not able significantly to offset financing decisions in the public sector.

If Barro were right, every time the government borrows people would have to decide to accumulate more so as to offset the burden of the debt on their own children. They would have to wish to leave their children an additional amount of wealth equal to the debt the government has issued, so that future generations might not suffer worse conditions than the present ones. Every time the debt increased, dollar for dollar, wealth would have to increase. This is tantamount to sayng that the amount of wealth minus the debt—that is, private real capital—is independent of the amount of the debt itself. But in a study of mine I have shown that the empirical evidence contradicts Barro and confirms my argument on the negative effects of the deficit, since it shows that the public deficit does not increase private wealth, as Barro claims, but instead reduces national wealth. Moral: The public deficit has an averse effect on the capital stock.

27   The Model for the Fed and Albert Ando

The years from 1960 to 1970 might be called the "golden age" of Keynesianism. Of course, I must specify that by Keynesianism I refer to the wise Keynesians: Solow, Samuelson, Tobin, Heller, and others of their kind. I leave out the sundry aberrations that are always bound to exist. In the mid-1960s the Federal Reserve Board asked me to build a model of the American economy that could be employed for forecasts and for analyzing economic policy measures. To comanage the project I immediately invited Albert Ando, a pupil of mine at the Carnegie Institute of Technology and coauthor, in 1963, of the first empirical test of the LCH at the aggregate level for the United States.

Historically, the method that led to modern econometric models was developed by the Dutch economist Jan Tinbergen and won him (in 1969) one of the first Nobel Prizes for economics. In the United States in the 1970s there were a great many models, some for teaching purposes, others for studying the use of alternative economic policies, yet others for forecasting long-term trends. In some cases the forecasts were not made public, especially those performed by government bodies or institutions responsible for economic policy, for example, the models of the Department of Trade and of the Fed. At that time, among the models whose results are periodically published, the first, and the oldest, used for annual forecasts since 1953, belonged to the University of Michigan. Until the oil crisis, the Michigan model seldom got its forecasts wrong: Only in 1970 did it predict a very slender expansion instead of the contraction (but a hardly perceptible one) that actually occurred. In thirteen years out of the two decades 1953–1973 the error was less than 1 percent, and only in one year, 1955, did it exceed 4 percent[28]. Lawrence Klein, who launched the Michigan model, later went on to a most ambitious project known as the "Brookings Model," at least ten times more complex than the former. Subsequently, Klein developed an even more ambitious, complex project. This was the Link Project, which started by ascertaining that all the industrial countries, and some of the developing ones, have one or more models of their economy, and that each of these contains a sector that covers international exchanges. Klein had the idea of putting these models together to obtain a model of the world economy, and in particular the international trade in goods, services, and capital. In Italy, Andreatta and his Bologna group took part in the project.

Ando and I developed our model of the American economy along essentially Keynesian lines—but our sort of Keynes, where money is very important. Indeed, we discovered that it was even more important than we thought, owing to the interaction between my consumption function and monetary policy. Since my consumption function shows that consumption depends on income and wealth, and since rates of interest influence wealth, we found an additional channel through which monetary policy can influence income. We demonstrated, moreover, that for our estimates, at least, this channel was faster than the traditional one that passes through investments and implies several delays.

The construction of the model was entrusted to us by the Fed in 1964, during the presidency of Chesney Martin, on the recommendation of Dan Brill, then head of the research section. Martin's successor, Arthur Burns, was less convinced. The model was completed around 1969, a little late because in the original version we had neglected to take account of the effects of inflation. This was justifiable because until the Vietnam War inflation had been low and stable. But the situation changed in 1966 and continued to get worse until 1970, when inflation reached 6 percent. We were thus forced to revise the model, making a more careful distinction between nominal and real variables. For example, concerning the interest rate, it became necessary to distinguish between the market rate (which influences the demand for money) and the real rate (the nominal one reduced by the rate of inflation, which influences investments).

The interesting thing about the affair of the American model is the decision by the Fed to entrust the development of the model to a consortium of American universities. The Fed wanted the model to be developed outside, the academic community to be aware of this decision, and the result not to reflect its ideas on how to operate. This has always struck me as a very interesting and farsighted decision for a public body. The Fed, then, granted funds for the research to an interuniversity organization, the Social Science Research Council, which coordinated the work of the faculties around common research projects. In so doing, there was the implicit assurance that the council would entrust the project to us at MIT under my direction.

The model was divided into two large sectors: the real one and the financial one. The real sector has to do with income, with the channels through which it is formed: consumption, public expenditure, investment. Some items of the real part, like private investment and consumption of durable goods, are plainly influenced by financial variables. Substantially, the financial sector links the real sector to monetary policy. The foreign channel was also taken into consideration—that is, international trade and the balance of payments. The variables and functions were divided into two large groups: the endogenous variables, those that depend on other variables of the system and therefore interact; and the exogenous variables, which can be taken as given from outside the system.

This was the first large, complete model of an open economy. There had already been some partial econometric models, like those constructed for countries by Tinbergen, which were more similar to the old Modigliani-Neisser model but that differed from ours because they included a very rudimentary financial sector.

Very interesting, too, was the ceremony of the model's presentation. For the Fed desired that there should be only two copies: One was delivered to the committee, the other remained with us, on the understanding that, according to their requirements, they would modify their copy, which would remain secret and confidential, while ours could be developed and made public, with periodic updates.

Onc of the indirect results of the model for the Fed was that in 1966 Guido Carli, the brilliant governor of the Bank of Italy at that time, asked me to head a group of members of the research department to build an econometric model for Italy. I accepted with pleasure because I thought, rightly, that it would help me to reconsolidate my ties with Italy and strengthen my knowledge of its real and financial economic structure, which at that time was not very systematic. What I less expected, but which gave me equal pleasure, was to establish firm friendships with several "young elements" in the research and management service of the bank (Ranier Masera, Antonio Fazio, Mario Sarcinelli, Paolo Savona, Ezio Tarantelli, Fausto Vicarelli, Guido Rey, Franco Cotula, Mario Filosa, Bruno Sitzia, and many others).

In those years, after developing the life cycle hypothesis, I wrote two papers, one of which was devoted to the test of the effects of the public deficit[29]. The other sought to test the LCH prediction about the importance of the income growth rate. The growth rate is normally very stable in an individual country—in the United States, for example, it has stood at around 3 percent for several decades; analysis of a single country is thus of no use for testing the effect of the growth rate. I therefore tried to collect data for a sample of countries, hoping to find very different experiences in terms of income growth rate. My research was most fruitful, thanks inter alia to the valuable assistance Antonio Fazio generously provided. We found growth rates that ranged from negative values (for example, in South America) to very high ones, in particular for Italy (5.3 percent) and Japan (9.9 percent). This evidence confirmed the forecasts of the life cycle hypothesis of saving beyond what I had expected; there was no shadow of doubt that the two variables that followed (and closely) the difference in the share of saving on private income were the rate of income growth and certain demographic variables. At the same time, there was also confirmation that the *per capita* income level explained nothing. The Japan of that time (1945–60) was one of the poorest countries of the industrialized world, but it saved 21 percent of its income, whereas the richest country at that time, the United States, saved only 9.9 percent. Italy, too, despite a very low *per capita* income, saved 14 percent.

28   Making Peace with the Monetarists? Or, My "Presidential Address"

To be elected to the presidency of the American Economic Association is considered the highest honor for an American economist. The vice-president will become president the next year. Hence, the choice of the vice-president follows a complicated path. The candidate is indicated by a committee chosen by the previous president. Through a series of meetings and communications by letter, the committee draws up a list of names that is then discussed with the executive committee of the association. When the choice has been made, the name of the candidate for the vice-presidency is placed in an envelope sent to the members, by which the vice-president is chosen, the president confirmed, and so forth.

The vice-president's main task is to organize the program for the congress to be held at the end of his tenure, selecting the topics to be dealt with and the persons to chair the various sessions, and these persons then choose the speakers. The year after that, all contributions are collected in a volume of *Papers and Proceedings*, edited by the president himself. The president has not many duties and can only press for certain initiatives. In my case, for example, I encouraged the performance of a task that had already gotten under way but was in difficulties—namely, the translation into English of Pareto's *Manuale di economia*. The other function of the president is to present the *Presidential Address*, a paper read to the annual congress. The *Address* is given on the evening of the first of the three days of the congress, and the sessions are interrupted in order to enable everyone to attend this key occasion.

I was especially keen for the session to be chaired by my dear mentor, Jacob Marschak, with whom I had always kept up affectionate relations, both personal and academic, throughout his peregrinations from Chicago to Yale and from there to the University of California at Los Angeles. For his eightieth birthday, a group of his students (including another future Nobel winner, Harry Markowitz) decided to make up a collection of testimonies in his honor. My own contribution consisted of three lines from the first canto of the *Inferno* in the *Divine Comedy* (a trifle presumptuous?) where Dante addresses Vergil:

> *Tu se' lo mio maestro e 'l mio autore,*
> *tu se' solo colui da cu' io tolsi*
> *lo bello stilo che m'ha fatto onore.*

> *You are my true teacher and my author*
> *You are the one from whom I learned*
> *the style that has brought me honor.*

During the months in which I had already been designated to the presidency of the association, the polemic with the monetarists had raised its head once more. At that time, the monetarists, headed by Milton Friedman, had returned to the attack with their suggestion to abolish any discretionary economic policy and replace it with a mechanical monetary policy: augmenting the quantity of money at an absolutely constant rate (3 percent). I felt it would be cowardly to avoid this topic in my address, and since cowardice is foreign to my character, I prepared a very full, passionate, polemical text. The effect on the audience was heartening. They broke into long, sustained applause. My colleagues and friends rose to their feet. I remember that the front rows in the hall were crammed with my pupils and friends. For me, that applause was a testimony of affection that I shall never forget.

I must say that my opposition to Friedman and his followers was never a preconceived attitude. I well understood the monetarist objections that stabilization policies are dangerous because we do not know enough about economics to calculate their effects or to recognize the shocks such policies may produce against the will of those who enact them. The monetarists start out from the consideration that we cannot claim to be sure that the stabilization measures will not ultimately run in the wrong direction. That evening, I replied to the objection with the following simile: Friedman's logical argument against stabilization policies and in favor of a rule of constant increase of money was, in my view, like saying that a person who wanted to take a trip from Saint Paul to New Orleans on very important, urgent business, should beware of going by car and should instead get hold of an old barrel, climb inside it, and have himself cast into the muddy waters of the Mississippi. In that way he would be sure of reaching his destination carried by the river current. Otherwise, traveling by car, he might lose the way and wind up in Alaska.

In reality, one must take into account the possibility that a certain policy, aimed at stabilization, may cause appreciable damage (in my view, the possibility exists but is a very slender one) and set it against the alternative possibility, that is, that not to pursue such a policy may lead to a catastrophe with long-lasting effects—as was the case in the great crash of 1929.

29   Our Vietnam War

Serena and I were uncompromisingly opposed to the war in Vietnam. It became a matter of commitment for the whole family, as well as for our friends. Whereas Kennedy had sent only military advisers to Vietnam, I well remember the "escalation" during the Johnson administration. It immediately struck us as an immoral war: Clearly, we had no right to impose our system of government and way of life on a people who plainly did not want them. We thought the interpretation given by the propaganda in the United States obviously false. The Vietcong were in no way the tools of a dictator who was forcing them to fight for communism. On the contrary, Ho Chi Minh had the consensus of the majority of his people, however little his ideas appealed to us. From the start, I was against sending draftees.

My first public protest against the war took place because at that time I was acting as counselor and academic consultant to the Treasury. MIT was expecting a visit from Treasury Secretary George Schultz, who was an old acquaintance, at least in peacetime, and former dean of the Faculty of Economics at Chicago. He was returning to MIT to visit the university where he had begun his brilliant career and still had many friends. His visit had the obvious purpose of asking us for help and advice about how to deal with the macroeconomic consequences of the war. When I learned of his coming, I took pen and paper and wrote him a pretty insolent letter, telling him I would be unable to attend the conference because I was already committed to take part, at the very same time, in a demonstration against the war in Vietnam. These were the very words I used. Sometime later, for the sake of consistency and without regrets, I wrote a letter resigning from my duties as official consultant to the Treasury.

We economists at MIT were opposed to the war almost *en bloc*, after the departure of Walter Rostow, who was considered to be the only "hawk" among us and who was, unsurprisingly, summoned by Johnson as assistant on the Security Council. We actually succeeded in getting the use of an important television station in Boston for a whole evening. All the faculty members volunteered to speak against the war and to reply to questions from viewers. There was Paul Samuelson, usually not very keen on being on show. There were Solow, Domar, Brown, and myself. We all called for a boycott of the war, and we explained that we were not dealing with a communist machination that had to be thwarted. The most fashionable argument at that time was the Domino Theory, the idea that if the communists broke through in Vietnam they would go on to swallow up all Asia; therefore, the war was in the nature of a mission to stem the global onslaught.

At the time of the escalation, our first son, Andrea, was about twenty-six. The draft was initially very selective, and for a while university students and young teachers were exempted from the draft. Only later was it extended to all (and, actually, that earlier exemption had struck me as hardly democratic). Our younger son, Sergio, was still at Harvard in 1967, scarcely over twenty years of age and thus fully eligible for the draft.

And here we need to take a step back to our beliefs as a family and the education we gave our sons. When our children were small, Serena and I immediately agreed that they should not be sent to religious schools, let alone Jewish ones. In Italy, our parents and some of our grandparents had already been free-thinkers and had cut loose from all religious bigotry, and we had no intention of relapsing. We have always been free-thinkers, convinced that morality must have its roots in conscience, not in dogma. Looking at our friends and acquaintances, we realized how much we admired and respected the Quakers, who in Europe are wrongly seen as a religious sect. In actual fact, the Quakers accept no dogma, are profoundly opposed to violence and most of them also to war, are abstemious and morally upright but also very respectful of individual convictions. All of them are free to think as they like, provided they remain true to themselves and to their conscience. They are brought up to be extremely tolerant toward others, yet very strict with themselves—the exact opposite of bigots of all species and religions.

In the United States almost everybody belongs to a religion or sect, and free-thinkers are not particularly understood or recognized as an ethical group. We decided it would be good for Andrea and Sergio to attend a Quaker school, so we sent them to a country school in Westtown, Pennsylvania, near Philadelphia, and we have never regretted the decision. An additional reason why Serena approved of this choice was that it would move the children away from me, for, in her view, I tended to encroach on them a little too much and my constant presence would not help toward the harmonious development of their characters. Serena said that in any intellectual discussion in the family I always had the first say and gave the answer, which very often had the effect of silencing the children. She may have been right.

Sergio, then, was at Harvard and had firmly decided to take no part in the war. After graduation, he agreed to return to his old school at Westtown to teach mathematics and thus postpone the draft. Sergio was very well known there because he had been president of the student body, a very important function in Quaker schools. Every year, during a fixed period, the president of the students takes the place of the headmaster and directs the school; the purpose of this is to encourage not only a democratic character but also a responsible attitude. During his last year at Harvard, Sergio decided to start the process for draft exemption as a conscientious objector, like many others of our Quaker friends. In this way I had the opportunity to make the acquaintance of this remarkable American institution, which allows an individual to refuse military service if he can persuade a commission created ad hoc that his refusal is grounded on an authentic question of conscience. The process lasted several months, but Sergio was successful thanks also to his connections with the Quakers and owing to letters from his teachers, from friends of ours, and a famous, ancient correspondence between Serena and our neighbor, a Protestant minister, in which my wife explained that we did not send our son to his Sunday school since we held that moral and religious education ought to come from the family rather than an external source, and our fundamental ethical principle was to be faithful to one's own conscience.

Incidentally, I remember recounting this "odyssey" of Sergio's one

evening among friends in Rome, taking some pride in American toler-
ance. But I also recall how it sparked a sharp exchange with a well-
known colleague, my former pupil and good friend. For, at the end of my
story, he said: "Well, more or less like in Italy!" "What do you mean?" I
wondered, knowing that in Italy at that time conscientious objection was
not admitted. "Because"—came the reply—"in order to be exempted as a
conscientious objector you need to write a couple of cultured, cogent
essays, and to do that in America you need to have been to college; and
to go to college you need rich parents. But in Italy, too, if you have rich
parents you can easily be exmpted from military service!" I was dumb-
founded, for he obviously meant it seriously. And I promised myself to
store this episode in my memory: There's yet another striking example of
the Italian habit of confusing questions of principle with pragmatic problems. I was proud that American law acknowledged the principle that
one must be free to follow one's own conscience over and above all duty
to one's country; but my friend cared only for the pragmatic result: to
sidestep, or not, the nuisance of military service. And he was satisfied
that this result could be achieved in Italy, too—even at the cost of brib-
ing a public official.

Serena and I took part in a great many quiet, peaceful demonstrations
organized by the Quakers, but our more passionate friends went as far as
to get themselves sent to prison for civil disobedience when they obstructed
troop movements or tried to bar the road to the Pentagon. I cherish a
memory of one of those demonstrations, which was based on the principle
that no one should conceal their own ideas. Each of us wore a tag with our
name on it. When crowds of strange photographers (probably FBI agents
come to register us) began snapping yards of pictures, we held up our
name tags to show our names and affirm our right as citizens to protest
peacefully.

It was a day of rejoicing when Johnson decided not to stand for reelec-
tion and the students marched through the streets of Boston, dancing and
shouting: "Hey, hey! What do you say? LBJ gave up today!" But the joy
was short-lived, and the euphoria of the people in the streets gave way to
a sense of torpor and sadness. In an article in the Corriere della Sera,
Wednesday February 7, 1973, I tried to explain to the Italians, too, this
mixture of conflicting feelings that possessed America, and then the world.

The doves who spent years awaiting this moment are still in
a state of shock at the indiscriminate terror bombing to which
Vietnam was subjected right in the middle of the Christmas celebrations, and not even the keenest hawks are able to deceive

themselves into thinking that an accord so laboriously achieved marks a victory for the United States or can in any way justify the dreadful cost of this war.

For, at the end of the war, Vietnam had lost two million dead, soldiers and civilians, with nearly half a million wounded in South Vietnam alone, towns razed, public buildings smashed, crops and forests destroyed, and huge numbers of persons displaced, either voluntarily or by force. The toll for the United States ran to 46,000 dead and 300,000 wounded. The total expense was reckoned at around $125 billion of that time. Then there were the indirect costs, of particular interest to economists: the wave of inflation that started in 1966. This inflation should not be ascribed to the fact that the war was, in itself, so expensive that it could not be financed by taxes and orderly recourse to public borrowing. Rather, the inflation stemmed from Johnson's decision not to have timely recourse to increases in taxation or in the cost of money, to hide the real cost of the operation from the public and thus to prevent public opinion from obstructing his policy. The inflation itself plus the huge increase in military expenditure abroad were also the principal causes of the massive worsening in the American balance of payments, which ultimately led to the suspension of the dollar's convertibility in August 1971 and the deep international monetary crisis that resulted.

30   *What We Did for Andreas Papandreou, or, When for Once, American Economists Found Themselves in Agreement!*

Around the mid-1950s the Department of Economics at Berkeley, California, offered me the post of professor. Offers did come along from time to time, but this one bore the signature of the head of the department at Berkeley, who was a well-known Greek economist, Andreas Papandreou. At that time we were not aware that he was interested in politics. But eventually he returned to Greece and entered politics.

Many years later, in 1967, Papandreou was arrested and put in prison by the fascist colonels who engineered the coup d'état in Greece. We felt we must do something for our colleague who was risking his life for his country in Europe. So, along with others, we organized a campaign to telephone all our fellow economists to convince them to flood President Johnson with letters, requesting him to intercede with the Greek military junta for Papandreou's release. Johnson is said to have replied: "Econo-mists never agree about anything, except about Papandreou." The presi-dent listened to us and sent Walter Heller, member of the Council of Economic Advisors, to Athens to negotiate the release of Papandreou, but before that he succeeded in obtaining permission for the American ambas-sador to Greece to visit him in prison and bring him comfort. We were overjoyed when he came out of prison.

Sometime later, he and his wife, Margaret, came to see us at Belmont to thank us for our support. Papandreou told us that while he was in prison, in complete isolation, he was sure that at any moment he would be hanged or have his throat cut, like many others, under the guise of suicide. But when the ambassador had been to see him and had taken him a cutting from the front page of the *New York Times* reporting our intercession with the president, he said, "I realized I was safe, because outside they knew I had been imprisoned." His fear was that no one knew he was in prison, in which case his life really would have been in danger.

31   *The Nobel Prize and Saint Lucy's Night*

The phone rang at seven in the morning. "Hello. Is this Professor Modi-gliani? Swedish Royal Academy of Sciences speaking. We were wondering if you would be prepared to come to Stockholm in December to receive the Nobel Prize." I was still dozing, and Serena swears that, startled out of my sleep, I mumbled: "Well, we'll see if it's possible. . . ."

Recalling what she had been told by Selma Arrow, wife of Ken Arrow, about the invasion of journalists a few minutes after his prize was announced, Serena said: "Take a shower and get shaved and dressed at once because they'll be upon us in next to no time. . . ." And behold, twenty minutes later, the doorbell began ringing and our house was besieged by radio and television reporters.

Serena phoned our son Andrea, professor at the University of Michigan, and began: "Andrea, sorry to wake you, but your father has won the Nobel Prize." This sentence appeared as the headline in the newspaper in Ann Arbor the following morning. Andrea's daughter, Leah, was at Oberlin College, Ohio, and the day following the announcement she went to buy the *New York Times* from her usual newsstand; she was thunderstruck when she looked at the front page and saw a big photo of myself in the act of kissing Serena, who was trying to fend me off, with all the reporters looking on. When she had recovered, Leah went back to the newsstand

and requested a second copy of the paper, to which the vendor replied: "But I've just sold you one, what have you done with it?" And so Oberlin, too, learned the news of her famous grandparents.

Serena prepared me to go to MIT, where a celebration had been organized, for I was almost out of my wits. And it was an incredible day, with crowds of photographers and flashbulbs popping. Dressed to the nines, I also had to improvise a press conference with the journalists in the hall of the institute. But what really touched our hearts was the response of Italian Americans. The butcher's shop sported the *New York Times* photo of Serena and me in its window, and when Serena went to buy meat she couldn't believe her eyes.

To put it briefly, I hadn't expected that phone call. There were some, however, who had given up expecting it. For you must know that economists lay bets on the Nobel Prize, and for a long time my friends had been saying that I was on the list of possible winners and many of them had therefore gambled on me, only to lose. The Nobel arrived when everyone had ceased betting on me.

The Nobel Prize for economics is not a Nobel in the strict sense, since it is not financed by the Alfred Nobel Foundation, which, wisely administered, is able to guarantee funds for prizes in the subjects originally specified. The idea of a Nobel Memorial Prize for economics came from the central bank of Sweden, which earmarked a sum to be entrusted to the management of the Nobel foundation. The first Nobel for economics was awarded in 1969.

From the moment I learned of the award the women of the family began thinking about their dresses, asking advice from Zella Luria, wife of my old friend and colleague, Salvatore Luria, who had already attended the ceremony for her husband's prize for biology. I invited Andrea to come along, and Sergio with his wife, Suzanne, and my grown-up granddaughters, Leah and Julia (their mother was divorced from Andrea), who were twenty-one and eighteen, respectively. My Italian nephews, Enrico and Paola, came too, with their spouses, plus my former student, colleague, and friend Mario Baldassari, who was entrusted with taking the photos.

We made two stops on the way to Stockholm. The first was in Rome, where the Italian president, Francesco Cossiga, and the government created me knight of the Gran Croce, an honor that gave me immense pleasure. We went to the Quirinal palace for the ceremony, and Cossiga had Antonio Maccanico show us round this magnificent building. And at a certain point in our tour, at the end of a corridor we saw a person running toward us. It was Cossiga, who had decided to make the tour with us. He said: "As I had nothing to do, I thought I might as well come with you." His courtesy was delightful.

Our second stop was in Brussels, where my fellow economist Jacques Drèze had set up an audience with the king of Belgium, Baudouin. I had been instructed in etiquette and told not to ask the king any questions, only to reply to his. But Baudouin was so charming and cordial that I forgot the etiquette and asked him how much he knew about economics. He admitted to knowing little, for he had ascended the throne at the tender age of eighteen, on his father's death. I therefore invited him to read Samuelson's textbook, and on our return to Boston I sent him a copy, inscribed with a dedication from myself and Samuelson. Serena scolded me for this breach of etiquette, but I defended myself by saying that the king had obviously enjoyed himself with me, as he had personally accompanied me back to the car in the courtyard!

At Stockholm we spent an enchanting week, with unforgettable parties and ceremonies. The first engagement is a press conference for all the Nobel winners. Then there is a visit to the Academy of Sciences, and, following that, on the first evening each prize winner goes to the embassy of her or his country. We were lucky in having two: the American embassy, where I went with the majority of the prizewinners, and the Italian embassy, where I went alone. The American ambassador gave us dinner, an informal and very cheerful occasion, with a great many guests, including children who chased each other merrily around the buffet table. The Italian embassy, on the contrary, offered Serena and me, along with other distinguished guests, a most refined lunch at a single long table, with delicious food and elegant china, crystal, and Murano glass, in an almost nineteenth-century atmosphere, in contrast to the American one and highlighting the different traditions of the two countries we held dear.

There followed the presentation ceremony by the king of Sweden of the certificate and the gold medal—but only after full rehearsals the day before, to avoid any mistakes or awkwardness. After King Carl Gustav handed me the certificate and medal and after the handshake and my bow to the king, I forgot all about etiquette and, with my hand, I blew a kiss to Serena—which evoked tremendous applause and, next morning, the approval of the Swedish newspapers, who wrote: "Professor Modigliani broke tradition and etiquette; you can see he was born in Italy. . . ."

All of us, myself and my family and friends in the audience, were moved by the ceremony. When a Nobel Prize winner is called to the center of the great hall, where the king awaits him, first the Swedish royal march is played, then the national anthem of the prizewinner's country. For me the "Stars and Stripes" of course. But on the vest of my tailcoat shone the silk ribbon of the knighthood of the Republic of Italy.

When the ceremony was over, I remember that the Italian journalists asked me what I was going to do with the $350,000 prize. And I replied that I would spend it just as the life cycle model predicted—that is, from then on, drinking a more expensive beer than hitherto!

The prize giving is followed by the grand banquet in Stockholm's splendid town hall, with the center table occupied by the king and queen, members of the government, diplomats, and the prizewinners with their wives, all surrounded by the other tables with about a thousand guests. The ceremony is impressive, because the hall opens on to a great staircase, down both sides of which come two lines of waiters carrying gigantic serving dishes on their shoulders. I sat next to the wife of the Japanese ambassador.

At the end of the banquet, each prizewinner is asked to make a short speech. Mine consisted of a simple profession of faith against nationalism: I said that during my life I had never believed in nationalism in the sense of "my country right or wrong." Though born Italian, I had left my country when my conscience told me my country was behaving in an immoral way, with race laws and then with the military alliance with Hitler. I disowned my Italian nationality at the worst moment of fascism when Italy symbolized the yoke round the neck of a number of other countries, however much the conscience of the Italians had prevented them from Nazism's cruelest excesses. But I was happy to feel myself Italian once again, now that Italy was a civilized country. I loved the America that had welcomed me, to study and to teach. But my Americanness was not to be taken as a blind endorsement of everything America did. To be loyal to one's country means being proud of it when pride is justified and criticizing it when it takes a wrong turn, in order to help set it back on the right path. And I wound up by saying that I hoped I might be allowed to add a third love: for the great country whose guest I now was, Sweden.

These words had a special significance because the Vietnam War had not long ended, and my family and I had refused to support our government for as long as it was in the wrong. Serena and I have always thought that states ought to be structures at the service of the citizen. We have never believed in blind, unconditional loyalty. When a state goes against the conscience of one of its citizens, she or he has the right to protest and must have the right to fight against its decisions. Our Fatherland is humanity, friendship, fair play—values that stem from deep within the conscience of each of us and that the state must respect.

Another prizewinner, an American biologist, told a memorable joke in his speech. A Nobel award winner, a famous academic, receives the phone call from Stockholm. In order to celebrate and to give journalists and friends the slip, he decides to take a short trip in the wild, deserted mountains in the interior. Off he goes with his wife, and, after many miles, he realizes that he is running out of gas. They look for a gas station and finally come upon a dirty, ramshackle place. Out comes a ragged man, covered with grease. He fills up their tank. But as the academic is about to pay, his wife jumps out of the car and starts kissing and embracing the man. Then she climbs back into the car and off they go again. Her astonished husband asks who the man was. And the wife says he was her fiancé long ago. Says he: "Well, you must be happy you didn't marry him instead of me." And the wife says: "Don't be so conceited. If I'd married him, he'd have won the Nobel Prize." Deep down, that's how I feel about Serena. But we were also amused by the reaction of Queen Silvia of Sweden, who was delighted by the joke and laughed heartily and with gusto.

During the Nobel week in Stockholm the really important dinner is the one held the evening after the prize giving in the royal palace for a mere hundred persons all seated at the same table, and it is confined to the Nobel winners and their spouses, the king and queen, and representatives of the court and the Swedish government. I was able to chat the whole evening with one of the queen's ladies-in-waiting.

Serena sat next to the prime minister, Olof Palme, who impressed her extremely and with whom she spent the entire evening talking about the pacifist friends we had in common, especially our colleagues on the faculty of nuclear physics at MIT. Palme was a close friend of well-known MIT physicist Victor Weisskopf, called Vicky; Jerome Wiesner, longtime president of MIT, and others. Their liking for each other grew during the dinner. Serena was fascinated by the wonderful plates: Each course was presented on a different service. Thinking that the underside would bear the manufacturer's mark, she asked Palme: "As you're at home here, please turn the plate over so I can see what it is." Palme did as requested, but there was nothing: "It's too old," he said. She grieved when Palme was murdered a few months later.

Talking after dinner with Princess Christina, the king's sister, Serena said to her: "What's so extraordinary about this dinner is the mixture of human warmth and hospitality together with the formality and elegance of the tall silver stands, the china, and the glass." To which the princess replied: "We don't dine like this every day, Mrs. Modigliani, only in your honor. . . ." The table was a huge one, and ever since then my wife continues to wonder whether the tablecloth really was the single piece it seemed, or was made up of sections. During the dinner we tried to detect the seams but couldn't find any. But however did they manage to wash it?

I was seated, as I said, next to the very pleasant lady-in-waiting to the queen. She explained a lot of things about the royal family to me: for example, that the queen had been a famous Brazilian beauty, and that she has a bodyguard all to herself—soldiers whose headgear is topped with a very tall peacock feather, seemingly decorative but actually stemming from an ancient and useful function. For it appears that centuries ago there was a very tiny queen who, if she got lost in the crowd, could be retraced by the feathers of her guards, which were easily visible above the people's heads.

Coffee was served at the end of the meal. That was the moment for me to be introduced to the queen. To my slight embarassment—but actually I was surprised and amused—she suggested: "Professor Modigliani, I would advise you not to sleep in the raw tonight, wear your pajamas, because tomorrow morning comes Saint Lucy." It was indeed the night between December 12 and 13; according to an ancient tradition, at the dawn of Saint Lucy's day, when it is still dark in Stockholm, the students go singing and dancing through the streets, the girls wearing crowns of lighted candles on their heads, and they go and sing before the houses of their teachers, and if invited to come inside they offer a rich Nordic breakfast of hot buttered rolls, jam, and coffee. It was indeed "Saint Lucy" who entered our room with her suite to offer us breakfast in bed, singing the song of Santa Lucia, which runs "Sul mare luccica l'astro d'argento. . . ."

We spent the next day at the university, where the Nobel Lecture is given, which has then to be presented in written form some months later. This consists of a summary of the contribution that won the Nobel prize for its author, and is given to a group of specialists in the field. I held my lecture in the aula magna of the faculty of economics. The citation of my prize mentioned two contributions, the LCH and the Mo-Mi and Mi-Mo theorems. I decided to devote my lecture to the LCH, among other reasons because it gave me the chance to recall Richard Brumberg's contribution.

I was touched and amused when the students of the faculty presented me with a most appropriate gift—a lovely racing bike called *Life Cycle*. The only problem was that it was intended for lanky Swedes: Perched on the saddle, I could hardly reach the pedals. The bike is now used by my grandson David, who luckily is six feet three inches tall!

It was hard to tear oneself away from this fairy land back to reality. But I was helped in this difficult task by the knowledge that in a few weeks' time I must hand in a polished copy of my Nobel Lecture.

32   Ronald Reagan, Inventor of the Peacetime Deficit

When Serena and I read in the Italian newspapers the distant rumbles of the ongoing arguments in Italy, we never cease to be amazed at the fact that, after so many years, the damage wreaked on the American and global economies by the Reagan administration is not evident. Reagan's success in foreign policy is, of course, undeniable. I acknowledge it without a qualm. Reagan scored a victory for the West against the communism that for decades reduced a part of humanity to slavery. He did so as a great actor, waging a technical battle with the enemy whose outcome was uncertain over Star Wars, which even in the United States failed to achieve the desired results but compelled the Soviet Union to admit its own technical and scientific inferiority, and led to the regime being dismantled; this was also favored by the slump in the prices of oil and gold, of which the Soviet Union was a leading producer. There are several ways of financing a war. Of all the possible ways, Reagan chose the worst: It did most damage to later generations and required tremendous efforts on the part of the presidents who came after him, Republican and Democrat alike, to heal the wounds inflicted by the eight years of his presidency.

In many respects Reagan can be said to have been the inventor of the deficit in the United States. Before him it had not really existed—or, rather, it had been used as an instrument of cyclical control of demand in periods of recession, but not as a structural phenomenon. Until then, Republican and Democrat presidents had always pursued a wise, moderate policy[30]. This analysis to some extent refutes James Buchanan[31] when he says that all democratic societies have an ineluctable tendency toward deficit. His assertion is not borne out by the history of the United States, with the exception of Reagan's presidency.

The deficit under Reagan actually reached 6.3 percent of GDP. This is an enormous figure if compared with the balance achieved under Clinton. Correcting for inflation, in the way I have proposed, the federal deficits from 1983 onward are the largest ever recorded in peacetime and showed no sign of falling until the last year of Reagan's administration.

In the discussion on the subject in America, we witnessed a very sharp clash in 1995 between the Republican-led Congress and President Clinton. But this clash did not concern the basic objective, shared by both sides: namely, to zero the deficit. It had more to do, if anything, with how the sacrifices were to be distributed, and how long the process would take.

The most surprising feature of all this was that Reagan stood for election saying: There is only one evil in the world, a real plague, and that is public deficit. During his first campaign, against Carter, Reagan adopted an economic model based on the so-called Laffer curve: If the state embarks on foolish expenditure, it will try to increase its income through taxation; but taxation contains in itself the beginning of its own end, for it cancels the incentive to produce; and in this way the government sees its tax yield dwindle, can no longer finance the expenditure, and thus takes to printing money; but printing money creates inflation, according to the monetarist model; inflation creates disorder, disorder creates unemployment and bad working of the system. And this was the situation in America as Reagan described it at the end of Carter's presidency in 1981. Reagan impressed the American electorate with the famous speech in which he said that if the deficit were piled up in one-dollar bills, one on top of another, the pile would reach as far as the moon.

No sooner was Reagan elected than he said, on February 5, 1981, that the United States was in the worst situation since the Great Depression. The monster deficit was devouring Americans' income. He claimed that since 1960 the percentage of income exacted by government in the form of taxes had doubled (actually, the increase did not exceed 20 percent and was entirely devoted to funding welfare expenditure). Addressing the seven million unemployed, he ended by saying that if they stood hand in hand they would form a human chain from coast to coast, from Maine to California.

Basing his views on the Laffer curve (which has never had any foundation in economics), Reagan promised he would reduce taxes so as to enhance the rate of saving, thus leading to higher growth, which would offset the lower tax yield. At the same time, he promised to fight inflation by pursuing a rigorously monetarist policy. In his view, inflation stemmed from the excess of money caused by the deficit. To eliminate inflation, all that was needed was to set a fixed rule for the increase in the money stock.

These were the programs stated in the election campaign. In the event, Reagan was successful in only one of his objectives, reducing inflation—an important one, to be sure. But I can show that this was the result of a monetary policy managed by Paul Volcker—appointed by Carter—who under a monetarist guise adopted instruments and policies that were anything but monetarist.

The economic model that underpinned Reagan's political program was wrong, but it had the advantage of appearing simple: Public expenditure produces inflation[32]. Thus, Reagan justified the first drastic reduction in social spending. A pity that the inflation of the 1970s had nothing to do with excessive expenditure and with a policy of monetizing the deficit: It resulted from the increase in oil prices. The central banks responded to this, as will be explained later, with a monetary policy that was not accommodating and caused a general rise in unemployment. The deficit was, if anything, the effect of increased unemployment, not the cause of it. Unemployment and inflation reached a peak during the second oil shock, in the two-year period 1980–81, during the presidential campaign. Yet in

1980 Carter presented a budget with a deficit equal to 2 percent of the GNP, which was more than justified by the situation of cyclical depression the economy was undergoing.

In that speech in February 1981, Reagan undertook to reduce taxes by 3 percent on all incomes in three years. He gave a distinct hint as to the policy the Federal Reserve would have to pursue, saying that he would aim at a "stable" monetary policy. There was no doubt about the monetarist accent. And it was made crystal clear in the 1982 report of the Council of Economic Advisors: "A key element for the policy of the government is support for a policy of continual and gradual reduction of the rate of growth of money, so as to reduce inflation."

Inflation shrank from 10 percent in 1980 to 2.2 percent in 1986, an excellent result. Yet in the same period there was no trace of a reduction in the rate of growth of the money supply—indeed, in some cases it actually increased. Headed by Volcker, the Fed acquired the habit of announcing monetary objectives, but, in the first place, it never indicated a single one, but four or five; in addition, it always suggested a target for growth of GNP in nominal terms. The monetary goals, surprise surprise, were always missed (except in 1981). The national income goals were always reached. The growth of the money stocks was always closely linked with the predicted growth of the national income in nominal terms. To sum up, in a political context that demanded a monetarist language and guise, Volcker conducted an excellent discretionary policy, keeping monetary income under control.

Disinflation took its toll, though this was carefully concealed. Unemployment rose from 7 to 11 percent, the highest since the war. Between 1981 and 1984 inflation fell by 6.7 percent, of which 4.7 percent could be ascribed to the increase in unemployment, the rest to the reduction in oil prices. When, eighteen months after the election, the president's economists realized what was happening, they hastened to take remedial measures. How? By a colossal increase of the deficit. The deficit was the cumulated result of a large drop in revenues—reflecting Reagan's tax cuts!—and a big increase in military expenditure.

Martin Feldstein, who then headed the Council of Economic Advisors, found a theoretical justification for the recourse to deficit in the theories of Barro and rational expectations. According to this model, as we have seen, people respond to a growing deficit by saving more; and they do so because they are aware that this deficit will in future lead to new taxes, necessary to pay the interest and the capital borrowed by the government. The increase in the stock of deficit would be accompanied by an increase in the stock of wealth, with the result that the funds available for investment in plant, capital, and infrastructures should not diminish. And, even if domestic saving should marginally fall, fresh capital could be attracted from abroad by raising the interest rates. In this way, the level of investment would remain unchanged, because the drop in domestic funds would be directly offset by the flow of foreign funds.

Feldstein provided a model to justify the sensational about-face of a president who had won the election describing Carter's modest deficit as the worst evil from 1929 to the present day. In actual fact, the tight money policy caused a rise in unemployment as a device for reducing inflation. Realizing this, Reagan began increasing the deficit in order to sustain demand, counting mainly on military expenditure. He would have liked to balance the increased expenditure with cuts in the welfare sector, but Congress prevented him from doing so. In order to allay the electorate's feeling that they were in a serious situation, Reagan had to cut taxes even more rapidly and more incisively than he had promised. The income tax was lowered by about 25 percent over three years, with a drastic reduction in the rates. In addition, there was an attempt at fiscal incentives to favor the formation of saving, lest the greater disposable income be entirely eaten up. The main device was the IRA (Individual Retirement Act), that is, restricted personal accounts (theoretically restricted for pension purposes), which allowed each family to set aside $2,500 per year, deducted from its taxable income and not subject to tax on the capital return. This instrument had an effect opposite to the one intended: Instead of encouraging the formation of fresh saving, it was used as a substitute for bank deposits and as a means to get around capital gains tax.

In reality, the combination of a tight money policy and a rising deficit inevitably caused real interest rates to soar. The real rate rose from 1 percent in 1976 (the average in previous years) to 7 percent in 1984, a leap that has few precedents in history. This was the real turning point that upset the entire global economy and left its mark on the 1980s. In the first two years of Reagan's presidency unemployment jumped from 7 to 11 percent. Over the next two years it fell from 11 to 7 percent, owing to a very high increase in demand, underpinned by an expansionary fiscal policy. At that time I never tired of preaching that much less would have sufficed to relaunch the economy—namely, an expansionary monetary policy, without needing to make the budget explode. The result was that in 1983 the economic recovery was so terribly strong that it had to be curbed by monetary policy in order to prevent a phase of inflation caused by demand.

That the deficit was not needed to sustain demand is proved by the fact that real interest rates remained very high even in the period of economic recovery. What did those interest rates reflect? The excess of demand that was contrasted by the monetary policy.

It makes me furious when I hear this foolish policy of Reagan's compared with those of JFK or Roosevelt himself. Reagan's policy was in no sense Keynesian. From the Keynesian point of view, an expansionary fiscal policy has a strong effect on aggregate demand, translating into: (a) an increased product; (b) higher inflation; (c) higher interest rates. Which of these results actually occurs depends on monetary policy? In the presence of unutilized resources, stagnation, and a permissive monetary policy, this propulsive force will tend to increase employment. This is the old, and unique, Keynesian prescription applicable to the Great Depression. But when there is no more room to create new employment, what can happen? If monetary policy allows it, this excess of demand drives up prices and fuels inflation. If, on the other hand, monetary policy is restrictive, in the sense that it aims at keeping the increase in monetary income within the limits of capacity, the fiscal impulse stemming from the expenditure will have two effects: increase in interest rates and reduction in investment, in the amount necessary to finance public expenditure. Thus it was that the real rates reached levels unimaginable until just before that.

Investors all over the world began to take advantage of this, purchasing American securities. And when people try to obtain dollars to purchase financial instruments, the price of the dollar rises. But in a system of flexible exchange, the only authentic way to obtain the dollars needed for investment in America is through the movement of goods. The rest of the world can invest in the United States if it has available net exports and uses the proceeds to purchase American financial assets.

By this oblique process the deficit caused interest rates to rise, and this increase in rates brought about the trade deficit. The rise in rates results in a greater request for dollars, which in turn causes the dollar to appreciate, and this leads to a net increase in the import of goods. The Reagan administration mounted a gigantic nationalistic propaganda campaign around the fact that the dollar was becoming a very strong currency, desired by all, and that investors throughout the world were taking their money to America. In reality, the level of investment fell much less than it would have done in a closed economy for such a huge increase in the deficit. The reduction in national saving was offset by foreign capital flows. But that is not the same thing: If the invested saving and the newly formed capital are foreign, the returns on that investment will also leave the country, worsening the balance-of-payments deficit.

A country that internally adopted the policy of "buy now, pay later" could not help becoming a debtor country at the international level.

Throughout the twentieth century, the United States had had the role of exporter of capital. And this was right, as the United States is the largest and richest economy in the world. But Reagan renounced this role, and this was to have very important consequences for the whole world.

There have been positive consequences. For instance, there has been a great expansion in the income of countries that were able to export to the United States. In this way the United States has involuntarily acted as a motive force for worldwide expansion. There have been negative consequences that have left their mark. The dizzying increase in the value of the dollar and the rise in interest rates have had a catastrophic effect on the developing countries that borrowed in dollars. The debt crisis, which has paralyzed Africa, Latin America, and several other areas of the world, has its source in the mistakes of Reagan's policy. Even Europe has suffered adverse consequences. High American interest rates have forced European central banks, the Bundesbank first and foremost, to choose between two paths: following the American rates or ignoring them. In the first alternative, there is a very strong incentive to purchase dollars; but this leads to greater devaluation, whose effect is not only to increase exports but also to create inflation. The European monetary authorities are choosing the second alternative and increasing rates; this is causing investment and domestic demand to fall, and the economies are slowing down.

With Reagan the United States abandoned its guiding role in the world economy and became the world's largest debtor. During a debate at Villa d'Este in 1984, I argued that the United States had the duty to resume its role of creditor country. How?

> In the long term this public deficit will have to return to zero, and the United States will have to return to being capital suppliers to the rest of the world. At that point the American interest rates will no longer be higher but lower than those of the other economies, the balance of payments will be positive instead of strongly negative as now, and the exchange rate of the dollar will fall sharply.[33]

The decline of the British Empire began when it started to be a net debtor, staying on its feet thanks only to the credits that came from its colonies, India above all. When a country becomes a net debtor, it can hardly maintain its role of central power in the global economic and political system for long. The United States ran this risk, but has surmounted it. Indeed, two presidents, one Republican, the other Democrat, have had to come to terms with the difficult legacy of Ronald Reagan and have managed to reverse the trend, thanks also to an excellent monetary policy that has favored expansion of the economy and employment owing to a spectacular reduction in real interest rates—even while the opposite was happening in Europe. The result is that at the end of the Clinton administration, the United States found itself in something like the situation I predicted at Villa d'Este. Both the president and the Republican majority in Congress wished to erase the deficit in the space of a few years. This would give a really important contribution to the American and world economies, for it would free a large share of saving for investment—a really imposing amount in absolute terms. This would wipe out the disgrace of the Reagan years, during which America prevented the countries that most needed it from borrowing on the international markets. Unfortunately the new Bush administration is threatening to undo all the good work.

II

⚜

EUROPE AND THE MONETARY ADVENTURE

1   Prologue

The 1960s were the time of the great (unsuccessful) attempts to reform the international monetary system devised at Bretton Woods at the end of the war and an increasing state of crisis. These were also years, however, when the pressure of the crisis in the monetary system and greater awareness of how the monetary mechanism discovered by Keynes worked helped us to understand more profoundly the logic of the monetary system then in force and of former systems—and, perhaps, to prefigure future systems.

In the classical model, the old gold standard in force during the first decades of the twentieth century functioned as an automatic adjustment mechanism that kept the price level, or at least the ratio between the price levels in all countries, stable. It was founded on the principle that in every country the quantity of money was linked to gold reserves and was based on the existence of high flexibility of wages and prices in response to excess demand or supply. For, if for any reason a country's prices rose, this would produce a deficit in the balance of trade that would have to be settled in gold, thus forcing a reduction in the money stock and thence in prices. If the quantity of gold in the vaults of the central bank grew at the same rate as the world economy, then not only relative prices but also absolute prices would be constant. Unfortunately, there is no mechanism that ensures such behavior, and this was one of the reasons for the creation of Bretton Woods, and for its subsequent crisis.

Before Bretton Woods—that is, after World War I—the gold standard underwent an important modification when the inflation and shortages produced by the war brought a flood of gold to the United States, which, by the rules of the game, ought to have increased prices to external levels; on the contrary, the United States let it be known that it would terminate its commitment to a fixed ratio between money and gold, even while maintaining convertibility of paper, thus inaugurating a policy of "sterilization" of gold. The result was that the separation between reserves and money spread in both directions; that is, a loss of gold did not necessarily lead the quantity of money to diminish, and with this the convertibility between domestic currency and gold at a fixed rate was suspended, as had happened before, but at least only for transitory periods.

Keynes suggested the creation of a new currency, the Bancor, managed by a New World Bank. But Bretton Woods sanctioned the existence of two moneys: gold and the dollar, which were initially real equivalents at a fixed parity, $35 per ounce of gold. Moreover, Bretton Woods encouraged international exchange by promoting the elimination of restrictions on international trade and capital movement. This led to an unprecedented increase in income and an even greater increase in international exchange, which grew more rapidly than the stock of gold. In this way, insufficient international liquidity developed—or, if you like, a lack of gold in the central banks' vaults—that was miraculously balanced by an increase in the dollar reserves stemming from a deficit in the American balance of payments, only partly due to a trade deficit and much more to the export of capital. This engendered the crisis of the system. On the one hand, it confirmed the old prophecy of my colleague Triffin on the insufficiency of gold as a means to finance international liquidity. It was therefore felt necessary to replace, or at least to accompany, gold by another means of payment or some credit instrument, and there was a lot of head scratching to devise the oddest sort of abstract currencies. On the other hand, several countries objected that the function of supplementing reserves could not be fulfilled through the rising indebtedness of the United States. They asserted that the United States enjoyed an extraordinary advantage from playing the role of central bank to the world, since it could buy goods or pay foreign firms by "coining" money. This argument was put forward by the French above all: To demonstrate their impatience with this American superiority, they refused to hold dollar reserves and presented the U.S. authorities with all the dollars they acquired through the balance-of-trade surplus to convert them into gold—the famous gold hoarded at Fort Knox. They also encouraged other countries to do likewise to, inter alia, force devaluation of the dollar against gold.

The search was on, then, for some fiduciary currency, somehow issued by an international bank, whose quantity could be regulated according to the needs of the system instead of being dictated by the producers of gold and by hoarding in the private sector or by the international balance of the United States. But who was to make the search and in what amounts?

2   A World Central Bank

Peter Kenen and I looked for an economist's solution, but one that would also function in reality[1]. There was the fear that if an international authority like the IMF were empowered to print money, it might use the power irresponsibly, with excessive issues that would make it more difficult to accept the new currency in place of gold[2].

Our mechanism turned on a scheme that would ensure that the quantity of the new instrument would be the appropriate one, not excessive so as to cause inflation, not insufficient so as to produce unemployment. And the solution we suggested for this problem was self-evident—that is, to allow each member country to indicate the amount of liquidity it deemed suitable to hold in its reserves, on the understanding that it would thereafter act to maintain this amount. According to our plan, this liquidity would be created in the form of a means of payment issued by a world central bank that would replace the International Monetary Fund. With a touch of academic coquetry, I proposed to call our reserve currency the "Medium of International Transaction," or MIT, a version of Keynes's Bancor viewed from the banks of the Charles River.

What we proposed was a game in which all countries accepted to play with their cards visible, without the asymmetry inherent in the current system in which a single country, the United States, had seignorage—that is, the power to print a currency that regulated the international exchanges of all the others. Each of the players of the game fixed a currency reserve target. This target took account of its foreign trade and of variability in the balance of payments. At the start of the game, a new MIT-bank would take the place of the International Monetary Fund and credit each country with a current account equivalent to its own reserve target (guaranteed by an equal amount of national currency).

The fundamental rule of the game was that all the players would have to undertake to settle international exchange balances only in MIT. On the other hand, none of them could hold foreign currency, except in very small quantities for daily exchanges. Each country undertook at all times to keep a level of reserves close to the target one, that is, that of the initial deal of

MIT. Reaching that level was the North Star by which to orient the economic policies to adopt.

We foresaw a sort of "band of oscillation of the reserves" around the central target, within which the deviant country was not expected to adopt any measure[3]. We amused ourselves, however, by imagining a full package of gradual sanctions for any country outside that oscillation band either by excess or defect. In the case of imbalances in the normal oscillation band, the sanctions were only of a negative sort: The offending country was forbidden to have recourse to customs duties and restrictions or to make its national currency unconvertible. It was also forbidden to devalue its currency against the MIT. This very strict rule could be relaxed only for a country that did not overstep the normal currency reserve band but that nevertheless suffered serious unemployment. In that case we thought expansion of domestic demand just, and to prevent this from leading to a loss of reserves the possibility of devaluation was envisaged. But, in any case, the decision to devalue was to be approved by a body of the MIT bank.

Two principles underpinned our game. The first concerned the imbalances in the target reserve: The imbalances in deficit were placed on exactly the same level as those in surplus. Both were to be condemned in the same way. The second principle was more general: The game we proposed implied that each country renounce its sovereignty in favor of the system. This was such a big step that we realized something must be done to make it acceptable. Our idea was as follows: to envisage a very full list of stabilizing measures, much ampler than the one usually proposed by the International Monetary Fund. A country with a positive imbalance might be driven to reflation (if it had weak demand and falling prices), to fiscal and monetary incentives, to export of capital, to revaluation of its currency with respect to the MIT. A country in deficit would be able to choose between fiscal and monetary deflationary measures (if it suffered from an excess of domestic demand, with rapidly rising prices), or it could be pushed to encourage capital imports, to devalue its currency, to subsidize the export of goods. In all cases, the most "expensive" policies, like unemployment or price rises, were to be considered as devices of last resort. A country that did not make adjustments—one, for instance, in excessive surplus—incurred a penalty with a yearly fine, which was then distributed among the other countries according to their currency reserves.

It should be recalled that the major trauma of the Bretton Woods system was the impossibility of achieving a generalized variation of the parities. Thus, over time, small imbalances became enormous and led to the breakdown of the system. My idea was to design a mechanism that would allow small but frequent adjustments of the exchange parities, revisions within 0.5 percent per month. If adopted, this mechanism would stifle large-scale speculation at birth and enable the authorities to govern the markets instead of being overwhelmed by them. We must always remember that in the 1960s the situation was very different from today, and monetary authorities still had far greater power and impact than the markets. But in the space of a few years the picture was reversed.

I explained my plan to the Italian public in a memorable conversation with my friend Paolo Sylos Labini, which was published in the weekly *L'Espresso* in 1968. This was just as the first signs of strain in the Bretton Woods system began to be felt, following the disastrous devaluation of sterling in November 1967:

> Personally, I feel no time should be lost in achieving an international monetary system in which the dollar (and also, of course, sterling) is a currency just like any other, without a reserve function. In order to finance worldwide exchanges, that are constantly expanding, it is necessary to create a global currency, whose stock should be increased in the right amount. . . . Each country, in proportion to the volume of its international trade, should have available an amount of credits with an international bank for the purpose, with which it can face its transitory trade deficits. But in general each country should as far as possible avoid both deficits and excessive accumulation of surpluses[4].

At that time I was very concerned at the tendency, begun by the French, then imitated by the Belgians and the Italians, to conceive of currency reserves, preferably in gold doubloons, as a sort of "chest of Uncle Scrooge," to be locked away in a safe deep underground. This struck me as a dangerously inward-looking, reactionary tendency that made nonsense of everything that the Western countries had learned since the war by following Keynes, thanks to American support. My view was, then, that as a general rule not too much importance was to be given to the American balance-of-payments deficit, and I tried to show that the accumulation of currency reserves was the mirror image of the same phenomenon, and that the faults were symmetrical:

> The solution . . . is not to reduce the American deficit but to reduce the reserves of Western Europe. The Western European countries must spend their reserves, stimulate demand, and invest more. They must import more, not only from America but above all from the rest of the

world. Only in this way will there be an increase in international liquidity, in world trade, and thus in the well-being of all[5].

3   1971, to Save Bretton Woods?

Our plan, alas, was too ingenious for its time. It was never seriously considered. The only thing that aroused admiration was the idea of calling the new currency MIT. So things went on getting worse with the hemorrhage of dollars. There was agreement that to halt this would require a devaluation of the dollar against the other currencies. But the apple of discord was gold parity: Should gold remain tied to the dollar and thus be devalued against the other currencies, or instead be revalued against the dollar along with the other currencies? The United States preferred the first solution as consistent with Bretton Woods, which did not envisage the possibility of a unilateral devaluation of the dollar. But the other countries, especially France, insisted that the dollar be devalued against all the other currencies, gold included.

This seemingly technical argument masked a purely political conflict. It was the central point of a sharp clash between the United States and Gaullist France, which sought to affirm its prestige against that of the United States. The devaluation of the dollar against gold desired by France was enormously advantageous to the latter and disadvantageous to the United States, since France had amassed large gold reserves whose dollar value would thus be greatly increased. In addition, the conversion of its dollar reserves into gold would demonstrate its wisdom in not trusting the United States by holding to dollar reserves. Last, there would be a loss, and a sharp lesson into the bargain, for those countries that had collaborated with the United States by not converting their reserves into gold as France had exhorted them to.

In my conversation with Paolo Sylos in 1968, I summed up the affair as follows:

> De Gaulle's aim is to create serious embarrassment for the dollar and achieve a revaluation of the price of gold; this would, among other things, represent a good bargain for the French Treasury, which has recently converted almost all its reserves into gold. The figure in question is a large one, for France's gold reserves amount to over 5 billion dollars. France would benefit handsomely from a revaluation of gold, whereas this would "penalize" all those countries who have put their trust in the dollar and have cooperated with the American government

to maintain a certain monetary stability. . . . For some time now, there has been a gaullist-inspired fashion in Europe for viewing American investments as part of a sinister American economic-imperialist plot. This view also has supporters in Italy. But in my opinion these investments, however advantageous they may have been for America, have also had very salutary effects for the countries to which they were destined, in bringing capital, increased employment, and technical and administrative know-how, and in revitalizing competition[6].

An explanation worked out in the winter of 1966 by my fellow economists Charles Kindleberger, Emile Despres, and Walter S. Salant[7] received some attention: They successfully argued that the American deficit so condemned by the French was in reality only apparent and stemmed from the fact that the United States was purchasing financial assets by borrowing funds from Europe (owing among other things to the scant development of the European markets); the United States was thus operating as the savings bank of a little country that financed its employment by borrowing from the depositors. The United States acted as banker to the Western world.

On my side, I attempted in an interview with Cesare Zappulli in October 1971 to explain to the Italians that the fault did not lie entirely with the Americans[8]. But I had already argued to this effect in my lively conversation with Paolo Sylos of January 14, 1968:

> The advantages of seignorage are not as evident as is supposed in Europe, and especially as the French claim. A country whose currency functions as a global reserve must inevitably be subject to serious restrictions in managing its economic policy. I think that a majority of the American governing class would be willing to take a very favorable look at a radical reform of the world monetary system[9].

The United States rightly complained that it could not reestablish an adequate level of exports by devaluing the exchange because it did not control that exchange. Volcker, Connally, and company told the Europeans: "You determine our exchange and balance of payments, you create our trade deficit, and then you insist we pay you in gold. If you wish to be paid in gold, we wish to control our exchange."

As no solution to the conflict was reached and the system was creaking more and more, I and my colleague Hossein Askari[10] tried to interest the authorities in a second plan, this time less radical and more feasible, with a view to providing a possible line of resistance to the wholesale breakdown of the international monetary system.

Our reform sought to respond to ill feelings toward the dollar while leaving intact the asymmetry that underpinned the system. The idea was to retain that asymmetry while preserving the seignorage the United States enjoyed in issuing the international transaction currency, but in such a way as to impose the obligations and costs on the United States. For anyone holding dollar credits, the United States was to guarantee either that these would be interest bearing or, alternatively, to insure against exchange risk, which was equivalent to fixing the United States debt in the currency of the creditor.

The compromise solution put forward by Askari and myself argued more or less as follows: "You Europeans continue to have control over the exchange and therefore over the accumulation of reserves; but you cannot then insist on being paid in gold; if you hold your reserves in dollars, the United States will pay interest on them." In this way, the United States would be able to control its indebtedness to the point it wished by varying the rate of interest. Or, its creditors would have a guaranteed exchange. If reserves were excessive, the other countries could reduce their surplus by unilateral revaluation.

But by now the system was past rescuing. To force the hand of the United States, France persisted in its policy of converting its balance-of-payments surplus into gold. This policy was gradually followed by several other countries, in the fear that America would suspend convertibility to avoid exhausting its gold reserves; but before this happened, the United States took steps to stop the run by suspending convertibility of the dollar into gold and allowing it to float.

This was the end of Bretton Woods and the system of fixed exchanges (which, all told, had given good results) and the beginning of a highly tormented period of fluctuating exchanges.

Just at the time when the article I had written with Askari was published, Guido Carli, governor of the Bank of Italy, was invited at my suggestion by the MIT economics department for a conference he was very keen to attend. The date of the conference was fixed a few days before the meeting of the International Monetary Fund. Thus it came about that Serena asked Carli and his assistants to a frugal lunch at our house. She prepared tomatoes stuffed with rice and artichokes. Carli was very nervous and ate, rapidly, only the tomatoes.

Rainer Masera and Mario Ercolani, too, followed the governor's example and confined themselves to the tomatoes. Rinaldo Ossola, a perfectly independent sort of person who couldn't care less, was in a good mood and ate everything. We made ordinary conversation, talking, for instance, about the squirrels that came down from the trees around our house to peep in at the windows. Judge how astonished I was, then, when in an article *"Processo al dollaro"* ("The Dollar on Trial"), followed by an interview on October 5, 1971, with my well-known journalist friend Cesare Zappulli, that meeting based on tomatoes and artichokes turned into a sort of secret summit to discuss the fate of the monetary world. Zappulli wrote:

> Not by chance, before the assembly of the International Monetary Fund began, a restricted monetary summit met, attended by Guido Carli, on the excuse of a meal at Modigliani's house at Belmont, to weigh up the causes of the decease of the first monetary republic and to assess which regime is most likely to succeed it[11].

There's no gainsaying the power of imagination! Otherwise, the interview with Zappulli was, as usual, precisely and faithfully reported.

My concern was that the disintegration of the fragile architecture of the world monetary system would lead to the ruin of international trade and would thus cause a terrible contraction of exchanges and income, along with deflation, impoverishment, and autarchic closure of trade frontiers. And, looming on the horizon, war and authoritarian governments, as in the 1930s. I took an unmistakably "reformist" line: The system needed revising, not destroying. But by then it was too late.

> The important thing was to develop the existing system, eliminating its defects and exploiting its virtues. Lacking such dexterity, America took a crude decision, in mid-August, declaring the inconvertibility of the dollar and imposing a 10 percent supertariff on imports . . . in a single gesture, the United States has demolished the twin pillars of western economic coexistence as regards currency and commercial exchanges, namely the IMF and GATT, abruptly bringing to a halt the trend of world trade toward expansion and stirring up the danger or the temptation of customs reprisals. The major risk is that the supertariff will become permanent, under pressure from protectionist urges that have never entirely disappeared. . . . It was preferable to devalue the dollar against the other reserve instruments (gold and special drawing rights), while inviting the other countries not to imitate the United States—i.e. to maintain their parities. . . . The devaluation would have operated on the two fronts of exports and imports: the supertariff affects only imports, and thus has the effect of shrinking the overall volume of international trade[12].

*   *   *

4   *The Waltz of the Currencies*

Hopes that the traumatic rupture of August 1971 would lead to a new world monetary system very soon evaporated. I remember the speech made by George Schultz, my old colleague and political adversary, to the International Monetary Fund in September 1972, which led to the efforts of the Group of Twenty supposedly in formulating a draft for the reform. Schultz pinpointed a compromise that was acceptable to the United States and included some elements from Askari's and my proposal. The dollar would have been forced into line with the other currencies:

> The dollar would have ceased to be the only intervention currency. All the member countries would have been encouraged to make gradual changes in their parity, going above or below it as reserves increased or decreased. Those countries which did not take sufficient measures to clear their deficits or had a chronic surplus would have been subject to sanctions. In particular, countries with a deficit, could have faced discriminatory tariffs from the other countries. Finally, all members would have been allowed to hold dollars in reserve in addition to other currencies[13].

At the same time, as I had already suggested in the plan written with Kenen, parity would have to be handled more flexibly:

> It was also recognized that market rates could vary within set limits from parity before the monetary authorities would have had to intervene. This would have assured each country more autonomy in choosing its monetary policy[14].

These ideas turned out to be written in the sand and were to be swept away by the first tide of speculation. It was during those years that I started to explain to the public how the markets worked without Bretton Woods in the new regime, a new world where savvy and cunning in handling currency were more important than they had been before.

In those months, a new actor made its appearance in the nonspecialized daily papers. Imaginary and yet very real, it was to generate much confusion in the understanding of economics. This was speculation. There is no doubt that before the oil crisis of 1973, speculation had played an important role in waylaying monetary reform. This was due not so much to its own intrinsic power as to the inadequacy of the monetary authorities of the Western world face-to-face with a new regime based on market forces.

On Tuesday February 12, 1973, a huge wave of speculation that cornered the German mark forced the dollar to be devalued by 10 percent against the gold standard and special drawing rights. It was a decision, I wrote, that was made at the wrong time because of market forces and represented an "abject surrender by the monetary authorities to international operators and speculators. It will not bring an end to the period of crisis." Of the markets that had been thrown into confusion by their own strength I wrote: "After having repeatedly routed the forces of order, they now feel that there is no longer any rational order on which they can rely."[15]

My first criticisms of the Bundesbank go back to the early seventies when it emerged as a new world monetary power. In my opinion, the February 1973 devaluation of the dollar, which had been the result of an unexpected flow of funds toward the mark, could and should have been avoided. Of the German central bank that did not choose to support the dollar, I wrote the following:

> To maintain the current level of parity, Germany should have been prepared to buy an unlimited quantity of dollars at the lowest price permissible by that parity. Contrary to popular myth, it would not have encountered any serious difficulty in following such a program. . . . To show strength in the face of bull speculation, the German central bank would have only had to sell marks which it is never short of as it mints them itself. . . . It is true that massive buying up of dollars, as it tends to increase the amount of money, could have created a danger of internal inflation; however, this danger could easily have been avoided by using means that the central bank has at its disposition or which it can easily procure.[16]

As far as I was concerned, speculation could have been beaten if there had been the will to do so. This would have demonstrated that, even in the new regime, the monetary authorities were able to keep the international flow of cash under control. But the will was not there. Behind the Bundesbank's unwillingness to support the dollar with the excuse that it could not take on such a huge increase in internal cash flow (which could easily have been neutralized on the open market), I perceive a structural constancy and a stubborn determination to play the loner. This emerged very clearly during the 1992 European monetary crisis:

> Only one risk was run by the German central bank. That was if the dollar were devalued unilaterally, resulting in bought dollars losing

their value. To avoid this risk, the Americans could have agreed not to devalue or they could have offered appropriate guarantees concerning the exchange rate until the operation was over. The announcement of such an agreement would have rapidly convinced any speculators that there were no fast easy profits to be made, thus putting them on the spot. As a matter of fact, much of the speculation on exchange rates, at least in the acute phase, is financed by short-term funds which cannot be held for long without incurring high costs and great risk.[17]

I tried to explain that without the safety net of a dollar that could be converted into gold, the new game looked pretty much like a system of gambling where the central banks would have to get directly involved in forming the expectations of the operators. Here, it was my old intuition about the theory of expectation that came to my assistance:

It was foreseeable that, in a short time, the wave of dollars on offer would halt. It would give way to some of the speculators attempting to get rid of their marks and buy dollars again. However, given that those dollars had been acquired from the central bank, it would be difficult to find people willing to buy marks with dollars until the central bank got involved in the market. The price of marks would go below that which most of the speculators had paid thus causing them a loss. It would only be then that the central bank would be able to start to sell the dollars previously bought, at a profit, and the flow of speculative funds would diminish. Only when the flow was largely stemmed would parity once again be reconsidered and, then, where it was opportune and on the basis of agreements arrived at gradually and inspired by common interest.[18]

It is not difficult to see the mistakes of yesteryear detailed in the mistakes of today.

5   To Float or Not to Float

The year 1973 was when fixed parity was finally abandoned and the age of floating exchanges started. It was also the year when the European governments made the first unfortunate attempts at floatation against the dollar with the so-called "Monetary Snake." The cautiously favorable position that I took on the floatation of money was strongly approved by Friedman and the Republican administration. It went as follows:

> There are two possible, rational solutions: Either we return to a system of official parity but avoid the previous problems by allowing adequate floating flexibility around the central core value and creeping parity based on objective criteria instead of speculative whims, or we wholeheartedly embrace the system of the floating exchange rate. The way I see it, the first solution is slightly preferable to the present stare of things. However, a system of floating exchange is not without its appeal, especially in talking about floating exchange between the big blocks; for example, the dollar block, a block within the Common Market, a Japanese block, etc., where there is relatively stable parity within each block. However, for a system of floating exchange to work, international operators and speculators who are relatively immune to panic or speculation fever are required.[19]

The failure of the authorities lay mainly in their inability to understand that, only by genuinely coordinating their actions in a spirit of unity would they be able to continue to govern the international markets. The Group of Twenty went to work enthusiastically for a year, during which time they agreed unilaterally to put off every decision until the spring of 1974. In their titanic effort, they managed to produce a fifteen-page document titled "First Outline of Reform," which was discussed at the International Monetary Fund meeting in Nairobi. The agreement did not get beyond these three points:

1. Members were obliged to maintain the market exchange rate, through official intervention where necessary, within the permitted limits of an "official parity" that was fixed but subject to gradual adjustments.
2. Currencies would all be treated absolutely equally in matters of duties (including convertibility) and rights (including modifying parity).
3. An abstract means of payment would be adopted and would become the unit of account and the main instrument of reserve and would also be a means of exchange between the monetary authorities.

"Gold, that glorious relic of the past, would remain at most an optional means of reserve and exchange."[20] In my analysis of the Group of Twenty's document in the *Corriere della Sera*, I remarked that the only progress seemed theoretical:

> To accept the principle that a country may, under certain conditions, temporarily abandon official parity and float its currency is to recognize that an excessive accumulation of reserves forces that country to take measures to correct its balance of payments . . . and in fact, for most western countries, surplus and deficit are symmetrical phenomena: one cannot eliminate one without eliminating the other.[21]

This went back to the central point of my article with Kenen:

> To improve how the system of international payments works, it was essential to dismiss the ideology of the past according to which having a surplus was deemed a virtue and having a deficit a vice, and consequently the full weight of correction should fall on the "guilty."[22]

The treacherous sands upon which all the reform projects would run aground were the vetoes that prevented the birth of an abstract currency as an international reserve. The Group of Twenty explicitly rejected the possibility of linking the value of the so-called special drawing rights (the International Monetary Fund's unit of account) to the basket of international goods rather than to a basket of currency.

6   Monetary Mururoa

I have already said that I have never found the French attitude, full as it is of nationalism, particularly convincing. I have never agreed with the notion that the blame for the monetary breakup lay with the American deficit. I find the accusations that the dollar is the main reason behind European inflation unconvincing. Neither was I convinced by the proposal that the devaluation of the dollar would be a panacea for all ills. Nor did I believe that the accusation that the Americans were lording it over everyone was justified. That accusation was based on envy of the role played by the dollar as the international reserve, which de Gaulle would have preferred be played by the French franc.

The first experiments in exchange floatation embarked upon by the Europeans were a failure. Still, the idea was a good one and indicated that a real possibility existed for restructuring the system of international payments on a homogeneous monetary area.

This was why I was overcome by fury when, halfway through the oil crisis in January 1974, Pompidou, after having maintained that the Snake offered the only hope for Europe, announced that France was leaving the fixed exchange system and was going to float the franc freely. I was so angry that I wrote a very strongly worded article about the selfish policy of Paris, which, as far as I was concerned, exemplified the sort of behavior that would end in catastrophe. Rereading my words today, it is very interesting to note that even then there was talk of national sovereignty, of grandeur, and of . . . nuclear experiments in the Pacific:

> The move to abandon the Community Snake . . . was taken, on the one hand, because of narrow-minded egoism and short-sightedness (if not downright blindness) and, on the other, the high-sounding preaching to others that France never tires of, about making sacrifices in the higher interest of the European and international communities (especially when they coincide with France's). . . . In recent months, we have been reminded of the pre-eminent role that France has played in nuclear explosions in the Pacific, in rejecting a lively common policy with the EEC, in solidarity with Holland and the unilateral French dealings with Arab countries to guarantee France a supply of oil.[23]

The basic mistake during the oil crisis was failure to understand that playing solitaire was a tactic that resulted in cheating one's neighbor instead of finding common ground with him, and also played into the hands of the monopolists who controlled the oil. Further, abandoning the Snake after having defended it so vehemently surely opened the door to devastating competitive devaluation. Were we going back to the thirties?

> The immediate, visible aim of the French move is obviously to avoid the danger that, by supporting the Franc during the present difficult times and to prevent a possible drain of capital, they would have to turn to their monetary reserves and, God forbid!, sell even one ounce of their gold. The loss of gold for France under Pompidou would have been far worse than the loss of its very soul. The real aim, however, was to devalue the Franc. . . . By devaluing the commercial Franc, it hopes to reduce or even eliminate its current deficit. However, it is absolutely naïve of France to imagine that other countries, which already have troubles of their own, will passively accept this last worsening of the situation. It is quite likely that they will have an irresistible temptation to behave like the French and answer the devaluation of the Franc by devaluing their own currencies. . . . If this race to devalue is not curtailed promptly, where will it all end?
>
> Firstly, much of the profit that France expects to make by devalua-

tion will be lost because the Franc will not be worth less than the Lira, the Peseta or any other of other currencies as they will be devalued as well in line with the French example. In order to improve the situation significantly, they will have to continue devaluing in leaps and bounds. . . .

Secondly, the countries that have devalued their currencies will be subject to inflation because the cost of oil will rise as will that of other raw materials from countries that have not devalued.

Thirdly, the oil producing countries will watch with glee as the race to devalue against the dollar gets under way because a barrel of oil whose price was fixed, let's say, at seven dollars, will be worth more in terms of goods coming from France, Italy and so on than what they had hoped for when they set the price at seven dollars. In other words, devaluation has had a negative effect on the trade exchanges between the industrial countries and the oil producers.[24]

7   Snake Relatives

The lesson of the oil crisis was that if the Western countries did not formulate exchange and monetary policies that were solid and well coordinated, they would be at the mercy of the sheikhs. This is the reason I was, already then, in favor of carrying out the initial experiments in a European monetary union, or the so-called Snake.

It was inadequate to establish fixed parity between countries whose economies were reacting differently to the oil crisis. The agreements had to establish a parity with an initial reasonable rate of exchange; but, especially, parity had to be mobile, with limits to the amount of flexibility allowed to each country and with a sufficient area for free fluctuation from the set parity at all times[25]. In order for such a system to work, a central institution was required to provide credit should there be any bursts of speculation and to withstand market forces. In the absence of a central bank or a European fund, an iron agreement between the central banks permitting them to act as a single block was essential.

In 1974, I suggested:

Maintaining the market rate within the allowed limits of fluctuation should be guaranteed by a solid agreement between the central banks who, in the case of speculative assault, would take it upon themselves

Franco, age 6, 1924 in Rome.

Meeting in Venice of 1937 Littori. Franco is seventh from left.

Franco at Gottardo Pass in the Italian Alps in our first
trip back to Italy after sixteen years in the U.S., 1955.

Serena, Franco, and André (5 years), in New York, 1945.

Serena and Franco, in Rome, 1938.

At home on Martha's Vineyard, 2000.

Serena and Franco, Bologna, Italy, 1938.

Receiving the Nobel Prize from King Gustav Adolph of Sweden (right), 1985.

At home in Cambridge, 2000

Serena and Franco, with Nobel
award in Stockholm, 1985.

Sailing on the Italian Riviera, 1999.

Martha's Vineyard with the President and Mrs. Clinton, and daughter, Chelsea, Summer 2000

Stockholm, December, 1985, from left: Sergio Modigliani, Leah Modigliani, (André's daughter) Franco, Queen Silvia of Sweden, King Gustav of Sweden, Serena, Suzanne Modigliani (Sergio's wife), André, Julia Modigliani (André's daughter).

to offer unlimited support, either directly or through appropriate means based on the International Monetary Fund.[26]

8   Inflation and Deficit

The year 1973 saw the arrival of the first oil crisis. The huge rise in the price of oil caused a fall in real wages; however, as real wages are rigid, this meant that wages go up as prices do. This creates an inflationary spiral, which can continue for a long time if the central bank is prepared to finance the maintenance of the M/P (money to price) relationship that existed previous to the crisis, thus allowing the quantity of money to follow the increase in the level of prices. However, if the central bank wants to stop inflation, it is forced to curb M while letting P increase. The central bank is forced to reduce real money as well as aggregate demand, thus creating unemployment while changing the relationship between money and prices.

In the seventies, all the central banks found themselves faced with the dilemma of accommodating or not accommodating. Not accommodating is a cure for inflation, which creates unemployment. This way, workers find they have to accept a reduction in their take-home pay, which they would not normally have accepted, while companies have to accept a fall in their profits. If the quantity of money is kept constant, inflation must, after a time, come to a halt. However, while it is coming to a halt, unemployment will increase, though temporarily.

It is interesting to note how Volcker's behavior after the second oil crisis, which occurred between 1979 and 1980, fits my Keynesian model to perfection. Volcker chose not to accommodate because accommodation would have meant postponing monetary rigor, which would have become tighter and tighter than had been necessary at the start of the process. What we may wonder is why Volcker voiced his aims in terms of quantity of money rather that interest rates.

Fixing interest rate had two negative results: (a) it was very unpopular in both the political world as well as in finance circles and; (b) neither Volcker nor anyone else knew exactly where to fix the interest rate without making a mistake.

Consequently Volcker chose another strategy: "I shall fix the amount of money. If the rates go up, it will be because the economy wants it that way and there is nothing I can do about it. It won't be my fault." And the rates shot up higher than they had ever been before. At one moment, they even briefly touched 20 percent. It is not true that Volcker had fixed the quantity of money without touching interest rates. Indeed, immediately afterwards, when inflation had been halted, there was a huge monetary expansion.

I remember having long conversations with Steve Axelrod, Volcker's strategist, about this reversal of policy. Axelrod and I were in Peking at an international conference on inflation. He spoke to me as if he were a marine: "I'm telling you the way it is. Block the growth of money and inflation will be destroyed. There's no other way."

In 1983, after the period of severe monetary tightening, there was a phase where things were even more unclear and less easy to decipher. The unions were more aggressive and continued to push for higher pay, even after prices had slowed down, because their aim was in terms of real wages. During this phase, monetary policy became difficult because wages tended to go up faster than productivity. It was in those years that the Bundesbank showed how unbending it was by openly declaring that it was not prepared to accommodate wage increases. The Bundesbank was as unmovable as Volcker had been. It maintained that it would make no allowances; it wished to keep money stable; it had no intention of financing wage increases that were higher than production growth. Their strategy was to make their point explicit and thereby take advantage of the financial markets.

Owing to the mechanism of the EMS's fixed rate and the growing freedom of movement of capital, the Bundesbank transferred high real interest rates and a scarcity of real money to all its European partners. Because of the fixed exchange rates and the free movement of capital, interest rates tended to rise to the level of the country with the highest rates. This effect was due to the fact that if a country keeps its interest rates low, operators will leave, selling bonds in their own currency so they can buy foreign shares. This increases the demand for foreign currency and leads to the loss of money.

But where does the money the operators need come from? There are only two ways to obtain it: by either (a) showing a positive balance of trade, or (b) by reducing the monetary reserves. Normally the balance of trade cannot react fast, so the only way to supply the market with the necessary money when the exchange rate has to be maintained is to take it out of official reserves. If a country has interest rates that are too low, it inevitably loses reserves. This situation can snowball if people start to believe that the central bank cannot defend its rate of exchange. Consequently, where capital is moved freely, in order to maintain the exchange rate steady capital must be prevented from making excessive movements. The only way to do this is to prevent one's interest rates from being lower than those of other countries.

During the 1980s, the Bundesbank managed to reduce demands for wage increases and also inflation and could therefore start to lower its real rates. For a two-year period, it appeared as if unemployment was actually going down. This had the immediate effect of increasing the quantity of money and aggregate demand.

To sum up then: (a) The economy is subject to external crisis; (b) If, despite the absence of a stabilizing policy, the effects of the crisis are absorbed quickly, intervention is not necessary. If, on the other hand, the situation remains unstable, then it becomes necessary to implement a stabilization policy.

9   The European Drama: Unemployment, a Situation That Should Not Be Accepted[27]

The reexamination of the collapse of the international monetary system made in the last few pages serves a purpose. It serves us to understand the causes, extension, reasons, and possible solutions to the crisis that today afflicts Europe.

What to an American observer seems incredible is how Europe has accepted frightening levels of unemployment for so long. Getting used to it runs the risk of having Europeans believe that such a condition is natural, whereas it certainly is not, and, in fact, may be explained in terms of Keynesian economic theory.

I am outraged by the scandalous lack of energy shown by the governments in dealing with such mass unemployment. Mass unemployment is by far the worst calamity that can befall a market economy. By no means is it an unavoidable fate. This is well demonstrated by the case of the United States, where a well-devised monetary policy has drastically reduced the level of unemployment and taken it back to manageable levels.

A situation where people can grow old without having a job that rewards them individually while adding to the collective well-being is morally unacceptable. It is something to cry out about. Perhaps it will be a cry in the wilderness; however, I would rather be misunderstood than remain silent. That unemployment is morally unacceptable can be illustrated by a careful economic analysis, which demonstrates rationally why it exists and how it can be corrected. Resigning oneself in the face of it is unacceptable. Likewise, it is simply not true that to behave as if the unemployment problem should be considered a top priority would result in the shelving of the Treaty of Maastricht and the Monetary Union. I can well demonstrate that there is one way of making the single currency compatible with full employment.

In the 1970s, the rate of unemployment in the countries that form the European Union generally stood between 2 and 3 percent. By 1997, the average unemployment rate had risen 10.5 percent with only two countries having a rate below 5 percent while seven had rates in excess of 10 percent and reaching as high as 21 percent. This sort of tragedy has never happened in the United States except, perhaps, during the Great Depression.

Thanks to the teachings of Keynes, students of macroeconomics have thought that they fully understand not only the causes of the malfunctioning of the market that produces unemployment but also the necessary action required to prevent such calamities from repeating themselves in the future. (Compare with chapter I, section 10, above.) And, indeed, it must be said that the United States has closely followed his teachings: Since World War II, the level of unemployment has only twice, and then by choice, gone slightly over 9 percent. Since 1982, unemployment has not risen over 8 percent and has often dropped below that level, recently returning to around 5 percent. On the other hand, in nearly all of Europe the rate of unemployment has constantly exceeded 9 percent. In spite of this situation, Keynes's teachings have been systematically neglected, especially by the central banks. What I have been teaching my students for the past fifty years has been ignored. This is that high interest rates, over the long run, when determined by an inadequate supply of money in combination with a tight fiscal policy, are incapable of compensating for the negative effects that that type of monetary policy leads to: a level of aggregate demand that is too low for the economy and therefore generates only limited jobs and results in mass unemployment.

It is generally held that it is Germany, which has imposed this disastrous monetary policy on all the countries in the EMS, as well as on the candidate countries to the single currency. It is a policy that has resulted in an insufficient money supply in real terms and one that, for the last fifteen years, has espoused high interest rates, which have been transferred to other countries via the fixed exchange mechanism.

My thesis can be summed up as follows:

*   *   *

1. Unemployment in Europe is the result of inadequate aggregate demand caused by insufficient money supply.

2. The low money supply largely reflects the policy of real interest rates applied by Germany, in particular from 1987 to 1995, and which was transferred to the other European countries via the fixed-exchange-rate mechanism.

3. The unemployment factor on the supply side is less important in Europe than one is led to believe.

4. Tight monetary policies are considered justified when viewed from a rigid real wage point of view rather than from that of the nominal wage, as seen in Keynes's analysis.

10   The Rigidity of Wages: Real or Nominal?

The general situation regarding what has happened in Europe over the last fifteen years is as follows: The labor unions have followed a precise strategy for real wages, demanding yearly nominal wage increases over which they generally have some considerable degree of control. Because of this, the monetary authority may find itself in the situation of not being able to change the real supply of money and thus achieve full employment. Thus, a restriction is created that impedes maneuvering the real supply of money.

When the unions, always with an eye to real wages, manage to get an increase in their nominal wages greater that the growth of productivity, the situation becomes serious. Demands of this type imply that an increase in real wages also corresponds to an increase in nominal wages.

It is impossible not to be reminded of that theoretical wild beast "the wage as an independent variable," when it was generally held that wages had no influence on economic variables apart from real wages and profits! Employers themselves have often given in to unreasonable wage increases, which upset the balance of the economic system, acting on beliefs as mistaken as those of the unions. These industrialists genuinely believe, deep down in their hearts, that they can control price increases and therefore can always pass the extra costs deriving from increased wages onto prices without suffering any loss in real terms. To offset the "wage as an independent variable," the industrialists used the markup as an "independent variable."

11 The Dilemma of the Central Bank: To Accommodate or Not to Accommodate?

Let us review the situation: In their quest for real wages, unions force nominal wages up to levels above that of the growth of productivity. This produces an increase in the unit cost of labor, because price levels are generally set by markups related to the unit cost of labor. The first reaction to the increase in labor costs shows up in prices. From this point on, everything depends on how the monetary authority, the central bank, reacts.

This is where the Hamlet-like dilemma comes into play: to accommodate or not to accommodate the increase in prices?

To all intents and purposes, accommodation signifies attempting to maintain the supply of money in real terms at a constant level while allowing the nominal supply to rise in line with price increases. A policy of this sort, if accompanied by an adequate devaluation of the nominal rate of exchange, allows producers, who largely control prices, to pass wage increases in toto on to prices without reducing profit margins. The drawback in this type of solution is that any real gains workers thought they were making with the increase in nominal wages is completely nullified. This is why, if the workers then insist on an increase in their real wages, push for further increases, and get them, a new wave of price increases is the result. This, in turn, leads to spiraling wages and prices.

The moral to be learned from accommodation is that it does not, in effect, produce a one-time increase but instead runs the risk of creating a permanent spiral of inflation, a situation that is worsened when indexed wages are introduced.

Let's have a look at the other solution: nonaccommodation. This solution is not impervious to negative consequences either. The decision to hold the nominal supply of money constant while allowing its real quantity to go down results in only a part of the wage increase being passed on to prices. Producers find themselves face-to-face with yet another dilemma: either reduce the markup or reduce sales. The results of fixing the quantity of money and the nominal exchange rate are as follows: (a) loss of market share in both domestic and foreign markets, as foreign competitors' costs have not risen so they have not had to raise their prices; (b) a constant supply of money on the domestic market and because of this, falling real income. This reduction leads to a fall in employment, which will probably be aggravated by a fall in profits.

Even if the central bank decides not to accommodate, price increases cannot be completely avoided; however, should they rise, the amount would certainly be less than the rise in wages, so workers would achieve a real gain. However, employment bears the brunt.

The increase in unemployment could persuade workers to limit their pay demands while encouraging entrepreneurs to be more careful in marking up their prices. These modifications could slow down inflation. But, in any case, the process is long drawn out and painful.

Where there is a fixed exchange rate, as in the EMS countries, if inflation in one of the countries, even if falling, is higher than in competing countries, this causes an increase in the rate of real exchange and related problems in the balance of payments, which worsen and eventually result in a further reduction in income. In cases like this, it is not unfeasible, when unemployment is rising and when there are problems with the balance of payments, for the authorities to set aside their nonaccommodating monetary policies and allow the exchange rate to float. Doubtless, this is far from the best solution, and leads to a period of only sluggish recovery, where demand increases while real wages fall. Generally, though, it pushes the country into another spate of serious, spiraling inflation.

12   The Main Road and the Short Cut

Until 1969, Italy was a flourishing country, fast growing and structurally sound. It is interesting to take a look at the period after that when the Italian economy staggered from one problem to another. It started at the end of 1969, when, over a period of very few months, wages rose approximately 30 percent, and continued until 1993, when the main labor unions signed an agreement with firms and the government aimed at bringing down and hopefully halting inflation. During that twenty-odd-year period, despite great leaps and bounds in productivity and *per capita* income (which had tripled since 1960), the country had to ride a frightening rollercoaster between times of accommodating policies and high inflation on the one hand, and periods of nonaccommodating policies marked by rising unemployment and balance-of-payments problems, aggravated by totally irresponsible fiscal policies, on the other. From 1960 to 1990, there was an almost twentyfold increase in prices while the unemployment rate rose from 3 percent to the present 12.5 percent.

When the lira joined the EMS and accepted the Bundesbank's strict discipline, the Italian accommodating policies were left behind once and for all. As foreseen, the decision brought a slight worsening of unemployment, but the inflation rate also fell both in absolute terms and as com-

pared to the other EMS countries. Inflation still remained higher than anywhere else, and this would cause gradual appreciation of the lira and a
growing deficit in the balance of payments, resulting in the drastic devaluation of 1992, which miraculously occurred after wages were unfrozen in
July of that dramatic year.

A glaring example of rigid real wages is offered by the two oil crises,
when workers set themselves the unachievable goal of holding their real
wages unchanged while the basket of goods, including oil, had gone up in
real terms because the price of petroleum itself had increased. In this case
the rigidity of real wages was to prove disastrous.

After 1973 and 1982, the monetary authorities showed increasingly less
propensity to accommodate. Even in Italy, people soon became persuaded
that stable prices were of paramount importance and that the central bank
had to impose them on the country. Consequently, inflation was met with
a fast increase in the interest rate while investments fell off as unemployment rose.

How this process unfolded can be seen very clearly in the case of France.
Taking 100 as the average of the index that measures the ratio between
investment and productive capacity at the end of the 1961–70 period, we
see a fall to 76 at the end of the 1972–82 ten-year period, a further fall to
69 between 1983 and 1990, and a slump to 56 during the two-year period
1991–93.

From 1961 to 1970, in what now seems like a golden age, the level of
unemployment seemed insignificant, inflation was modest, and interest
rates were low in both real and nominal terms, stimulating spending on
investment, which grew quickly, enhancing income, and keeping unemployment low. With the oil crisis, wages rose quickly, feeding the inflation
caused by the rise in fuel and domestic prices, which in 1975, reflecting
wage increases, reached a dizzying 19 percent. Interest rates shot up to 11
percent. Real interest rates, when calculated conventionally by subtracting
current inflation, did not go up; however, this means little because the
times were marked by considerable turbulence, suggesting that much of
the inflation was transitory. By 1975, investment had fallen by 9 percent
while production, as compared to the productive capacity, had gone down
5 percent.

Because of the turnabout in the oil-price trend and probably also
because of the high level of unemployment, which tends to put the brakes
on price inflation, the end of 1975 saw wage inflation start to slow down.
At the same time, the central bank's nonaccommodating policy and high
interest rates saw investments and production fall, which, in turn, led to
further unemployment.

High inflation and high unemployment caused what came to be called stagflation. It should be noted, however, that stagflation was the result of the failed efforts of the central bank to lower inflation through its nonaccommodation policy and to rising unemployment. Monetary policy that aims to keep the money supply low in real terms will succeed in putting more people out of work; however, it is not very successful at lowering inflation. Inflation, therefore, does not spring from low employment and excessive demand, as traditional wisdom will have it. Rather, it springs from the tight money policies pursued by the central bank and the cause-effect relationship of inflation to unemployment rather than that of unemployment to inflation.

At the end of 1979, investment had sunk by 17 percent and overall production by 7 percent. The rate of unemployment had gone up to 5.8 percent, while inflation held on stubbornly at 10 percent.

The second oil crisis set inflation spiraling off again. This time, a nonaccommodating monetary policy shot interest rates up to 11 percent. Between 1981 and 1982, real interest rates, calculated traditionally, rocketed to 14 percent, investments went down a further 24 percent, production sank 12 percent below capacity, and 8 percent of the workforce was out of work.

13   The Puzzle of the 1980s

The end of 1982 marks the start of the most complicated and significant phase in this whole story. In 1983, very high unemployment coupled with inflation in net regression suggested that the monetary rigor that had been adopted up to that point would loosen. And, in effect, nominal interest rates would slide down uninterruptedly until 1989. Nevertheless, real interest rates were very high when compared to those of the so-called golden age (around 5 percent as compared to 2 percent in the 1970s). In fact, real interest rates actually tended to rise, going from under 4 percent in 1982 to nearly 6 percent at the end of the 1980s. The consequence of this tendency was that investment continued to fall. Between 1985 and 1989, it lagged at more than 30 percent under productive capacity; production managed to hover at around 20 percent under actual productive capacity, while unemployment rose to record levels above 10 percent. These causal links are shown by the fact that, for a short period before the fall of the Berlin Wall, between 1988 and 1989, a slight reduction in the interest rates was followed by a strong recovery in investment spending.

However, with German reunification in 1990, interest rates, both real and nominal, started to rise again rapidly, signaling the start of the period from which Europe is still painfully trying to exit. Investments fell again, and production fell to a minimum.

To sum up, then, this backward glance shows that the high levels of unemployment in the second half of the 1970s were justified by the need to stop the inflationary spiral that had been caused by a real phenomenon, the increase in the price of oil products; however, it also shows that the increasingly higher levels of unemployment after 1983 were due to a tight monetary policy, that is, high real interest rates, which suffocated investment and the growth of future income.

The crucial questions are these: What was the reason for the tight money policy? What was the reason behind the high interest rates? There is no obvious answer because it is increasingly evident that the tight money policy does not appear to have been justified by any real reason or, conversely, by a serious threat of inflation. How could such restrictive measures taken by the European central banks in concert be justified when unemployment was very high and still rising steadily?

Two explanations can be offered: The first is that the European central banks, under the influence of Germany, sought at all costs to maintain prices at a stable level. Under those circumstances, any wage increase that would have pushed inflation above 3 percent would have been considered untenable. This gave rise to increasing unemployment. The second reason could be that the European central banks had decided that they would, willy-nilly, keep exchange rates within the EMS on an even keel, as per their agreement, once they had set sail for monetary union. This, however, happened at the same time that the European countries allowed capital complete freedom of movement, even for short periods, when monetary reserves were limited. The only way to hold the exchange rate stable was by linking it to the German exchange rate, which, however, stayed high throughout the entire period. As far as Germany was concerned, this was not necessarily a case of self-inflicted suffering, for although interest rates had a lesser negative influence on production growth in the country where they had originated, they certainly cut into the job market. Consequently, Germany was able to handle the high real interest rates she had imposed on her European partners better than any of them, with the exception of Holland.

There is no doubt that the process set off by wage increases in response to the oil crisis is by far the greatest cause of the inflation seen in the 1970s. But there is no evidence that demand played any role whatsoever in the process. To corroborate the first of these conclusions, two observations can be made: (a) during the whole period, markups maintained a steady level; (b) although pressure on prices due to excessive demand always tends to go hand-in-hand with a notable increase in jobs and low unemployment, this is exactly the opposite of the situation in Europe in the mid-1970s.

14   The Intertwined Fates of France and Germany

Between the second half of 1989 and the beginning of 1990, because of the reunification of the two Germanys and the decision of the German government not to finance the annexation exclusively by increased taxation, both long- and short-term interest rates started to go up quickly. The raised interest rates, although greeted with some measure of dismay by the other European countries, were undoubtedly justified by the Bundesbank's desire to reduce to a minimum the inflationary pressure caused by the effective and expected increase in demand. And in effect, although long-term interest rates had already gone up to 7 percent by the first half of 1989, and were already over the 9 percent mark halfway though 1990, where they would stay for the whole of 1992, short-term rates had gone up even more. Yet despite this, there was a genuine boom in investment in Germany in 1991 and 1992; incomes increased steadily and unemployment figures went down. The tight fiscal policy would only be felt in 1992, when investment in machinery and equipment went down, productive growth slowed, and unemployment started to gather strength.

Why were rates allowed to go up to 1992 levels? For an answer, we have to look at how wages and prices were behaving. By 1990, German wages had already gone up around 6 percent, a level well above that of productivity, and had increased the unit cost of labor, which had been largely passed on to prices. In 1991, wage increases went over 7 percent, only to rise again in 1992, when they would push inflation over the 5 percent benchmark, which the German public found acceptable. And all of this despite unemployment's creeping upward. In 1992, the Bundesbank was no longer able to brush off the rising inflation. It adopted an ever tighter policy, which caused productivity to fall and unemployment to rise dramatically, passing the 8 percent mark in 1993. The central bank's action had the desired effect of containing the movement of wages, which, between 1992 and 1993, once again grew at a rate of less than 2 percent, in line with prices, which had also stabilized. The moderate way that prices and demand were moving along should have induced the monetary authorities to implement a process of rapid reflation by increasing the supply of money and making significant cuts in interest rates, and, indeed, at the end of 1992 both short- and long-term rates did go down. However, it was not enough to avoid a fall in productivity in 1993 and very low growth rates in 1994. German unemployment had meanwhile reached the previously unthinkable level of 11 percent (9 percent in the eastern part of the federation). In the other EMS countries, unemployment was even higher than in eastern Germany, except in Holland, where it stood at 7.2 percent.

The hypothesis I advanced and for which I found empirical proof is that the unemployment that scourges Europe is clearly Keynesian in nature. This is because it is the result of inadequate aggregate demand caused, in turn, by an inadequate supply of real money, the latter depending on the fact that the monetary authorities in the EMS countries persist in following the narrow road of high interest rates set by the Bundesbank. Nevertheless, the reasons for following the policy before August 1993 and afterward, when the crisis between the franc and the EMS occurred, are different.

Until August 1993, the umbilical cord linking the monetary policies of the EMS countries with Germany was set by the exchange agreements according to which exchange rates could fluctuate within a narrow area around fixed parity. As a result, from September 1992 onward, all the interest rates danced to a German tune, except for the British and Italian rates when the pound and the lira were forced to leave the EMS exchange agreement.

At the end of the 1970s and for much of the 1980s, many of the European countries found that having to toe the German monetary line scrupulously was, in fact, a good thing in terms of keeping wages and prices down. After the mid-1980s, though, the requirement started to feel like a straitjacket to many of them, a handicap that became ever more hampering as the 1990s approached. After the reabsorption of East Germany, the tight monetary policy and the high interest rates that Germany found it necessary to impose became a burden to most of the countries in the EMS.

France, in particular, suffered heavy consequences. Her inability to free herself from the chains of German monetary policy during the two-year period 1987–88 meant that France lost a golden opportunity. This was not merely because, at that time, the Germans would have accepted a unilateral revaluation of the mark, which would have avoided the devastating increases in interest rates. However, France's inability to break loose after the Germans had again increased interest rates in 1991–92 proved nearly suicidal. Paris should have immediately expanded her money supply in real terms until long-term interest rates had reached those of the so-called golden age. That would have produced an increase in income and the rate of growth through more investment in and exports to Germany, which, in turn, would also have helped that nation, once it had recovered from its reabsorption of the former communist country, to put the brakes on price increases resulting from internal demand (and therefore on inflation) and to acquire resources for the eastern territory. Even if other countries had followed France's example in breaking loose from the Bundesbank, not all of the competitive edge would have been lost, for in any case exports would have expanded because of increased income caused by the reduction in interest rates.

From what I can gather from those who were responsible for European monetary policies between 1990 and 1992, Germany was prepared to take this type of approach, both to alleviate unemployment in France and to lighten the pressure on Germany's and the Bundesbank's partners, thus slackening the reins of the monetary policy as fast as Germany's interests would allow.

Unfortunately, the French would not budge from their position. The socialist government clung to the franc, going so far as to dub it the "francfort," and doggedly opposed any decision that even faintly hinted at devaluation. For this, France would pay very dearly in terms of unemployment and reduced income growth. The reasons advanced to explain this apparently self-destructive behavior were these:

1. It was felt that devaluing the franc would mean leaving the EMS and interrupting the process of European unification, which had become a matter of life and death for France and the other European countries, especially after Germany's reabsorption of her eastern territories.

2. The devaluation of the franc might have put the credibility of the EMS and the franc itself into question.

3. Far more important, it would have hurt French pride and cast aspersions on la grandeur de la France at a time when Germany was fulfilling her dream and freeing herself once and for all from the constrictions of the past.

The events that followed the affair demonstrate that French obstinacy in not devaluing the franc forced the whole system toward a parity that was at odds with the new cyclical situation and the recession that was taking hold everywhere. It damaged the EMS and the credibility of Europe as a monetary block and pushed the possibility of achieving a single currency further off than if the opportunity offered by German reunification for a general in-depth review of monetary parity had been taken. There is yet another consequence that has not been granted the attention it deserves. The "franc-fort" policy removed the (less painful Keynesian) possibility of using monetary policy to lessen unemployment. This meant that, as they could not simply increase the supply of money to maintain aggregate demand, there was nothing they could do other than adopt an expansive fiscal policy and a growing public deficit.

In the face of this catastrophe, a group of MIT economists, including myself, published an appeal in the Financial Times in August 1993 in which we exhorted the French authorities to put unemployment ahead of national pride and to reduce interest rates fast. On the other hand, the markets, which felt that a monetary parity that carried such ruinously high social costs was no longer sustainable, forced France to abandon its Maginot Line—which, once and for all, put paid to the system of central parity in Europe.

There were two options in the solution we suggested. They were either to lower interest rates drastically or devalue the franc and perhaps withdraw temporarily from the exchange agreement and float the currency; or a general devaluation of all of the currencies in the EMS against the mark, which would have allowed considerable reduction in German interest rates.

What did happen in the end was completely different and, in some ways, totally unexpected. The EMS was saved by a hair's breadth by enlarging the area of fluctuation to 15 percent, a measure that permitted the various member nations to reduce their interest rates without leaving the system. The most incredible and unexpected thing was that, notwithstanding the wider margins allowed by the new agreement, over the next days, weeks, and months interest rates were still kept within the old tight area of movement, a policy supported in particular by France, which still gave priority to maintaining its links with German interest rates without entertaining any concern for the enormous costs they entailed.

15   Why Does Unemployment Increase in Europe But Not in the United States?

One widely acclaimed theory concerning the mysterious way unemployment stays very high and tends to increase in Europe as compared to how it faithfully follows a set cycle in the United States was advanced by my friend and colleague, Jacques Drèze[28]. In his theory, the two economies behave differently because their real wages are traveling in opposite directions[29]. The picture emerging clearly from a graph very much in vogue these days illustrates that in the United States, wages have increased very little since the 1970s. In fact, they have only risen 12 percent over the whole period, or about 1 percent per year. This markedly moderate pace has gone hand-in-hand with the creation of a very large number of new jobs each year, about 2 percent, or 50 percent over the whole period. In Europe, on the other hand, we have the inverse situation. While wages have gone up steadily at about 3 percent a year, the number of new jobs on the market did not change until the mid-1980s and, overall, has increased only 15 percent during the entire period. This, when compared with the American situation, provides a rather disconcerting picture.

In Europe, the generally accepted explanation for the diversity in the two economies is that the increase in real wages has reduced employment for three reasons: (a) it has favored substituting employment with capital; (b) it has accentuated international competition from countries with lower labor costs; (c) it has reduced the profit margin, thus discouraging investment. Another difference lies in the fact that the European labor unions are far stronger than in the United States and have been able to push for wage increases much faster, meaning that job creation has grown far more slowly.

I have one basic objection to raise against this apparently solid argument. Why is it that in both areas the growth of real wages and productivity occurs at exactly the same rate?

My impression is that the tendency of real wages and employment to diverge in the two areas is merely coincidental on the graph. We can use a different starting point; that is, although the labor unions manage to control nominal wages, it is the entrepreneurs who control prices. Under these conditions, given that profit margins are relatively stable and the spread of income is stable between wages and profit, the difference between the rates of growth of real wages in the two areas is the result of the fact that, in Europe, productivity grew far quicker than in the United States. On the other hand, the difference in the employment rate is the result mainly of aggregate demand, which is obviously related to the size of the workforce. I would further maintain that, in the United States, the increase in employment is the end result of conscious and efficient management of aggregate demand developed in line with potential income, which is the sum of the growth of the labor force and productivity. Consequently, the increase in employment, which equals the increase in income minus the growth in productivity, is the same as the increase in the labor force. In Europe, the growth in income, which runs at approximately 3 percent, has been much lower than the growth of potential income, which has equaled around 5 percent (2 percent for the labor force and 3 percent for productivity). This is why unemployment began to increase over the period and only recently peaked. A closer look at the "infallible" graph reveals, on the one hand, a simple coincidence but, on the other, leads to a really important conclusion: The failure of all the European countries to achieve growth equal to their labor force and productivity is the result of insufficiently developed aggregate demand.

16   The Mistake of the Europeans: This Unemployment Is Due Not to Supply But to Demand

When my American colleagues and I ask why on earth Europeans accept these levels of unemployment, we find a whole series of commonly held theories in Europe that argue that the level of unemployment depends on structural factors, most of which have to do with supply. The prevalent idea among European politicians (spread in part by official EU documents such as Jacques Delors's *Livre Blanc*) is that, at any level of aggregate demand in the European economy today, there are legal ways and means of reducing the ratio of employment to manpower[30]. Let us briefly review them:

1. One generally accepted reason for the limited amount of work available is that unemployment benefits in Europe are quite generous. Calculation of the net sum of pension and social contributions paid by workers and employers would suggest that the difference between staying at home on unemployment benefits and going out to look for a new job is very small indeed. However, whether these benefits are in fact more generous than they were in the 1950s and 1960s and whether they are really higher than those in the United States is highly questionable.

2. One must remember that there is a far larger number of chronically long-term unemployed persons in Europe than in the United States. The supply-siders conclude that these are the least desirable candidates for new jobs and tend to seek new work less and less. But the American experience suggests a different and simpler explanation: A high level of unemployment extended through

time tends to generate an increasing number of chronically unemployed persons. When aggregate demand reduces unemployment, the number of the chronically unemployed returns to normal levels.

3. There is also the mismatch argument, which is very popular among enthusiasts for technological innovation. This assumes an increasing tendency for work offers to be incompatible with demand because the modern job environment calls for new technical knowledge and professional experience that the present workforce is hard-pressed to offer. Proof of this situation is apparently found in the fact that among the increasing number of people out of work there is a disproportionate ratio between poorly educated workers (on the increase) and highly educated people.

   The first in-depth study of this phenomenon was undertaken in the United States in 1961, when unemployment reached a postwar peak, bouncing from 4.1 percent in 1956 to a then frighteningly high 6.7 percent. Extensive research showed that, when African-American unemployment was taken into account, the level of unemployment rose to from 8 to 12.4 percent. These statistics were interpreted to mean that the new age of computers was sweeping away jobs for less-qualified workers; however, this explanation failed when increasing demand due to the Vietnam War saw African-American unemployment fall quickly to 4.5 percent.

   The next explanation was a little more sophisticated. When unemployment rises, the loss of work is felt more among the more poorly educated people because their jobs are given to better qualified newly unemployed people. As demand rises again, these move on to better jobs, thus making space again on the lower rungs of the labor market. The conclusion to be drawn is that the problem is essentially one of demand: When demand rises the problem of the less skilled workers is mitigated.

4. Another widespread theory says that developing countries take up the workload of the far more expensive European countries in what is called globalization. This argument came out forcefully in the final, propagandist stage of the GATT negotiations; but it is a well-known fallacy and indicates a clear ignorance of economics. If third parties want to sell us goods and services for less than it would cost us to produce them, this is to our advantage if they improve our balance of trade.

5. The only apparently genuine curb on the supply of labor in Europe is created by the minimum wage. In this viewpoint, the larger numbers of workers and the greater growth in employment in the United States can be put down to modest productivity in industry and extremely low real wages. This conclusion is borne out by the above-mentioned evidence. In the United States, the dynamic employment situation is counterbalanced by very low growth in both productivity and real wages. In any case, this difference need not necessarily be linked with the existence of the minimum wage in Europe, a situation that is neither new nor exclusive to the old continent.

In conclusion, then, it is very difficult to measure how far these factors that limit supply really contribute to the rise of unemployment.

My own explanation, based on the Beveridge curve, is radically different. As we saw in the first chapter, this function is valuable in that it enables us clearly to distinguish whether a certain trend in unemployment and the number of jobs available in an economy depend on the effects of supply and demand.

17   An Emergency Plan for Europe, or, When, for a Change, Italy Sets the Good Example

I am in favor of the Maastricht agreement because, in order to stay in line with Germany and the Bundesbank's monetary policy, many countries these days are having to accept overly high interest rates. Ever since the start of 1999 and the introduction of the single currency managed by the Central European Bank (where the Germans certainly play a preeminent role but, nevertheless, have to confer with the other members), it has been possible to introduce rates of interest and monetary policies that are more conducive to full employment than those at present being adopted.

As against the wording of the treaty, I am convinced that the only way the euro can work is through a mechanism linking wages to the rate of programmed inflation; but the Europeans have shown no intention to implement such a mechanism. This problem, though, can be shelved. But Europe has a far more pressing need that requires absolute priority. Stimulating demand and finding an efficient way of handling unemployment are not problems that can wait for even a single month. By now, all Europeans accept the need for an emergency plan to return unemployment swiftly to historically acceptable levels while maintaining prices stable. Can it be done? I think it can.

1. The member countries of the economic and monetary union, perhaps with the exception of Germany and Holland (but as time goes on they, too, are stepping into line), must set up a program to rapidly expand the supply of money in real terms, cutting short- and long-term interest rates drastically. To reduce unemployment, aggregate demand must be stimulated. To support monetary policy and to carry it through, the countries with the healthiest public balance can make room for fiscal expansion, especially in investment and public works.

2. The act of relaunching demand requires an expansion of the money supply in real terms. The part that hurts is that the central banks are really capable of controlling only the nominal expansion of money. Herein lies the danger that an expansion of the money supply in nominal terms could be accompanied by a wave of increases in nominal wages, which would lead to a return of inflation. This would put the real objective, the increase of the real money supply, at risk, and would, instead, generate nonaccommodating action by the central bank, which would in turn result once more in undesirably high interest rates.

This perverse mechanism, by which monetary expansion in support of demand actually brings about a loss of demand, lower employment, and a reduced supply of real money, thus causing both inflation and unemployment, can be avoided in only one way. It was the route taken by Italy in 1992 and 1993. It involves tripartite agreements between labor, business, and the government and aims to guarantee stable prices through the even pacing of prices, wages, and investment. First of all, workers have to accept that their wages be frozen in line, if possible, with their current contracts, or that wage increases be no higher than productivity growth. Similarly, businesses have to freeze their profit margins, their markups, so as not to redistribute income to their advantage. The government may intervene to support these agreements by blocking taxes and transfer programs. The freeze should stay in place until unemployment has gone down to acceptable levels. This type of agreement assures that prices remain stable and the purchasing power of wages is not affected. Indeed, workers win in terms of real wages through increased productivity.

Of course, miracles do not happen every day, so it is unlikely that the case of the tripartite agreement signed in Italy in July 1993 will occur again. Yet that is the road that must be taken by the other European countries, starting with Germany. Obviously, the agreement signed between unions, businesses, and government will have to guarantee that real wages be protected and that there is a definite goal of increasing the number of jobs. A time limit could be set for achieving the aims stipulated in the agreement. And whichever of the parties caused the enterprise to fail would be responsible for a huge rise in unemployment.

To sum up then: In Europe today, a decisive, rapid reflation program is feasible. It would increase the money supply in real terms in order to stimulate aggregate demand and would not cause any inflationary side effects, provided that an agreement to preset and direct the wage and price structure toward programmed inflation were orchestrated at a European and, especially, German level. In a sense, it has been Italy leading the way, showing the path that Europe should follow. The agreement signed in 1993 and strongly supported by the Ciampi government provided the wherewithal for sorely needed monetary expansion in Europe while staying on the rail tracks of monetary stability as agreed in Maastricht on May 2, 1998, when the euro was born.

18   The Economists' Manifesto Against Unemployment

Unfortunately my preaching for an effective, fast program to fight unemployment has produced only scanty results. Occasionally, the European Union members have expressed their concern about unemployment but then have failed to agree on a common working program to deal with it. At the 1997 Luxembourg meeting devoted to unemployment, they ignored the importance of measures aimed at increasing aggregate demand and, in consequence, at creating new jobs. Instead, they concentrated on measures regarding the labor market but that had no way to make any significant impact on unemployment. Furthermore, they even denied the relevance of such a policy, maintaining that the solution to unemployment is domestic and lies in the hands of each member state—and this when they were well aware or should have been aware that each country no longer had the power to force demand. A policy of this type is based on two fundamental elements: monetary and fiscal policies. Control of these two elements has been removed from the individual member states by the fact that, in Europe, monetary policy is preset and the same for everyone, while fiscal policy is heavily influenced by the parameters set at Maastricht.

In the meantime, unemployment gave no sign of falling, even if there were some signs of recovery in the job market.

I was pained and discouraged by these developments, and, realizing that I was not the only person who was worried, I decided to get up a manifesto against unemployment with various colleagues from different American and European countries in the hope that many others would promote it. The manifesto criticizes the measures, or lack of measures, that have so far been taken to solve the problem. It also makes a series of concrete proposals.

First, there should be a quantified program to expand investments, which have fallen by one third over the last twenty years and which should increase by 50 percent in the coming twelve. This program should involve all the countries in simultaneous expansion, for it is more effective that way than if undertaken by countries singly. It should produce many new jobs.

Second, a complementary program should be undertaken to improve the way the labor market functions in assuring that new jobs be taken. This would act on regulations that overprotect insiders from dismissal and that were originally conceived to protect employment but, in reality, have promoted unemployment of outsiders, especially the young. We propose that the undertaking be carried out, not in an antiunion spirit, but for the benefit of everyone, so that measures liberalizing contracts be introduced progressively as the program to expand demand unfolds new job opportunities.

Further measures should be taken to motivate the unemployed to take existing jobs. These could include linking unemployment benefit payments to the number of unfilled jobs: When these become numerous, the time will be ripe for fully encouraging people to seek and accept jobs. Another fairly novel measure would be to use unemployment benefit payments, or part of them, to finance companies offering jobs so as to help them cut their costs.

A preliminary version of the paper, "An Economist Manifesto on Unemployment in the European Union" was recently completed and signed by seven noted economists from five countries. Apart from myself, there were Fitoussi, Moro, Snower, Solow, Steinherr and Sylos Labini, and we were greeted with rapidly increasing support from other economists. The manifesto was presented at a conference held in mid-October 1998 at Lake Iseo in Italy, and was attended by leading figures from the world of economics, the business world, and the workforce and was covered widely in the press. It also appears to be receiving some attention at government levels.

19   *The Unwritten Part of the Maastricht Treaty*

It is my profound conviction that the euro and the Maastricht Treaty can work. However, success will come about only if the governments and central banks realize that the success of the euro depends on their ability to control wages and therefore prices. Monetary policy is not capable of doing this except through restrictive means. These only aggravate the unemployment disease, a disease that threatens to kill the European Union. For the day will come when the whole unification design will be blamed for the tragedy of an entire generation being excluded from the productive processes and, in consequence, the destruction of capital and future income. There is not a trace of an income policy in the Maastricht Treaty; however, an income policy coordinated at a European level is the only one that can make the single currency viable. The model to follow, then, is that formulated by Ezio Tarantelli. His intuition in this matter was the reason he was assassinated by the infamous Red Brigades on March 27, 1985, after a class held at the Economics Faculty at the University of Rome[31]. Tarantelli, who had been a student of mine at MIT, was barbarously murdered precisely because he voiced the need for tripartite agreements based on predetermined nominal wages within programmed inflation.

Tarantelli's brilliant intuition would take concrete shape only many years later with the Amato and Ciampi governments, and from all the signs it has been a complete success. For the first year and half, wages and prices were kept to the narrow path outlined by the agreement. This allowed Italy to handle an unexpected, severe devaluation at the start of 1995 confidently. It was caused, not as in the past by excessive wage demands, but by a lack of confidence illustrated by the clashes between the parties when approving necessary public finance measures. The unplanned devaluation caused a net loss of purchasing power by the laboring class and a reduction in real wages. The basic tenor of the agreement regarding the cost of labor prevented the unleashing of inflation as in the past.

A theoretical conclusion: The very possibility of a tripartite agreement is based on a fundamental equation. This equation establishes that the percentage variation of the price level, in other words the inflation rate as calculated annually, is equal to the percentage variation of the nominal wage (wage inflation) minus the percentage variation of real wages (wage inflation minus inflation). This means that the negotiating table consists of two distinctive components: one that defines the objectives in purely nominal terms, while the other defines them in real terms and thus sets the objectives of real wages. This passage is very important and very subtle because it explains that if one adopts a system of programmed inflation, it is possible to program very low levels of inflation, even zero inflation, without cutting into real wages. Indeed, once the real wage level has been selected, we can achieve any inflationary aim simply by choosing a wage level at the desired inflation rate minus the desired growth rate of real wages. At this point, the labor force finds it is in its interest to accept any objective in terms of nominal wages inasmuch as this will have no effect on the real wage that is set separately. The nominal wage only affects the inflation rate. In other words, the labor force has nothing further to gain—indeed, it could only lose—should nominal wages rise faster, inasmuch as this is reflected in price increases, higher interest rates, and diminished purchasing power of publicly owned financial assets.

These considerations lead to the conclusion that, if one chooses programmed inflation, the best inflation to program is zero inflation.

III

ITALY AND ME

1   *Should We Return to Italy?*

To understand how we reacquired our stable relationship with Italy, we have to go back to the war years. Serena and I had learned to love the United States because of the way we had been welcomed and how we had managed to fit into the university world. However, despite this, we kept our Italian nationality from 1939 to 1946, when we grew dismayed at the dwindling of the opportunities for hope and renewal that the struggle for liberation had brought. I have already mentioned that the final straw that made us decide to opt for the United States was the appearance and success of the "Common Man" movement.

During the war, Serena and I followed the tragedy of our country under the Republic of Salò (the reconstituted Fascist puppet regime established at Lake Garda in 1943) from afar, terribly concerned about what had happened to so many friends and relatives. I was especially worried about my brother, who had stayed in Italy with his family. To our horror, we learned that Rome had been occupied by the Nazis. We read about the revolt against Mussolini by Badoglio's supporters and the Fascists themselves, and our fears for my brother increased daily. We knew that he had made many attempts to leave the country but had been prevented each time. From September 1943 until the spring of 1945, we were unable to get any news of him or his family.

Finally, on the day that Rome was liberated, we received a military dispatch informing us that they were all alive and well. What happened? Well, that day, Giorgio and the family had literally captured an American soldier who happened to be passing close by them. They had taken him to their home, where they had uncorked for him a bottle of very old, extremely fine wine they had been saving especially for that occasion. They persuaded him to send us a phonogram military dispatch immediately. It was what they called victory letters, and we still have it today. Our joy when we got that little letter was indescribable.

Only later did we learn that Giorgio and his family had passed months wandering around the Roman countryside, trying to escape the Nazis who were combing the area. Every night, they slept in a different hayloft. The Roman peasants never betrayed Giorgio's family, who would come straight out with the truth: "We are Jews. The Germans are looking for us so they can take us away or kill us. Can you give us somewhere to sleep?"

The answer was always the same: "Yes, but only for one night." They were afraid, but they never refused to help. Every night, Giorgio and his wife tied a rope to the window of the hayloft and showed their seven-year-old son how to climb down while holding his sister, who was only a few months old, in his arms. If the Germans started to go up to their hiding place, he was to run to a nearby house with her. Only in the final months of the war did Giorgio realized that the anonymity of the big city offered more safety than the countryside. So, after he had managed to get false, but official papers through a state office, he went back to Rome.

When we managed to contact him, we immediately suggested that he join us in the United States. We would find him a job. They would be very happy living with us. Giorgio's reply was that in those months of wandering around the Roman countryside, with the wonderful help of so many simple folk who had exposed themselves to grave risk knowing well what the penalty for hiding Jews was, he had understood that his country was Italy and he had no desire to leave.

During the first months of peacetime, my father-in-law returned to Italy, passing through Paris to see whether he should take up the option that the publisher Mondadori had offered him at the time of his departure. The Messaggerie's bill of sale included the option that, within a certain number of years, my father-in-law could exercise his right to repurchase the business. However, the picture that he drew for us upon his return was not particularly rosy: Corruption was still rife and the political situation was very confusing, so we decided that it would be madness to leave the United States.

* * *

2   *Paolo Sylos Labini and Gaetano Salvemini*

For a long time, contacts were few and far between. In the meantime, though, I met many Italians in America. As early as 1948, when I was at the University of Illinois, I had the pleasure of meeting Paolo Sylos Labini, who had come to Chicago (and Harvard) to study with Schumpeter and other great men. We took an immediate liking to each other, and between us a brotherly friendship sprang up that has continued until today, strengthened by the enormous similarities in the way we view economics.

Paolo had only recently moved to Harvard when I was invited to the famous interview with Burbank; so I organized my visit to Harvard such that I could have an afternoon break with Sylos. I had just written a long article that had been published in the *Giornale degli Economisti*[1]. It had been an exercise in forcing myself to imagine how production was run efficiently in a socialist economy and how it handled the absence of a market so as to achieve the desired result. At that time, I was very interested in the theme of price controls, which was, in fact, a way of understanding how prices were formulated. Controls, rationing, and food cards were very commonly used in all the Western countries immediately after the war. The question entailed understanding whether the market economy system with its competing private producers had been the only efficient way of formulating prices throughout history. It was a classical theme that found its source in one of the writings of Enrico Barone, "Il Ministro della Produzione nello Stato Collettivista"[2], but which had influenced great economists like Oskar Lange, Abba Lerner, and Dickinson. My conclusions, which were absolutely theoretical, did not paint a negative picture of socialism; however, the reasons that could, in theory, have supported the socialist economic thesis were light-years away from those actually being used by communist propaganda. Thus in 1947, I wrote:

> The same old repeated slogans like "production for consumption and not for profit," or "the firm must be run in the general interest," are completely meaningless where there are no clear, objective, verifiable means of achieving them. Even though it is not perfectly efficient, the capitalist system works because the people running the firms have a clear task to carry out: they must make as much profit as possible for the firm. If, in socialist countries, once firms have been socialized, there are no guidelines other than some vague ethical principles for managers to follow, the economic machine will function arbitrarily or not at all.

I believed that there could be a set of logical rules that socialist countries could apply so as to make their economics plausible. Theoretically, "Socialization of firms is not necessary when perfect competition exists." So, when does socialization actually become legitimate? When competition is not perfect or when a single firm is in a position to influence the market price. In this case, which is common enough in many capitalist economies, what happens is that "the system of private enterprise often cannot guarantee the use of all the available quantity." In my opinion, the important thing was that, if the companies were socialized, "one could do no better than to order the company's managers to run production as if they were private entrepreneurs," because they would otherwise have no direction at all and would produce goods that consumers and society had no desire for.

The only known meeting point between goods and consumers is reached via prices. "Whether in the private capitalist system or in the socialist one, prices of consumer goods largely play the same role. They serve to guarantee that the goods produced are assigned to the precise individuals who most intensely desire them." In retrospect, we know that socialism failed because it was unable to carry out the task of creating a mechanism for formulating prices. At that time, however, we were more interested in the limitations and failings of a capitalistic-style economy:

> In the private enterprise system, the all-important price function in consumer goods is highly distorted. This is because the ability of each consumer to fulfill his needs depends on income, but the income is distributed unequally among consumers, so the secondary needs of a rich person carry more weight than the more urgent requirements of a poorer individual.

The seeds of the economic catastrophe of the socialist countries can be found right there, in the very concept of price formation.

We have deduced that the absence of a capitalist-style price system means that economic resources cannot be used intelligently or efficiently to satisfy the needs of society. This is because prices offer the only objective criterion for evaluating the economic requirements of society and for establishing the most economical way of satisfying them.

Over the years, we have often seen price controls applied in market economies. They have nearly always been catastrophic experiences. This is not because they were necessarily morally wrong but simply because they obstructed the price-formulation mechanism. And that is the only way so far discovered by humans to allocate the resources of society efficiently. This is why I have never tired of suggesting solutions that, while letting the market determine its own prices, enable governments to reallocate resources throughout society by fiscal means.

Of course, the long conversations I had with Bruno Pontecorvo in the cafés of Paris as the Nazi armies were taking up their positions along the Maginot Line had, in spite of everything, left me with some soft spots for socialism.

During my years in America I had been completely occupied with my studies of classical economics and the Keynesian revolution. That article had also been an attempt to interpret socialist economics in the light of classical economics. Perhaps it had been too enthusiastic. Sylos considered it somewhat romantic, typical of my character and worthy enough to be the reason for a meeting with his teacher, Gaetano Salvemini.

After the meeting with Burbank and after lunch with Schumpeter, Sylos took me to see Salvemini, who had a carrel, a tiny room where he could study in peace at the Wiedner Library at Harvard. I recall that when we entered, we could hardly find him, half buried as he was by an incredible number of books, piles of which rose from the floor and were stacked in every corner. All the available space was taken up with journals, papers, and magazines.

It was an important meeting, and I left him my article on socialism. But conversing with him and, later, reading his books would distance me, once and for all, from whatever sympathy I had entertained for socialist theories and lead me to embrace democratic liberalism unreservedly. I, who loved the United States and who had just become an American citizen, found it very comforting to hear Salvemini speaking about democracy: "The United States is the oldest democracy in the world and the youngest nation in the world." The secret of democracy lies in its assumption that no one is infallible and no one holds the secret of good government. Salvemini was very bitter about fascism and the weakness of the Italians, and I did indeed find him terribly pessimistic.

After that field day at Harvard, my friendship with Sylos grew ever stronger and became an important reference point. It was during my sabbatical year at Harvard in 1958 that, using an important book by Paolo as a starting point, I developed an article on the theory of oligopoly. In the article, I developed a simplified model to explain how prices behave in an oligopoly.

At the end of the 1950s, it was Ferruccio Parri himself, who then ran the magazine *Astrolabio*, who invited Paolo Sylos Labini and me to a very interesting debate on the conflict between General de Gaulle and the United States. This conflict involved every field, including monetary and economic policies. During the debate, Parri coined a very amusing term when he accused de Gaulle of wanting to set up Gaullshevism in Europe. I remember how we laughed when we were sent the issue of the magazine that included the transcript of the debate. An overzealous but dull editor had amended Paolo's term, writing Bolshevism instead, completely removing the subtlety from the phrase.

3   *The First Time I Go Back*

It was because of Sylos pressuring me that I decided to apply for a Fullbright scholarship to lecture for six months in Italy in 1954. I won it and so was able to spend some of 1955 in Rome and Palermo. That was when I renewed my contacts with the Italian academic world and felt not a little pleased that I had chosen to live in the United States. The impressions I received were very bad indeed. I had forgotten just how great the differences between the American and Italian university education systems were. At that time, the Italian system had a three-level hierarchy. At the top, immediately below God, were a few, mostly elderly professors; in the middle was a good-sized group of assistants, hopeful and servile, while at the bottom of the pyramid and ignored by everyone were the students. I will never forget something that happened when I was at the University of Rome. Professor Papi, who was then the rector and living symbol of the institutional system, invited me to speak at a seminar held in his faculty. He introduced me (I was then thirty-eight years old and had been a full professor for several years) as a "promising youth." I thanked him but pointed out that, in the United States, I was already considered a bit outdated!

Another emblematic episode had occurred sometime earlier during an international economics congress held in Washington. On that occasion, Jacob Marschak himself introduced me to the famous professor Corrado Gini. I recall him, elegantly dressed with a cummerbund. He shook my hand and, seeing that I was a young man, immediately pulled a watch out of his pocket and said: "Look, I broke my watch yesterday. Would you be kind enough to get it fixed and bring it to me at my hotel?" I could not believe my ears. I answered him, "Of course I could, but I think it might be more appropriate if you asked the bellboy at the hotel to do it for you." He appeared a bit surprised and put out by my answer because obviously that was the sort of relationship Italian professors had with their younger colleagues.

This was how they tested you, to see how much you would put up with to get into the boss's good graces. And this is one of the reasons for the structural inefficiency of the Italian university system as compared with the American. It is also one of the basic reasons for the Italian crisis, because a ruling class that is chosen on the basis of its ability to put up with humiliation and to have no self-respect is in no shape to guide Italy. In the United States, professors and students have always thought together, eaten together, and lived in the same places. If a good idea comes from a student, then the professor needs to work with him, perhaps even put their names together on an academic paper. I remember the total silence of the students during my classes in Rome. Once I got fed up and said to them: "For heaven's sake, don't you have anything to say about the things I'm telling you?" One of the few students who took up the invitation to speak was Paolo Leon.

During my year in Italy, I went to Milan several times at the invitation of an important research center for public economics run by Professor Giorgio Mortara. He was a highly competent and kindly person but he was also a bit shy. He rose to fame among our American friends after a Chinese dinner held at a congress for economists. At the end of the meal, the fortune cookies with their little paper slips inside arrived. Everyone broke the cookies open and joked about their fortunes. The only person who was not enjoying himself was Mortara. Then, somebody asked him what it said on his slip, and he answered falteringly, "I . . . ate it."

Among the circle of very bright young economists that had formed around him, Siro Lombardini and Nino Andreatta stood out. I recall that we gathered at Bellagio on Lake Como to prepare research material on the economy of the area.

In the same year, I met Giorgio Fuà who would afterward invite me, time and time again, to seminars at Ancona. These would often finish at the marvelous Passetto restaurant and lead to a tour around the beautiful Marche region. It was on one of those occasions that we first went to Recanati to visit the Leopardi sites and to see the famous Holy House at Loreto, which, according to legend, had flown there directly from Palestine!

My contact with Fuà's group, as well as with Andreatta and Lombardini's Milanese one, was very close. There was an intense exchange of experiences, data, and work from both sides of the Atlantic. And I started to be a regular visitor to Italy. I remember one trip I was invited on by Fuà in the spring of 1964 when I was able to talk to Antonio Giolitti, the minister of Budget and Planning. I explained to him that the proposal, then under discussion, to tax interest with a onetime tax instead of combining it with other income subject to income tax was not consistent with the concept of progressive taxation, which was supposed to be a fundamental aspect of socialism. I recall that Giolitti understood perfectly what I was saying but he was not able to apply it. This is the reason behind the profoundly unjust system that allows people who invest in national bonds to pay 12.5 percent tax a year while most taxpayers pay between 20 and 30 percent.

I took up this position thirty years before Fausto Bertinotti (leader of the Rifondazione Comunista Party) was to include it in his political propaganda. And propaganda it has to be, for, now that Italy is a member of the European Union with the complete freedom of movement of capital which that entails, interest income cannot be taxed the same way as other personal income unless all the other countries agree to do the same. Not only will Bertinotti have to fight for an increase in the way BOT (Treasury bonds) are taxed, but he will also have to persuade all the other EU countries to accept the principle that interest must be taxed in line with all other personal income.

When we went to Palermo, Serena and I were honored with great celebrations and much human warmth. I was asked to make the inaugural speech in the main lecture hall of the university. The head of the department sent the janitors to collar any students who happened to be passing by and herd them in to hear me. I also remember high-society receptions. At these, the same thing would always happen: A professor, a liberal, for instance, would come up to me and say: "Be careful, professor, here the Mafia is run by the Communists." Then a Christian Democrat would come up and whisper in my ear: "Be careful, Professor, here, the Mafia is run by the liberals." And so it would go on until they had run out of political parties. I found the complications of Sicilian politics totally incomprehensible. Once, for example, Frisella Vella, a university professor who made no secret of his desire for autonomy, said he favored Sicily becoming the forty-eighth state of the United States.

4   Ugo La Malfa and Electricity

Among the Italian politicians I met was Mario Ferrari Aggradi. But I greatly admired Ugo La Malfa, with whom I shared many fundamental ideas. These included his stance on economic policy, and in particular his preaching about an income policy that otherwise fell on deaf ears. It was through his son, Giorgio, who had become a student of mine, that I met him in the 1960s.

There was one action taken by Ugo La Malfa that I have never understood: the so-called nationalization of electricity. In economic terms, it is doubtful whether it made sense to remove the production and distribution of electric power from the private sector, considering it was already run as a concession. There is no clear argument as to why it would have been better run as a centralized, public enterprise. The only defensible reason that can be adduced is a pragmatic one. The electricity companies had developed a concentration of pressures that the political world—or, to be more precise, the center-left led by Fanfani in 1962—considered excessive and distorted. However, if the idea had been to remove the excessive power that the electricity companies had accumulated, then the solution chosen made absolutely no sense at all. Indeed, if the aim was that—and I repeat, it is the only defensible one—the state should have expropriated the companies by the simple act of a forced takeover from the shareholders, paying them off according to the number of shares they held. Instead, the companies were kept alive artificially by the government's paying for the value of the plants and systems and handing over an incredible amount of cash to the companies, which instead of curbing their pressuring power only increased it out of all proportion. The aim had been to limit the excessive power of the electricity companies, but they had instead been showered with money and didn't even have the uncomfortable task of having to produce electricity!

I shall never understand how that decision was made. If Carli had suggested the technical solution, as he appears to admit in his memoirs, why he did so remains a mystery to me. However, the political onus of the whole operation fell on La Malfa. Despite this, I consider him to have been one of the best politicians Italy has ever known.

Some years later, during a long trip to Europe in the summer of 1973, I made an enthusiastic stop in Sweden, the country with the greatest *per capita* number of economists in the world. During my stay I wrote several pieces for the *Corriere della Sera* comparing Swedish socialism with the nationalization policies adopted in Italy[3].

Perhaps the most intriguing and paradoxical aspect of the Swedish success story is that, for the last forty years, the country has been governed by a social-democratic system. The brilliant results I have reported have been achieved by keeping the system of free enterprise intact. Remember, in Sweden, the amount of nationalization of the means of production is very small—much smaller, for instance, than in Italy. Here, socialism is not about the sterile nationalization of the means of production inspired by some abstract ideology. It is about being pragmatic; thus, it exploits the efficiency and flexibility of the profit-making private enterprise system by making judicious use of incentives to guide production in socially useful ways. In addition, it takes the form of a gradual reduction of economic inequality via redistribution of income in a complex, advanced social security system.

5   *Giorgio La Malfa and I Criticize Carli*

In 1964, Giorgio La Malfa and I were very dismayed by the monetary squeeze and the recession caused by the Italian central bank. Long discussions with Giorgio resulted in the idea that, together, we should write an article that would illustrate the econometric models implicit in the behavior of the central bank's actions that we felt were deserving of criticism[4].

In the bank's behavior, Giorgio and I saw the emergence of decidedly traditional ideas. They followed the classical line wherein money has a direct effect on prices. As good Keynesians, we argued that, on the contrary, money would have an indirect effect. This was because it acts directly on investment through the interest rate. Investment influences income, and it is the effect on income, and that alone, that causes the price level to change. The classical route was just a little too simplistic. Our basic criticism was that the bank had used excessively violent monetary tactics. In our model, monetary policy affected investments, whereas it was fiscal policy that had a direct effect on consumption and thus on the structure of demand.

Looking back, the article contained a technical mistake that Nuti later pointed out; but, above all, I think the article was too critical. I believe that it was a mistake to criticize Carli's heavy hand so severely inasmuch as, in the previous two-year period, the central bank had set course on an overly expansive monetary route. This had been an error, but once the bank had started down that road, it had to implement a very tight money policy; otherwise, it would not have been able to stop inflation from spiraling and, later, would have found itself in an even more severe recession and having to adopt even more restrictive measures.

In any case, La Malfa and I were right to say that the monetary rigor and loss of jobs could have been avoided if an income policy had been implemented. After the central bank had let prices run away in 1962 and 1963, it should have prevented price increases from transferring to wages, which only served to push prices up again.

The Bank of Italy had accommodated inflationary pressure because it thought that, by doing so, it would not curb investment, allowing the rates to fall with the increase of liquidity and of money, which was created to accommodate prices. In our view, monetary policy could not directly control prices. But they thought it could. They therefore argued as follows: "We do not wish to pursue a policy of high interest rates, in order not to discourage investments; since we don't wish in any way to discourage investments, accordingly, we must first accept inflation, then apply a monetary squeeze."

6   The Ghost Review

The story concerning my article with Giorgio La Malfa was tortuous but, to some extent, meaningful. While we were getting heated up over Italian affairs, we received a phone call from our friends in the research department of the Bank of Italy. Carli's team of young lions, especially Antonio Fazio, Mario Sarcinelli, and Guido Rey, wanted to publish our study in the first issue of a magazine they were secretly putting together. Much as the Fed does, the Italian central bank wanted to open a window onto the world of economics and offer a view to Italian universities and scholars from all over the world so as to be able to discuss issues unhindered by monetary policy. I thought it was a very long-sighted view, in keeping with the times. All we had to do was phone the Rivista Economica. As I recall, our friends in Rome did an excellent job of editing the Italian version, even helping us to criticize them better. The drafts were printed and we were sent a copy. But then, as the weeks went by and the magazine failed to make an appearance, I understood that something had gone wrong. At a certain point in our correspondence, we found out that the top management of the bank had decided to block publication and to render our courageous, innovative initiative void. They wrote to say that they would see to its publication as soon as possible in the BNL's "sister" magazine, then edited by the admirable Luigi Ceriani. And so they did. But the Bank of Italy probably missed a good opportunity.

In 1966, the article came out in the September issue of *Moneta e Credito*, and along with it came family troubles for my friend Giorgio. We had written the article as economists in the true sense of the word, with no political intentions. Certainly we were Keynesians and we were fighting for the Keynesian revolution. We were convinced that that was the only way to make heads or tails of the complex monetary phenomenon that had come into being.

But it has to be understood that, in Italy, everything that Carli, governor of the Bank of Italy, said was interpreted as being either for or against the center-left. Now, one of the center-left's leading lights, if not the leading light,

was Giorgio's father. Ugo La Malfa was obliged to blow his top about our article because he felt that it might have been interpreted as a criticism of Carli
made indirectly by himself through his son Giorgio. He was wrong, of course,
but Giorgio stayed in a foul mood for quite a while after that and, for a time,
did not telephone his father. However, our criticisms had been sincere, and
the bank itself had explicitly encouraged us to formulate them as fully as possible, so my feelings toward the occupants of the institution in Via Nazionale
remained warm despite the magazine's not being published.

There was one other aspect of the informal model being followed by the
Bank of Italy that perplexed me. By allowing prices to rise, the economists
in Via Nazionale thought they would reduce the real wages of workers by
changing the distribution of income in favor of those who lived off capital
or their business, with the effect of increasing the aggregate saving rate.

This idea was flawed in several ways. If prices had not gone up because
there had not been enough money available—in other words, if the central
bank had not kept money tight—wages would not have risen. But, the
bank was convinced that if they could hold prices down by not increasing
the money supply, a process would have been set in motion whereby
income would have been redistributed in favor of wage earners, whose tendency to save and accumulate capital was more limited. My frequent meetings with my friends in Via Nazionale on this theme were often very heated.
I never managed to persuade them that their Kaldor-style consumer function was clearly nullified by my model and related tests. The economists at
the bank believed that investment (and therefore employment) was determined by the spread of income between wages and profits. But empirical
tests on the life cycle hypothesis clearly demonstrate that aggregate savings
depend on the rate of growth of income rather than *per capita* income, and
that how income is distributed is fairly unimportant. In any case, at that
time, there were not sufficient estimates. Giorgio and I rejected the idea
that the savings rate was determined by income distribution. We also criticized its internal consistency. For, in order to account for investment, not
only the propensity for saving but also the interest rate must be taken into
consideration—which, in 1962 and 1963, Carli tended to underestimate.

7 Carli Calls Me to the Bank of Italy

At the end of 1966, when I was asked to take part in developing their
econometric model, my relationship with the Bank of Italy gradually
became one of the closest cooperation. It was during those years that stu-

dents started to come from Italy to take my courses at MIT. Some were brilliant, and many were to become dear friends. Previously, I had had students like Antonio Fazio, and later, Paolo Savona, Franco Cotula, and Bruno Sitzia. They had been followed by Tommaso and Fiorella Padoa Schioppa, and of course I would also like to mention Fausto Vicarelli, Ezio Tarantelli, Mario Baldassarri, Mario Draghi, Franco Bruni, Francesco Giavazzi, Tullio Jappelli, and Marco Pagano. Every one of them left me something. I learned something from each of them.

My own students and then Alberto Ando's students at the Italian central bank are too numerous to count. The first person I met there was the then economics counselor, Salvatore Guidotti. A delightful Neapolitan, he unfortunately left the bank suddenly. There was also Rainer Masera leading the handful of very young economists who, starting in 1968, would become my friends, counterparts, and workmates as we developed the econometric model. I only met Guido Carli and Paolo Baffi later when I explicitly asked for a meeting with the other people working on the model so as to understand what the bank's concrete aims were. I wanted to make the econometric model spring out of a Socratic-like process that would force us to reflect on the new ideas we were trying to construct. And I had the pleasure of meeting two exceptionally intelligent and lively people.

The length of time we spent with the Bank of Italy meant that we were able to enjoy Rome in its marvelous extended springtime. In 1969, we were the bank's guests at Villa Einaudi, which it owned. I can recall our amazement when we entered our room and saw the bed entirely decked out in pale blue velvet. Serena immediately said that she felt like the queen of England. We were served and spoiled by the housekeeper, the caretaker Giovanni, and their whole family, who insisted on bringing us bunches of fresh flowers every morning. It was just incredible.

When the apricots were ripe, I climbed the tree without a ladder, something I have always loved doing since I was a child, and picked the fruit and threw it down to Serena. When Giovanni the caretaker realized what was going on he was dismayed: "But, Professor, you mustn't do things like that. That's my job. If you'd told me, I would have brought you a basket of apricots every morning."

Italy during those years was still a very closed country. The Italians had not yet started traveling all over the globe. They looked at us askance, as if we were Martians, when we showed surprise at habits and beliefs that we did not understand. One thing we couldn't stand was the steady line of people who came asking to be recommended for jobs, even as ushers, at the Italian central bank. Seeing that we were living at Villa Einaudi, they felt that we must have a lot of influence.

At the beginning of the summer, Andrew Brimmer, an African-American governor at the Fed, came to see us in Rome with his wife and daughter. Brimmer was absolutely amazed when he went to the zoo with his family. As they were about to go in, they found themselves at the center of a huge crowd of excited children, accompanied by a few nuns, who had never seen anyone with black skin before. They were so curious that they wanted to touch the little girl's skin. Brimmer told us that he had never, in the whole wide world, ever seen such curiosity about people of a different color.

I don't know why, but Italians then were completely misinformed about what was going on in the United States. They would often come up to us and ask us aggressively: "Why is there so much racism against the black people in America?" Serena would always give the same answer. "Well, yes, it's there, but the Italians in America are the worst racists of all." It was in those years that the Italian community was beginning to do well, opening restaurants, barbershops, and cobbler shops. It was also the time that parents stopped teaching their children Italian because they wanted them to be only American.

8   "The Horse Won't Drink": My Dialogues with Carli and Baffi

The fundamental experience that enabled me to restore many severed links with Italy, during which I understood so many new things, so many crucial problems in the Italian economy, undoubtedly coincided with the period in which the econometric model was given its first organic arrangement. Though the first draft of the model was not completed until 1970, we had worked it out with our friends in the econometric research department in the winter of 1967–68. That was on the eve of the student protest that started with the Paris May events and was to set all Europe alight. Traces remain at the Bank of Italy, in written records, of three meetings in which I and all the coworkers on the model met the governor, Guido Carli, the director general, Paolo Baffi, and some functionaries who were expert in various fields[5].

The meeting resembled a long session on the psychoanalyst's couch during which, as often occurs, the analyst (myself) finds himself being asked questions by the analyzed. It is quite exceptional for an economist to have available for several hours two persons responsible for the monetary policy of a country, and to be able to question them as to the real goals motivating their decisions, the implicit models, the instruments available to them, and the ones they prefer.

Recently published under the title Dialogue Between a Professor and the Bank of Italy, the written records of those meetings bear unmistakable witness to two exceptionally qualified persons, Guido Carli and Paolo Baffi, certainly among the most remarkable I have ever encountered in my life. They were intimately acquainted with modern economics, and thus with the Keynesian approach, and were moreover, to my delight, Keynesians in the specific sense of the term, for they held that full employment could not be maintained simply by flexibility of wages and prices, but required intervention on money and/or interest rates. Their goals, however, differed from what Keynesians could typically declare, that is, to maximize income by reducing unemployment to the minimum possible, and to maintain the price level as stable as possible. Their fundamental objective, instead, was substantially to maximize investments and thus "to bring the level of income in Italy close to the level prevalent in the other countries" of the European Community. Since investment is limited by saving, which depends in turn on income, that objective could be seen as equivalent to maximization of income. But that is not exact, since investment may also increase by reducing the consumption for a given income. This explains the Bank of Italy's aversion to easy credit for consumers, which tends to favor consumption (especially if this includes consumer durables, as the governor certainly thought, even though this is a highly debatable thesis).

For the same reason Carli did not favor raising pensions, which permanently increase consumption, nor raising wages at the expense of profits, based on the view that the amount of profit saved is considerably greater than that of the wage. This view was strongly rooted in Carli, in the Bank of Italy, and also in conventional wisdom in general, including many fellow economists. I have never shared this view because it is not consistent with the spirit of my saving hypothesis (the LCH model), and the empirical evidence seems to bear me out.

With regard to the trend of prices, stabilizing them in the absolute sense did not appear to be among Carli's intentions, but only to stabilize them in relation to foreign prices—this because it was necessary to maintain competitiveness with a fixed exchange, which was considered to be highly desirable.

After the initial ice had been broken, there was no doubt that Guido Carli greatly enjoyed my impertinent questions and relished the scrutiny of his activity in past years. Baffi, who replied to my questions in the very technical way of a pedigree economist, seemed more tense than the governor, cautious perhaps not to hint at any disagreement with Carli, but he displayed an unmistakable sense of humor.

Our task was to formalize the behavior of the Bank of Italy and to render the monetary variables exogenous—that is, to explain them with other variables as part of the model. To see the discussion in a proper perspective, it must be borne in mind that monetary variables are normally taken as exogenous and thus not conditioned by the other components of the system.

One of the main topics of discussion was the instruments the bank intended to use to achieve its goals. Should the quantity of money be fixed? If so, it was accepted that the interest rate would oscillate, wherever this was necessary to reestablish equilibrium in the bond market at that quantity of money. Or would it be better, instead, to fix at every point in time the rate of interest at which the bank was prepared, without limit, to purchase or sell bonds and give credit to the banking system? In that case, the bank would have to give up direct control over the quantity of money, since the rate would determine income, and rate and income would determine the quantity of money desired by the economy, which the bank would have to satisfy in order to maintain that rate.

For about eighteen months by then, Carli had been following this path, fixing the rate and allowing the quantity of money to fluctuate. The stability of the interest rate, and hence of bond prices, was felt to be a guarantee for selling government bonds, which was thought to be essential after the financial crisis that had loomed in 1964. This stability was also favored as discouraging waves in capital movements—especially in the light of the widespread conviction that once capital had been transferred outside Italy it would never return. But it is important to bear in mind that, in actual fact, the income and the quantity of money did not entirely depend on the rate fixed, for, at that time at least, the bank had a huge arsenal of instruments to control the volume of investments and the demand.

> MODIGLIANI: . . . Let me mention one thing that strikes a person like me who is accustomed to the American central bank: the profound difference is how many things the Bank of Italy does and can do. Briefly, it would never occur to an American firm to ask the central bank if an investment should be made or not . . . you have fifty thousand instruments at your disposal.[6]

These instruments were, in part, sanctioned by law, such as the control over the flow of issues of equities through authorization by the interministerial credit committee, with further discrimination by the bank as to when to put them on the market, or the rationing of credit to the banks. But the majority were based on moral suasion, such as pressure on the government regarding public investments and issue of bonds, and directives suggested to the banks. In like manner, the Bank of Italy was able to exert important influence on capital movements, and thus on the movement of currency reserves, through the amount of foreign indebtedness of the merchant banks, protecting them against exchange risk by means of swaps.

But immediately underlying that highly theoretical discussion (all of us really knew that the central banks always have, at the same time, a certain idea of the appropriate trend of the rate of interest and of the quantity of money) there was one fundamental point: the Bank of Italy's autonomy and independence from political authority.

The Bank of Italy had a great many "improper" instruments of monetary policy, but lacked the most ordinary one, the possibility of exerting a monetary squeeze by maneuvering the money stock, owing to its role as Treasury banker—which began to change only many years later with the famous "divorce" between the Treasury and the bank. In addition, given that there was a very extensive area of easy credit, since public-sector and public enterprises were always able to borrow, a hypothetical monetary tightening would have had undesirable distribution effects: It would have favored expansion of the public sector, which was less sensitive to the trend of rates, and would have concentrated its effects of reducing investments and income on the private sector and especially on small and medium-sized enterprises. This concern was evident in what Carli said, but was also expressed by Baffi. Indeed, I would say it was at the center of their thoughts. At bottom, their ideal would have been to create a short-term money market, mainly with treasury bonds (BOT), in order to link the banking system with monetary policy through the variation of short-term interest rates. To achieve this, of course, the Treasury would have to give up the direct creation of money through the central bank's line of credit to the Treasury.

During those meetings in January 1968 Carli said:

> I think we must move gradually towards a short-term money market and must therefore dissociate the rates on the required reserves from the rates of the Treasury Bonds; we must maintain the position of the Treasury close to zero and therefore, given a certain level of liquidity, allow the rate to rise and fall, and must then tie it to the bank rate. But this must happen very gradually.[7]

We know how the story ended. The "long hot autumn," the disintegration of the international monetary system, and then the two oil shocks caused a huge inflation in Italy and elsewhere, and the divorce from the Treasury was postponed till the 1980s.

During these conversations there were also various implicit references to the criticisms made by Giorgio La Malfa and myself of the monetary policy in Carli's first period as governor. The mechanism of development had become jammed. We felt that the squeeze was too violent and, above all, that after the crisis had ended the reflation had been too meek, the increase in the money supply insufficient to produce an adequate reduction in interest rates.

Carli and Baffi never thought this criticism valid, but their defense was grounded on two arguments inconsistent with one another. One of these, respectable in itself, centered on the problems of the balance of payments. After the 1964 crisis, the Bank of Italy felt it vital to reconstruct an adequate amount of reserves; and a moderate increase in income contributed to this goal by reducing imports. Moreover, Carli thought that, despite the administrative restrictions on capital export, a reduction in the Italian rates, even a moderate one, would cause a lot of capital to go abroad and a loss of reserves, with scant effects on the rate of investment:

> CARLI: All things considered, the fact that reserves have been built up once more enables us to face up to future eventualities. . . . There is an open frontier, across which capital moves in both directions, and so an excess of uncontrolled liquidity may cause an outflow of capital and thus fail to promote production.[8]

There was an additional motive, but it was one my friends were a little less eager to talk about: The interest rates at which the banks could borrow from the central bank could certainly be lowered, but since the banks formed an oligopolistic cartel, there was no guarantee that they would lower the rates for their clients and thus transmit this expansionary impulse to the economy.

But Carli showed much sympathy with the banking cartel and the way it exploited the rest of the economy: "I prefer a banking system that works with the widest possible margins and indeed in this respect it is an objective in itself, other things being equal, to widen the profit margins of the banking system."[9]. And a little further on: "All provisions that restrict the possibility to earn are of great concern to me, since they are reflected in a diminished elasticity in the administration of credit, with resulting damage to investments and so damage to the primary objectives."[10]. For this reason he was happy to see the cartel squeeze deposi-

tors and firms with frightful intermediation margins. And he stood firm
on this position even under my criticisms and my doubts as to his "idea
of the great efficiency of the banking enterprises . . . according to which
if the costs diminish all the wider margin goes in saved profits, whereas
in my view if the costs diminish a goodly part of the increased margin
often ends up wasted."[11]

The experience of the subsequent thirty years has proved that I was
right and Carli was wrong. My American experience told me that monop-
olies and cartels never do any good. I have never believed that saving can
really be increased by making the poor poorer and the rich richer. That
mistake of Carli's is probably the only serious one that can be laid at his
door. Still, it was not a small one. It had grave consequences; it produced
a grasping, inefficient banking system, overloaded with redundant staff
that today is one of Italy's eyesores.

But while the arguments expounded above seemed to suggest that the
feeble recovery had been deliberately designed to rebuild reserves, many
other arguments appeared to acquit the Bank of Italy from any intentional
guilt in the weakness of investments and the economy as a whole. The real
reason was that "the horse wouldn't drink," in spite of the sufficient liquidity provided by the central bank. In order for investment to recover sat-
isfactorily after the crisis of 1963–64, it was necessary to allow firms to
reestablish their profit margins; in that way, they would resume investment. Carli accepted the traditional opinion in Italy that investment occurs
only if it can be financed from profits. To me it seemed obvious that this
was true only in the (unreal) case where firms were completely averse to
taking bank loans or other outside financing. If the level of profits fell, then
it was all the more necessary to institute a monetary policy that, by reducing interest rates, would maintain the level of investments unchanged, at
least within the limits allowed by the foreign rates. But that operation con-
flicted with the existence of the banking cartel, which determined an element of downward rigidity for interest rates. Carli, instead, gave more
importance to the scant demand for loans, an insufficient demand that
could not and must not be tackled by an increase in the money supply.
Once again, the problem was that "the horse wouldn't drink." Italy was
never the same after the 1964 crisis. The entrepreneurs were weary. There
was a flight of capital. Families sold their shareholdings and bought villas
in Italian Switzerland.

However, at the end of the long discussion over whether investments
had diminished because "the horse wouldn't drink" or because, deliberately,
there wasn't much water around, it seemed to me that Carli and Baffi were
after all in agreement with the Modigliani–La Malfa view: The main expla-

nation was the second one. At least, this is what one can infer from the following exchange:

> MODIGLIANI. So, when it was said that the horse wouldn't drink?
>
> CARLI. We never said so.
>
> MODIGLIANI. Then I find there's a certain inconsistency, because one says: I'm glad things have gone as they have; and then says . . . it's lucky he hasn't drunk.
>
> CARLI. I think there's an intermediate situation. That is to say, we were also going to set ourselves the goal of reconstructing the reserves.
>
> BAFFI. I never said it was better if the horse didn't drink. But at a time when this attitude is helping me to rebuild the reserves, which are abnormally low, I don't think a central banker should stick a pipe into the system ("horse") and pour water down the horse's throat.[12]

To conclude, the poor old horse wasn't very thirsty, but according to "old daddy" Bank of Italy (but not according to us) this was ultimately good for its health, so there was no point in bending over backward to make it thirsty!

I have never learned so much about the Italian economy as I did in those months—and, I should say, about the real economy and the political-institutional interlacement that runs through it. The work on the econometric model took a long time. All things considered, the part that functioned right from the start was indeed the real part. But what really fascinated me and the governor was the monetary part. And my right hand in that task was Antonio Fazio, who a few years previously had been my pupil at MIT. It was Fazio who first introduced the concept of "monetary base," thus substituting a model founded on liquidity flows and on a concept of total liquidity of the banking system that came to him from Dutch models of the later 1950s. In the United States one was fairly clear about what the monetary base was. In Italy it was much harder to define. There were securities and financial assets of uncertain nature and difficult to categorize. I recollect an epic (but substantially futile) argument I had with Mario Ercolani on whether or not to include bonds and post office deposits in the monetary base (resumed at length in Dialogue Between a Professor and the Bank of Italy). The Bank of Italy preferred to extend the notion of monetary base much more broadly to demonstrate that it could not control it. (No one can be expected to do the impossible.) But I had the impression that they were not quite sincere on this point and that, at least at that time, the control they exerted was actually very tight.

9   *Myself and ISTAT*

During our discussions about the model, I remarked that Italian national accounting was different from that of the rest of the world. I thought it would be useful for the Bank of Italy group to have a talk with Professor Barbieri, then head of ISTAT (the Italian national bureau of statistics), and so they did. I was critical of Italy's decision to exclude public expenditure from the calculation of the gross national product. This decision descended from a noble tradition in Italy, from a famous polemic by the liberals of the school of Ferrara and Einaudi, who argued that public expenditure did not represent a "product" but, rather, a necessary cost to enable national production. From the theoretical point of view, the question is controversial. From an abstract perspective, the Italians were perhaps not necessarily wrong, provided public expenditure did not include transfers, which cannot be treated as production costs.

I said to Barbieri: "All the OECD countries do differently, but I don't think that's a reason to start a war of religion, so long as the choice is followed consistently. Let's go on to another point. . . ." It was Barbieri himself who did not want to leave the subject. He said to me: "No, no. All the others are wrong on this point, only we are right. Let's talk about it some more. . . ." So I took off my jacket and showed him just why his view was wrong. Not only that, I also demonstrated that, once it had been decided to exclude public expenditure from the gross domestic product (GDP), the Italian accounting method was inconsistent. The argument lasted the whole afternoon, and some of my young friends at the Bank of Italy still remember it. After my return to the United States I learned that, sometime later, ISTAT had replaced its method of calculating GDP with the standard OECD one.

10   *A Lesson from Mario Sarcinelli*

During our interminable, sometimes quarrelsome meetings, Mario Sarcinelli would come in and out. He is one of the most intelligent and honest people I have ever known. And it was in one of those conversations, during which we would often get sidetracked, that Mario explained to me one of the fundamental features of the Italian legal-political system. "To understand how this country works you must always remember that while Italy has laws, their enforcement is optional." And, in effect, this optionality gives the holder of the option immense power; in other words, the bureaucrat has the option, and therefore the right but not the duty, to apply the law. This means that laws that have remained unapplied for years can suddenly be enforced by someone who has the power to do so. And this takes on all the more importance from the fact that Italy has thousands of laws that are habitually not enforced, if they ever were, but may suddenly be so enforced by a functionary who can exploit his power to decide whether or not you are within the law, with the purpose of blackmailing you. In my view, this is one of the sources of Tangentopoli ("Bribe City," as the investigation into corruption in Italy is popularly called). And this is why—as when I had stoutly defended Sarcinelli against the judges who had sent him to prison—I have sometimes felt afraid to return to Italy. This in spite of the American ambassador's assurance that he would get me out of jail at once! I had already caught a whiff of what was to become obvious—namely, that in Italy many judges wield much more power than do their American counterparts.

In the United States, the League of Women Voters, a respected association that exists in every state and almost every city and town worthy of the name, has fought for years and laid down the principle that an unenforced law should always be repealed. This is one of the advantages of not having a rigid civil code like the Code Napoléon. The league has often succeeded in establishing that laws cannot exist merely on paper, and through its efforts many have been repealed.

11   The Experience of the "Observatory"

In 1972, as the result of a simultaneous "attack" by the editor of the *Corriere della Sera*, Piero Ottone, and Nino Andreatta, a well-known professor of economics and former secretary of the Treasury, I undertook to write a regular column in the *Corriere* titled "Observatory." This entailed economic comments that Nino Andreatta, Bruno Visentini, former minister of finance, and I took turns writing. As it was a weekly column, each of us would have to do a little more than one article per month. The experience was a very pleasant one, for it enabled me to keep well up-to-date with the ongoing debate in Italy and to develop a comparative perspective that was probably of use in Italy, too. At that time, the Italian left may not have welcomed my American liberal point of view; but I don't think it was a waste of time on my part to try to explain the significance of the conflict between Nixon's and McGovern's campaign platforms, or to expound the American view of the monetary clash between France and

Europe, which in Italy was seen from a slightly old-fashioned standpoint.

The first of my articles appeared in November 1972, under the title "Fair Taxation and Full Employment, the Paths to American Prosperity." I explained how the economic ideas of the defeated McGovern would prevail over the victorious Nixon's election promises[13]. Actually, McGovern's proposals had been supported by a good 1,300 American economists, who had paid to publish a manifesto in the *New York Times* in support of the Democratic candidate. Serena, too, took an active part in the campaign for McGovern, visiting the old first-generation Italians in the working-class districts of Boston's North End. They were overjoyed to meet a person who spoke their language, even though some of them remembered only their dialects. In any case, Massachusetts was the only state McGovern won. In consequence, when the Watergate affair exploded, very many cars in Massachusetts sported a sticker on their bumpers saying: "Don't blame me, I'm from Massachusetts."

12   The "Grand Tour" of Europe

The year 1973 saw the triple crisis: money, oil, and Western morale. It was the year of my grand tour of Europe, which I took from March to August, beginning just after the tragic February when the dollar was devalued by 10 percent, Europe closed its exchange markets, and the monetary "snake" began—which was supposed to guarantee a joint fluctuation of European currencies against the dollar. The journey ended before the oil crisis, which introduced a new, unforeseen element into our history. All considered, it was a journey of reflection on the European economies, on the model of growth they had followed from the end of the war up until then. And just as well, for a few months later we would be compelled to rethink everything.

The Bank of Italy, with whom Ando, my former student, coauthor, and friend, was busy perfecting the model, leapt ahead of the other European central banks and was rather envied for the quality of research it began to produce.

At the beginning of the 1970s I received an increasing number of invitations to come to Europe as adviser to central banks, financial institutions, and governments. For this reason I concentrated all my engagements into six months of sabbatical leave from MIT. In the first half of 1973 Serena and I zipped through Europe, from south to north, in an eternal spring from February to the summer. It was almost as if I was an ambassador for the American econometric models.

In February of that year I paid my first visit to the marvelous country of Spain. The dictatorship of Francisco Franco was still in place. Nonetheless, I accepted an invitation by the Bank of Spain to help them work out their econometric model, and spent a few weeks in Madrid. Why did I do so? For political reasons, I had never wished to go to Spain while Franco was still dictator. But my Spanish students at MIT were at pains to persuade me that I was wrong: "Never mind the regime in power now," they said[14], "it is important that you help Spain to get up-to-date so that, as soon as conditions allow, in the near future, it will be ready to join the European Common Market." It was beginning to be evident that, beneath the blanket of its Fascist dictatorship, Spain was growing and was headed for the European Community. A good economic and monetary setup would enable it to ensure against extremism of any kind.

13   An Anarchist Upstairs

Two things happened that convinced us that the regime was really breathing its last. The palace that houses the Banco de España is a sumptuous, solemn, formal building, with majestic rooms full of elegant portraits, tapestries, carpets, and statues—but its attic held a surprise! While I was at work with the young men in the research department, one of them took Serena on a tour of all the works of art. At a certain point he asked her, "Do you like etchings?" She replied suspiciously, "Well, it depends on the etchings." "Look, I ask," he said, "because there's a good deed to be done. On the top floor of the building, in the old granary, we are giving shelter to a young anarchist who has just come out of prison and earns his living by doing engravings and etchings. I can introduce you to him, if you like." So, up they went to the top floor to see the engravings of the young anarchist hidden in the Banco de España! The etchings weren't bad, but much too violent in their symbolism against the regime. There was a young peasant pinioned between two enormous black-uniformed gendarmes, and so on. Serena said frankly that they seemed too obvious as symbols. She selected a more traditional one, of a charming wrinkled old peasant woman, that now hangs in our summerhouse at Martha's Vineyard. I hope the artist, who signed himself Cuadrado, had success in Spain in later years.

Some days later, the head of the research department, Rojo, who is now governor, invited us to dinner at a fine Madrid restaurant. Earlier that day, we had visited the Escorial, and we told him that on our return journey the driver had taken us through the celebrated Valle de los Caídos, Franco's monument to those who fell in the Civil War (and his future tomb). "What a bad idea!" cried Rojo. "Why?" we wondered. Rojo explained that the monument had been built by political prisoners condemned to hard labor: "I am sure they made it weak on purpose, one day it will fall down." We were most alarmed at the way our friend let himself go in public, and we asked him if it wasn't dangerous. "No, no, in English you can say anything aloud. But not in Spanish, that would bring you trouble."

Spain was a marvelous place, with its historic and natural beauties, its colors, its people, but it was also most interesting for my understanding of the Italian model of growth. I gathered data and explained them to the Italian public in an article in the *Corriere della Sera* of April 4, 1973, "Spain resembles the Italy of the boom." Though one country was a democracy, the other a dictatorship, their stories were strikingly similar.

In the golden period of Italy's economic miracle, running from 1952 to 1963, income grew at an average annual rate of 6 percent. Growth suffered an initial setback with the inflation of 1963 and the restrictive policy of 1964. It then recovered, returning to rates of around 6 percent until 1969, the year of Italy's "long hot autumn," characterized by serious labor strife, and everything took a turn for the worse. The Spanish economy reached the same miraculous growth rates, an annual 7 percent, between 1960 and 1973. But the similarities did not end there. It was the form and nature of the process that converged: In both countries, the lightning increase in income between 1953 and 1973 stemmed from a very strong growth in *per capita* productivity, above all in the industrial sector, but also in others, accompanied by an appreciable, but not excessive, rise in employment in the high-productivity sectors.

Both increases were made possible by a high rate of investment, financed in turn by a very high rate of saving and, in part, by import of capital and know-how from abroad. The rapid growth of income was accompanied by an enormous increase in imports, but these were financed by an equally enormous increase in currency earnings, which, in turn, stemmed from a rise in exports, since both economies were placed in a favorable competitive position by the growth of productivity and the relatively low wage level. Italian and Spanish growth was also fueled by an increase in remittances from migrants, who had found work in other European countries, and from the huge increase in foreign tourism.

The analogy, as I pointed out in my article in the *Corriere*, was confined to the boom period. At the time I was writing, the quiet I found was a calm

before the storm. Spain felt as if wrapped up in a time prior to the catastrophe coming from the Middle East to fall on the heads of the industrialized countries. In Madrid I encountered enthusiasm, a sense of euphoria
that always goes hand-in-hand with rapid economic improvement, even
though the absolute level of well-being was far behind that of other
European countries, especially the northern democracies. "To be sure," I
wrote, "for many people the economic euphoria is clouded by discontent
with the present regime, but the latter is rendered more bearable by the
conviction that the situation is only a transitory one"[15]. In Italy that sense
of euphoria had long since vanished. Indeed, from the restless but creative
atmosphere that pervaded the 1960s they had reached the rock bottom of
1969, the year when the growth mechanism broke down. The miracle had
ground to a halt. After that year, the growth rate scarcely touched 3 percent (which in those days looked tiny!).

Why did the mechanism stop? My opinion at that time was strongly
influenced by civil commitment, not a technician's response. I wrote
frankly:

> The rapid process of growth and modernization of technical struc-
> tures and equipment has not been accompanied by an equal adaptation
> on the part of the democratic structures, legal institutions, and above all
> ways of thinking, and politicians bear a heavy responsibility for this.[16]

With respect to Italy, I remember as if it were yesterday the severe figure of Carli explaining how the inability to spend all the amounts budgeted
was a reproach to public administration. It resulted in an accumulation of
unspent credits, which could act just like an alpine glacier melting in hot
weather—in this case suddenly causing a flood of unpredictable expenditure. It was already evident at that time that the bureaucracy was Italy's
core problem, with its inefficiency and its feeble commitment to the public good. Interpreted from a Keynesian perspective, the concern that was
very strongly felt at the Bank of Italy at that time was that the clogging of
the administration prevented the possibility of promptly increasing public
expenditure with the early signs of a slowdown.

> As regards the inadequacy of the bureaucratic structures, one of its
> most deleterious features is its proven inability to make rapid invest-
> ments in public works, such as schools, hospitals, housing and trans-
> port, for which funds have been earmarked. If such investments had
> been made during the recent period of economic stagnation, partly due
> to lack of private investment and lack of profits, this would have sus-

tained demand and employment. From this point of view, the Spanish system appears to have a clear advantage over its Italian counterpart. Public investments have responded flexibly to allocations.[17]

The essential point was that the Keynesian model envisaged the central element as real wages. I found little sympathy for the workers' rebellion of 1969, culminating in the wave of wage claims over and above any parameter of productivity growth. It struck me as a selfish act on the part of those who had jobs, redounding to the disadvantage of society as a whole, including themselves:

What has not yet penetrated the general awareness is that a complex and advanced economic system allows a high level of remuneration only on condition that the employees show an equal amount of commitment, and that individual cunning can only translate into collective damage.[18]

Absenteeism and a wage behavior aimed at snatching as much as possible to swell one's real wage, with no thought for anyone else, have been the cancer of Italian society—even though at the time much play was given to the ideals of justice and egalitarianism.

14   Northeast Passage

On May 16, 1973, I wrote in the *Corriere della Sera*:

I have left Madrid and Spain, to follow the spring season on its march through Europe, and traveling northwards I have ascended the rising scale of *per capita* income: from Spain to the United Kingdom, to Denmark, to Sweden, the country at the summit of Europe. It's fascinating, too, to note that the order in which I have visited the various countries chimes with a very different criterion of classification, a political-economic criterion ranging from the capitalism of a right-wing dictatorship to the most advanced form of democratic socialism.[19]

And Italy? Well, from reading those travel notes perhaps one wouldn't say much progress has been made in certain areas, such as corruption. For us Americans scandals like Watergate were very upsetting, but they were also a moment of truth and great hope: the attempts to cover up the affair had failed, the truth had taken its course. It was a step forward for democracy. In Italy, on the contrary, what was happening?

The Watergate scandal with the skulduggery of the Republican party staff in getting funds for the recent electoral campaign was not of much concern. What is really worrying is the headline in the Corriere della Sera of May 12: "Telephone Tapping Investigation Shelved."[20] And even more alarmingly, under the headline "Impunity for Senators in the INGIC Scandal" we read that "absent-minded embezzlement on behalf of a political party does not constitute an offence, according to the majority of senators" because "the failure to solve the burning and ever-present problem of financing the parties . . . has often placed their representatives under pressing need to procure the funds needed for the functioning of what are ultimately the pillars that uphold the entire Italian constitutional system.[21]

On that occasion, "Tangentopoli" (as the big corruption scandal of the 1990s was to be known) was covered up quite easily.

I remember how in those months I amused myself by being not only an economist but a sociologist, too. Reading the Italian newspapers in those years one had the impression that the United Kingdom, under the Labour government, had sunk to one of the poorest countries in Europe. The dynamic of the growth rate was, of course, unsatisfactory, below the European average. But did it justify speaking in terms of crisis? I had serious doubts, and these were fully confirmed on my arrival in London. This was why I suggested to the Corriere the heading, "Quality of Life According to Britain." I went ahead with my comparisons: Between 1960 and 1970 the Spanish national income had doubled and the per capita income had risen by more than 90 percent. In the same period the Common Market countries had seen their total income grow by 70 percent and their per capita income by 50 percent. But the UK's national income had risen by only a third, its per capita income by a mere quarter: "This feeble growth of the British economy has by now become proverbial and it's the fashion to commiserate with this country over its problems." But one had only to look around one to feel grave doubts about this argument.

Spain, traditional home of the siesta, is now gripped by euphoria and a feverish activity stemming from an explosive growth that, in the space of a few years, has led from age-old poverty and consequent fatalism to relative well-being and a new awareness that "if you work, you eat" and if you sweat you eat more. But in Britain there's a feeling in the air of calm and tranquillity, of the order and stability of a country where the average citizen, on reaching a decent level of well-being, sees no need to drudge for something extra and is, on the whole, satisfied with and proud of his institutions, his social achievements, and gives great importance to the quality of life.[22]

That these two attitudes implied different economic costs in the strict sense seemed obvious to me.

I noted two examples of an ecological kind:

> The air in Madrid is often polluted but few people worry about it and almost everybody prefers to ignore the phenomenon. In London the air is surprisingly pure for a metropolis of that size and everyone proudly mentions the fact that, about ten years ago, the proverbial London fogs became rarer and rarer until they vanished altogether. Another contrast that set me thinking is between Madrid's botanical garden and London's [Kew Gardens]. In the rush towards material prosperity, the botanical garden in Madrid has clearly been forgotten by all, government and citizens alike. Its walks and flowerbeds are neglected, the erosion of the soil that impoverishes the centuries-old exotic trees gives ample proof of the inadequacy of the funds allocated. Kew Gardens, with its fine beds of rich black earth abounding in artistically arranged flowers, with its ancient trees tended with infinite love by an army of expert gardeners and horticulturists, is a sort of earthly paradise that enriches the life of the Londoner.[23]

The calculation of the growth rate takes none of this into account.

It was a time when we were all becoming aware that the growth wouldn't go on forever. Since the war it had galloped along wonderfully, with small, frequent, and, all considered, beneficent recessions. The turning point for Italy was 1969. For the world as a whole it was the breakdown of the Bretton Woods system. The hike in oil prices, which exacted impoverishment from outside for all but which instead caused wages, and so prices, to surge, fell like a bombshell in a situation where the model of growth hitherto adopted was already showing its limitations.

The last of my stops as special envoy in the European economy was, as I've said, Sweden. I am deeply attached to this country, above all because of my admiration for the quantity of great economists it has produced, from Knut Wicksell (who, way back at the end of the nineteenth century, made a fundamental contribution to the theory of inflation in his Interest and Prices) to Karl Gunnar Myrdal and Bertil Ohlin, who also became ministers. So my last travel reportage for the *Corriere della Sera*, June 13, 1973, was headed "The Role of Economists in Well-off Sweden." Unlike Britain, Sweden, though starting with a very high income level, maintained a strong yearly rate of growth, at around 4 percent, throughout the 1950s. Along with the excellent, free public services, I remarked that the Swedes had already dealt with the problem of pollution that Rome has yet to solve: Domestic heating, which is highly polluting, was replaced by plants utilizing heat generated by electric power stations.

Sweden's problem stemmed from being a very open economy, therefore dependent (like Italy) on the trend of international trade, which is by its very nature subject to considerable variations that are beyond the control of the country's authorities. The variations in volume of exports have been important sources of instability, neutralized with stabilization measures aimed at generating a compensatory tendency in other components of world demand. What impressed me about Sweden was the vast number of economic policy instruments available for intervention in and stabilization of the cycle.

One in particular I considered extremely interesting: This was the system of special investment reserves:

> The system consists in allowing firms to set aside up to 40 percent of their profit in a special account with the central bank. This sum is exempt from the tax on profits of companies quoted on the stock exchange, which amounts to about 50 percent. When the government thinks it timely to apply a strong stimulus to investment to counterbalance the fall predicted or under way of other components of global demand, the firms are authorized to use these funds provided the spending is begun and completed within a period specified by the government. The investments so financed can also be immediately amortized in toto, and in some cases the firms are also permitted to deduct a certain percentage of the expenditure from their taxable profit.[24]

15   The Eve of the Oil Crisis

I wrote those notes under the tepid midnight sun in Scandinavia before returning to the sweltering heat of Rome, whence I was to set out homeward for the United States, from which I had been absent for almost six months. On the day I came back to Italy a new government was taking office. Rumor replaced Andreotti, and the presence of Ugo La Malfa, minister of the Treasury, was for me a ray of hope. After a few days deep pessimism returned. The newspapers even talked of a strike by the bakers in Naples that brought famine to the city. I went to see my friends at the Bank of Italy.

I spent a few days on the top floor of the bank in oppressive heat, leafing through statistical data. There could be no doubt that a net increase of global demand was under way, more than 4.5 percent, but accompanied by wage increases above productivity. I noted:

> An increase in demand of that size would, of course, have an adverse effect on the current account balance, especially if imports of certain foodstuffs were facilitated in order to contain prices. . . . Nothing wrong with a rise in net capital import if it finances a recovery of domestic investment.[25]

The conclusion was in flat contrast to the hypothesis I had heard going round at the Bank of Italy: a monetary and credit squeeze to act as a cold shower for the overheated economy. Like my colleagues, I very clearly appreciated the risk that a perverse wage-price spiral might be initiated. In spite of that, I was opposed to a squeeze, since a deflationary policy had what at that time seemed to me excessive costs. It would be better to control wages directly, calling for moderation by the unions:

> What I think should certainly be ruled out is the solution, tried on other occasions, to contain wages and prices through monetary and fiscal measures aimed at reducing demand and increasing unemployment. As well as being socially unacceptable, an operation of this kind to reduce inflation is of doubtful effectiveness and is very slow when the cause of the inflation is not an excess of global demand.[26]

The alternative to Carli's policy, that is, a monetary and fiscal squeeze, was the traditional solution of blocking nominal prices by an administrative decision: price control. Not that I was opposed to it out of prejudice. The point was that the Italian administrative machine had already then gotten out of hand. The question, then, was: Who would have enforced the agreements?

> Many people say they are in favor of price control, but this generally refers to other people's prices! The American experience suggests that a system of price and wage controls may be of some limited assistance in slowing down the inflation spiral, in presence of appreciable margins of capacity. But this experience is of doubtful relevance for Italy where no adequate administrative structures exist, and one cannot rely on the

habit of citizens to respect the regulations. This is why I doubt the effectiveness of blocking prices, especially at a moment when the costs of raw materials are rapidly rising and further wage increases are inevitable, if nothing else because of the working of the wage indexation.[27]

This argument, too, belonged in the category of "useless sermons," and before I set out for Boston and home on the Michelangelo at the end of the month, the government pegged the prices of major commodities, rents, and industrial products for the public. The return journey was complicated by pneumonia, which attacked me no sooner than I had embarked. But I was expertly treated by the ship's doctor, first with antibiotics, then with rare-cooked steaks and champagne!

My return to the United States was somewhat of a shock. During my long absence the situation had deteriorated awfully. Price controls were so badly managed by the Nixon administration as to turn into a disaster.[28] In Boston, one month before the Yom Kippur War, things already seemed to be going downhill. I described my dismay in an article of September 12:

> As I wrote in my column of January 10, the economic prospects at the start of the year looked rosy and well-founded, as did the political prospects for November's presidential election victor [Nixon]. Rapid but orderly economic growth was expected, at an annual rate of 6–7 percent. Inflation, the bristling problem of Nixon's first four years, looked to be almost under control. But by mid-August everything seemed to be going to pot. The general price index had climbed in the first two quarters to a yearly rate of over 7 percent; the foodstuff segment by almost 30 percent. Wholesale prices recorded an even more catastrophic rise: The general index had jumped by 22 percent, that of farm products by almost 70 percent. Some food products (meat and allied goods) were hard to obtain, there was talk of scarcity of other items like building materials, and of hoarding that further contributed to the sense of scarcity. On the international markets the value of the dollar continued to dwindle. . . . And this atmosphere was faithfully reflected in the stock exchange by a drop of around 20 percent, even though profits had risen by 20 percent in the first two quarters.[29]

The fever that gripped American society was not merely economic; it stemmed from monetary disorder and the feeling of dismay that came with the end of the war in Vietnam. But the error that unleashed that situation was a human one, an error of the administration: The devaluation of the dollar, deliberately brought about, was a sign of disorder that left the West weak and prostrate when, a month later, the mad hike of oil prices began.

16   The "Long Hot Autumn" and Its Aftermath

Italy had hardly emerged from the devastating crisis of 1964 when the "long hot autumn" arrived, a period of serious disturbances that ended with a crazy wage increase of around one third in the space of a few months. This marked the end of the "Italian miracle," a hectic growth starting in 1952 and only briefly interrupted by the crisis of 1964. The latter year initiated a phase in which the unions, selfishly concerned with their members' wages alone, used their great power to obtain wage increases above productivity, thus producing inflation and unemployment. The essential mechanism (explained in more detail above, chapter II, section 11) is that when the nominal wage rises more than productivity, this leads to an increase in the cost of labor per unit of production, which producers tend to shift onto prices. Since, however, the union's aim of obtaining a wage increase is nullified by the rise in prices, the union is driven to fight for further wage increases, which are reflected in further price rises, and so on. This lays the groundwork for an inflationary spiral that reflects the fact that the union can, at least partly, control the nominal wage, whereas the real wage depends on the prices, which in turn are determined by firms.

The development of the spiral depends on the policy of the central bank: If it "accommodates" inflation by creating money, so as to hold the real money supply constant, and allows exchange to devalue at the same rate as inflation, the spiral may continue indefinitely and even get out of control. Inflation can be halted only with a "nonaccommodating" policy—that is, by maintaining a fixed exchange and allowing inflation to diminish the real money supply. For, in this case, producers cannot shift the wage increase entirely onto prices by means of international competition, and hence real wages grow more than productivity, but at the same time producers will find it convenient to reduce production and thus also employment.

A further fall in domestic demand occurs through the Keynesian mechanism: The reduction in the real money supply drives up the cost of money, thus reducing investment and income. In addition, the worsening of the trade balance due to the rise of domestic prices as against foreign prices may lead to a current deficit that can no longer be financed; this leads to further restrictive measures and increased unemployment. At a certain point it becomes necessary to revitalize employment by devaluation and accommodation, and so inflation resumes.

In this way, in 1969, Italy moved into the infernal cycle of unemployment–devaluation–inflation–wage increases[30], which plagued Italian life for a quarter century—until, that is, the unions learned their lesson in 1993.

With the parenthesis of 1964, Italy's economic miracle lasted precisely from 1952–53 until the "hot autumn" of 1969. As was shown in a paper I wrote with Fiorella Padoa Schioppa, up until the latter date productivity continued to rise and thus enable wage increases, although for that same reason unemployment did not increase. In spite of which, serious, pathological unemployment started only in 1975. According to the official data, the unemployment rate hovered around 4–5 percent throughout the 1960s and the early 1970s, but afterward rose steadily to reach 9.7 percent in 1983. The workforce, which shrank at the start of the 1960s and remained more or less steady until the early 1970s, showed a substantial acceleration in the decade 1974–83, increasing at an average annual rate of 1 percent. A growing workforce together with steady employment from 1980 onward accounts for the increased unemployment of this period. In order to analyze well the trends of the Italian economy we calculated the cost of labor per unit of output, which measures productivity. And it can be seen that up until then the real cost remained constant, if deflated with the wholesale price index.

Another result is that, in Italy, the cost of labor must be calculated in terms of foreign prices or, better, based on a basket of currencies representative of the composition of Italy's foreign trade. For it is the increase in the real wage expressed in terms of foreign currencies (and adjusted for competitiveness) that causes problems in the balance of payments.

What characterized Italy in the 1960s was a phenomenal increase in productivity. In the same period, employment remained stable while the workforce continued to swell. This means that employment should and could have grown. Why didn't it? Because that period witnessed an enormous rise in wages (deflated with the consumer price index), equal to 350 percent (and even more with respect to foreign prices in lire). And this enormous rise in real wages was partly due to the increase in productivity, and partly to an independent wage surge. The ratio of wages to national income grew. Wages grew more than productivity and increased the cost of labor per unit of product; this phenomenon reduced the national product, diminished net exports, and diminished the profits of enterprises, which are a proportion of income. It follows that, if wages rise by more than productivity, firms must accept a reduction in their profit margins, the markup, or must raise their prices rela-tive to the prices of their international competitors. In either case, they reduce their profit. The most probable solution is a combination of the two options. This behavior by firms leads to a shrinkage of jobs. And that is exactly what happened in Italy from 1969 onward–slowly at first, then, with the first oil shock, more violently.

In that way, Italy entered a tunnel of continuous inflation, rising unemployment, and recurring crises in the balance of payments. From this stems the attempt to explain it all by the unions' drive to continually increase real wages and peg the increases by means of ever more rigid, more absolute indexation devices, culminating in the wage-indexation scale with recovery of 100 percent and more of inflation. With wage indexation fixed, the W/P ratio must remain fixed, and W must rise together with P. This was the scenario up until 1975, when much worse was to happen.

17   Bancor and the Squeeze of 1974

Italy had already started on that downhill path when the great oil crisis of 1973 exploded. All that was needed to cause the gigantic surge in oil prices—a strategic import item for the industrialized countries—was a modest reduction in supply, owing to extremely rigid (inelastic) demand. This posed three knotty problems for the economy and challenged the economist to solve them with the minimum possible damage:

1. How to prevent the strong initial increase in energy prices from turning into a generalized inflationary spiral? (This objective had to be attained without relying on "monetarist" mechanical solutions that would produce mass unemployment.)

2. The price increase and the resulting deterioration in the exchange rates of the importer countries would diminish all other consump-tion: how to stop this fall in demand from causing a drastic shrink-age in production and employment?

3. The importer countries would be saddled with a large balance-of-payments deficit: How would they pay? (This was the so-called "transfer" problem.)

These were the problems debated by many economists at the end of 1973, and I, too, discussed them with my students—in particular, with promising young men freshly arrived from Italy. Discussions with them were partly stimulated by a series of articles we read in the press. In Italy at that time there was much talk of the articles published in the weekly *Espresso* under the pen name Bancor, the name Keynes would have liked to give the world currency he proposed at Bretton Woods. Bancor was said to have been the governor of the Bank of Italy, Guido Carli, but was more likely Eugenio Scalfari (later editor of the daily *Repubblica*), who, with Carli's consent, turned their conversations into articles. Baldassari, Draghi, and other Italian pupils of mine used to buy *Espresso* in Harvard Square and often brought it to MIT, where it was discussed in lively fashion. With reference to the solution of the three problems we were working out, the economic policies suggested in those articles appeared to us way off the beam and dangerous for Italy and her partners.

Our solution to the first problem, inflation, was logically very simple, though certainly not easy to put into practice. To understand it well, it must be recalled that none of the industrialized countries, with the possible exception of Japan, succeeded in finding a satisfactory solution. What happened was that the jump in the prices of energy and allied products immediately sparked a rise in the cost of living, which reduced the purchasing power of incomes. But people did not, as would have been rational, accept that impoverishment, which reflected the enrichment of the "monopolist sheikhs." On the contrary, workers tried to make up the loss by, successfully, requesting wage increases. But the effort was in vain, as it led to an inflationary spiral. For, since the productivity of labor in terms of domestic product had not changed, the wage increase drove up the cost per unit of production, which was shifted onto prices, leading to a rise in production prices and thus to a domestic inflation that was added to the imported one. Fresh wage increases then arrived to offset the annual price increases, and so on. The resulting inflationary spiral drove the mean wage increase in the EC countries up to 19 percent in 1975, and the mean price inflation from 6.5 to 14 percent.

These developments brought the central banks face-to-face with the classic dilemma of whether "to accommodate or not to accommodate" inflation. As we saw above, accommodating—that is, letting the money supply increase at the rate of inflation—involves allowing inflation to grow uncontrollably. Responsible central banks cannot passively accept a development of this kind, so at a certain point they had to initiate tight money policies that would diminish the "real" money supply. As was shown in the previous chapter, these policies, by colliding with the inflationary process that had built up considerable inertia, could not fail to produce a rise in unemployment. The latter, in turn, jointly with a certain reduction in the imported inflation, returned inflation to 10.5 percent in 1978, but at the cost of an increase in unemployment by 2.5 to 5.1 percent. Owing to the presence in Italy of strong wage indexation and highly aggressive union behavior, inflation passed 20 percent and actually touched 25 percent.

Thus, the oil crisis of 1973 and the one immediately following, in 1979–81, produced a very costly period of stagflation, that is, high inflation coexisting with high unemployment, a phenomenon unknown until then. It stemmed from the fact that while restrictive monetary policies were effective in reducing employment, they had a much slower impact on inflation.

This tragedy could have been prevented by a "rational" wage policy. The first necessity was to shape public opinion, explaining to dependent workers first of all that the leap in oil prices had made them poorer beyond all remedy, and they would therefore have to agree to keep nominal wages stable and resign themselves to the loss of purchasing power, which, in effect, was the visible sign of their impoverishment. In essence, as the distinguished Italian economist Nino Andreatta rightly remarked, the increase in the oil price was fully equivalent to a tax on consumption destined to transfer resources from the consumer to the collector of the tax—in this case, not the government but the sheikh. Governments should therefore have undertaken an "income policy" aimed at containing pay rises within the limits of productivity. This approach would have made it possible to avoid the first increase in domestic production prices and thence the whole spiral of prices and wages, without needing to diminish investments and without causing the sad waste of resources due to unemployment. In the light of this argument the solution aired in the articles by Bancor seemed to us completely off the mark—namely, a monetary squeeze that would have been appropriate for an inflationary process resulting from excess demand.

Instead of discussing the one thing needed—an income policy—Bancor's article at the end of January 1974 and the comment by Scalfari that accompanied it dealt with how to pay for a large increase in the cost of oil imports and suggested a devaluation that would go hand-in-hand with the monetary squeeze: "Exports in any case appear as the most indispensable instrument for rebalancing our foreign accounts: An implicit or explicit devaluation of our currency could work in this direction." This, too, seemed to us a serious mistake, since it would further increase the price of oil along with that of all other imported goods, thus reinforcing the inflationary spiral and stagflation, especially in the absence of an income policy and in the presence of wage indexation.

We had a radically different solution, which we saw as part of a plan to solve, at the international level, the twin problems of lack of demand and the balance of payments of the Western countries. Our recipe was published in the *Espresso* of February 3, 1974, under the title "Reply to Bancor." I must add that the young students Mario Baldassarri, Franco Bruni, and Mario Draghi, who signed the article with me were torn between a feeling of joy at the idea that an article on the burning topic of the moment appeared with their names beside that of their professor, and a certain apprehensiveness at the fact that they were about to take issue with no less a person than the revered governor of the Bank of Italy!

Here are some passages from the article:

> Let us first reiterate that the automatic effect of the increased cost of oil will be to reduce the domestic demand for goods and services, the domestic supply of which will, in real terms, be in any case in excess. If that "demand vacuum" should be replaced by the demand of the oil producers resulting from their increased purchasing power, as both Bancor and Scalfari seem to suggest, the system would return to equilibrium without need of restrictive monetary policies. Such a replacement is, however, most unlikely to take place immediately and automatically: The increased value of our imports will, instead, have to find its main counterpart in credits from the exporting countries. In this case, the economic policy will have to be such as to stimulate the most opportune way of dealing with "the demand vacuum": Among the available alternatives, stimulating public and private investment seems the most desirable, since the indebtedness is directed at improving productive capacities, which in the medium term can also provide the basis for servicing the debt and for an increase in exports or a reduction of imports. Of course, this solution relies on general acceptance of the fall in income and real consumption stemming from the increased cost of energy sources.

How to stimulate investments? In that situation, was it possible to contemplate reducing interest rates? We thought so:

> A reduction in interest rates would necessitate an expansion of means of payment, which, however, would not have any inflationary impact owing to the accompanying reduction in the velocity of circulation. Secondly, a policy of low interest rates would obviously be hard to pursue unilaterally, since it would lead to an outflow of capital that would worsen the deficit. It ought, on the contrary, to be the result of

an agreement among the industrialized countries, which would above all draw advantage from it, since they would reduce the cost of their indebtedness to the producer-creditor countries.

But the matter on the agenda was devaluation, which seemed to be unofficially announced in the article by Bancor and Scalfari. To this we were firmly opposed:

> An attempt to relaunch exports by devaluing the lira would translate into a further worsening of our terms of trade. In addition, it would encourage a process of competitive devaluation by the other importer countries, which also face serious deficits in the current account balance. The effects of such devaluations would obviously cancel each other out and advantage would lie only with the producer countries, whose terms of trade would be further improved. Devaluation, then, in whatever technical form applied, does not appear advisable to us, at least for the time being. In the longer run one must hope that the increased revenues of the producer countries will be used to purchase goods—for example, for the industrialization of the Third World. In the meantime, in order to incentivize the producer countries to finance the deficit of the West in presence of probably not negligible rates of inflation, the possibility could be canvassed of creating "indexed" international debt instruments—that is, instruments whose nominal value, linked to an appropriate price index, would retain a constant purchasing power.

Shortly after that argument with Bancor I had the delightful opportunity to meet Romano Prodi, currently president of the European Union, who had been invited to take the De Bosis chair at Harvard for a semester. (The chair, initially set up for Gaetano Salvemini, takes it name from the brave, unlucky opponent of fascism who flew over Rome to drop leaflets against the regime and never returned.) We rapidly appreciated each other and sympathized so that we invited him to our country house in New Hampshire. There, a comic event occurred that has remained famous in our family annals. It was spring. My wife told us it was time to plant the peas. Peas were scarcely contemplated in our economic lore, so like good academics we had recourse to a manual of horticulture. We read that, after preparing the soil, we must set the peas at a distance of about one inch and a depth of a quarter of an inch. So we took the sack of peas and a ruler and set about measuring the one-inch distance: At that moment a country neighbor arrived and burst out laughing: "Here's how you plant peas . . . ," and she took a handful and sprinkled them on the ground just as they came. The sowing was soon done. Romano set off home to Italy and the peas sprouted, grew, and matured. We ate them and sent him a sample by mail.

18   1975, or, The Folly of the "Uniform Point"

The year 1975 remains etched in my memory for the senseless agreement on indexation with a uniform point negotiated by the unions and the *Confindustria* (Confederation of Italian Industry) led by Giovanni Agnelli, the president of Fiat. In the annals of the Republic of Italy it will stand as the year of folly, of self-destruction, of condemnation to an economic crisis that might have led the country to disaster and was only averted by a fluke, thanks to the sangfroid of a few persons who continued to reason calmly while everything was falling to pieces around them.

In those years Ezio Tarantelli was living in the United States and studying at Boston College. Together, we made repeated attempts, by letter and during our brief stays in Italy, to convince the unions that real wage increases, not justified by productivity, and protection of them by a 100 percent wage indexation could only lead to Italy's ruin, with mass unemployment. Our efforts in the 1970s were quite unsuccessful.

On January 20, 1975, I was in Italy for a conference of economists, and I went from the airport to my brother Giorgio's home. When I entered the house, I asked for news of the talks between the unions and the Confindustria that I knew were under way, and my brother said they were discussing a fixed-point wage indexation, a system by which an increase of 1 percent in the cost of living would entitle all workers to a pay increase by the same amount—that is, 1 percent of the average wage, regardless of one's individual wage. I couldn't believe it: "It's not possible, there's no sense in it." Giorgio told me that a press conference had been fixed for that afternoon and so, if we liked, we could go to the EUR and hear about what was going on from those directly involved. We did, and that afternoon I witnessed, thunderstruck, the rehearsals for a tragedy. I saw Agnelli and expressed my incredulity that he should be ready to endorse an agreement like that. "But after all, it's right," he said, "because when the cost of living goes up, it does so for everybody."[31]

I had to get back to Boston. A little later, at our house at Belmont the *Corriere della Sera* of January 26 was delivered, with the milk, announcing that the deal had been signed. The fatuously laudatory tone of the headline made me even more furious: "Important Confindustria-Union Agreement Creates New Prospects for Relaunching Production." I felt I would go mad with rage. I tramped angrily round the house telling Serena, "It's the craziest thing that's ever been done!"

It is easy to show that the aim of the fixed-point wage indexation has nothing to do with protecting real wage indexation from inflation. Quite the opposite, it represents the intention to use inflation to change income distribution: The higher the inflation, the more egalitarian must the distribution of income become. Inflation becomes a device for redistribution between rich and poor: If the cost of living rises, the poor receive more than they are entitled to in proportion to inflation, and the rich receive less.

When I had calmed down a bit, I took up a pen and dashed off an incensed article. I rang the *Corriere* and spoke to the editors. Without enthusiasm, they agreed that I should dictate a critical comment. Which I did accordingly, with much heat, to a stenographer. When you dictate an article to a newspaper, the stenographer often interrupts if there is difficulty in understanding a word or the spelling of a name. I clearly recall how, at the other end of the line, the poor man's voice became more and more feeble and anxious. When we had done, I asked him furiously: "Have you understood?" and he answered wearily: "Yeesss, I've understood." The article was politely headlined, with the obvious intention of toning down the explosive content: "Beware of the Hazards of the Fixed-Point Indexation.[32] The editors introduced my comment with a note of warning: "From Boston, where he teaches, Professor Franco Modigliani has sent us this critical comment on the recent agreement between Confindustria and unions." As if to say: We didn't ask him for it . . .

In what I had written I did not conceal my irritation at the article describing the agreement of January 25: "After reading it over and over again, rubbing my eyes, it looks to me as if the way to salvation [for Italy's economy] has run into a new impasse." Then I tried to explain where the mechanism had gone wrong as simply as I could—because I knew that I would be alone in that conflict:

> The most upsetting aspect of the new agreement is that the indexation has a unified point. Over recent months I often heard talk of this request by the unions, but I thought it too absurd to be taken seriously. I supposed it was just a scare, put out to obtain other concessions. It is plainly ridiculous to argue that when the cost of living rises it does so for everyone and so everyone must receive equal compensation. Suppose for a moment that all prices rise in the same proportion, say

ten percent. If a family earns one hundred thousand lire and spends this amount in consumption and saving, in order to enable it to purchase the same basket of goods . . . its income must increase by ten percent, or ten thousand lire. Likewise, if the family earns three hundred thousand, its earning will have to increase by ten percent, or thirty thousand lire. If now we unify the "wage indexation point" at the highest level and give the family with one hundred thousand another thirty thousand, what we have done is not to compensate it for the increase in prices but to give it a net increase of nearly twenty percent.

How could everybody have joined in this total conspiracy of silence? How was it possible that newspapers, parties, even academics held back from indignant protest at this catastrophe? Many were annoyed by the interpretation I gave in my article:

> The truth, as I see it, is that the unions gave small importance to the false argument set out above, but, in fighting for the fixed-point wage indexation, their intention was first and foremost to raise wages and then to level them. For, as is plain from the example given, each time the cost of living rises (not such a rare phenomenon in Italy) the lowest wages will climb considerably more than the cost of living; that is, there will be an increase of real wages for the lowest-paid workers, who are by far the most numerous. As a result, the average wage will also rise by more than the price index. The leveling stems from the fact that the lowest wages would grow, in percentage, by more than the highest ones.

To compound the absurdity, even had it been right to reduce income inequality, the instrument chosen was the worst:

> In a free-enterprise economy, wage differences largely reflect the mechanism of supply and demand. In particular, the experiences of other countries suggest that attempts to narrow the wage range by raising the lowest wages are soon followed by a reenlargement of the range through a general rise in the level of money wages. Income equalization can only be efficiently achieved through the tax system and public services. I agree that the tax system in Italy is still extremely unfair and public services inadequate; but that is where the battle should be fought, as I have for years been trying to persuade my friends on the left. Lastly, it is quite absurd that wage leveling should rely on the amount of inflation, because inter alia the moments of inflationary tension are those least appropriate for operations of this nature.[33]

The only person who immediately gave me his support was Ugo La Malfa, who at that time, however, held the office of deputy prime minister and as such had obviously been unable to prevent the worst. Substantially, La Malfa said he hoped my dismal prophecies would not come true but that in any case he blamed the atmosphere of unconsidered pressures and mutually contradictory claims that have characterized our national life for some years now. You cannot go on demanding that inflation be combatted and public and private investment restimulated while, at the same time, calling for commitments that openly contrast with the fight against inflation and the policy to revitalize investments. In an atmosphere like this, everyone, the government included, is in difficulty.[34]

And in an editorial on February 5 in the *Voce Repubblicana*, La Malfa came to my aid: "[It is surely] no sign of concern for the workers to worry about their money wages but not about the purchasing power that effectively corresponds to these wages."

Accusations came thick and fast, especially from the left, but as I tend to be highly stimulated by polemics and the battle of ideas, I gave as good as I got in a long and carefully thought-out article in the *Corriere della Sera* on March 9, 1975. In it, I drew up an overall balance of what might be the consequences of the disastrous agreement. Among other things I noted:

> If the mechanism has the effect of increasing the average wage and hence the total cost of labor out of proportion to prices, the effect is destabilizing. Suppose, for example, that the rise in the cost of labor is double that of prices: If in one quarter wages and prices increase by 1 percent, in the next quarter the cost of labor will rise by 2 percent, which, assuming productivity is constant, will tend to drive prices up by 2 percent; so in the quarter following that, wages and prices will rise by 4 percent and so on. The phenomenon will of course be curbed by the monetary authorities, but at the expense of jobs.[35]

At the macroeconomic level the agreement posed a frightful dilemma: either to accept devaluation and inflation without limit, or to uphold the exchange rate as far as possible but to lose the market share, which would be replaced by foreign goods, and in addition to risk a restriction on consumption. For, if the exchange rate held steady, what would happen? Domestic prices would rise, though by less than wages, relative to the lira prices of foreign competitors, which would remain stable. There would thus be a tendency for domestic and foreign demand to shift to the latter, with an inevitable fall in the volume of exports and increase in imports.

The reduction in net exports would reduce aggregate demand and employment. But also the current balance of payments would tend to worsen, which would be unacceptable for an Italy that had just received loans from the International Monetary Fund. And thus the increased current balance deficit would lead to a monetary and fiscal squeeze in order to reduce consumption and imports through a further drop in income and employment. The alternative? Obviously a devaluation, which (if accompanied by an appropriate money policy) would enable firms to shift the bulk of their wage increases onto prices without losing competitiviness—but this, through wage indexation, would entail further wage increases, further price rises, and a fall in the exchange rate.

Later on I remarked that, aside from its effect on income distribution, the fixed point also worsened the effect of the wage indexation on prices.[36] That is, with a rise in prices, by virtue of the fixed-point mechanism a given inflation would be accompanied by an even larger percentage increase of inflation, paving the way for yet more inflation.

If prices rise and, through fixed-point indexation, all wages rise equally, the price/wage ratio (W/P) of the various categories changes. For the highest categories the amount diminishes, and thus when prices rise they lose purchasing power in comparison to the lower-paid categories. With the leveling of the wage range firms realize that they can no longer find highly skilled and responsible staff, and the result is that for a more difficult or responsible job the employer must increase wages by a greater amount than indexation entails. If, say, the general wage has risen by 10 percent, in order to maintain the incentive for the most skilled workers they must be offered a 20 percent increase. Thus, the average wage increases out of proportion to prices, just as if the indexation were actually more than 100 percent!

When indexation takes the traditional form, in which the adjustment is proportional to the wage, it has been shown to have the effect of stabilizing the system if a demand shock occurs, and to destabilize it if the shocks are on the supply side. The reason for this is that in a demand shock there is no need to vary the markup, but with a constant markup you can allow a price increase to shift onto wages. A supply shock, on the other hand, requires an increase of the markup. If you need a change in the markup it is necessary to increase prices with respect to wages; if there is indexation, when prices rise wages do the same, and the inflationary spiral starts.

*   *   *

19   Conversing with Micha

My friendship with Ugo Stille, "Micha," is of thirty years' standing. When he was the correspondent of the *Corriere della Sera* he often phoned from New York at eleven o'clock in the evening because, having to work late, he was accustomed to sleep mornings. He phoned to find an angle, almost always confidential, on American and Italian matters to discuss with Serena and me and to scout out an independent opinion. He frequently came to Boston and every now and then dropped in on us. He was unfailingly pessimistic, shaking his head in perplexity.

His appointment as editor of the *Corriere della Sera* pleased him on the whole; it was an immense acknowledgment of his long and glorious career. He adored that newspaper and never once thought of leaving it despite the offers that had rained on him throughout those years. He would have liked it to resemble the *New York Times*, setting one opinion against another, giving them authoritativeness. The last time we saw him was in New York, and we went to a restaurant together. He was pessimistic, as always. But very proud of his son, Alexander, who had just published his first important book.

Of all my public interventions, perhaps the one that has given rise to the most debates, polemics, articles, accusations, and ripostes is the interview I had with Micha shortly after the meeting of the American Association of Economists held at Dallas over Christmas 1975, at which I took up the post of president. The interview was published a few days later on January 3, 1976, under an unmistakably provocative title: "In the Year of Economic Recovery the Italians Will Have to Live Worse." But the situation had become so serious, owing to the agreement on fixed-point wage indexation, that the only way then to get free from the spiral of barter was to reduce real wages. A very nasty medicine to hear about, let alone to swallow. And I certainly didn't mince matters. The year began with excellent prospects for all except Italy. I likened Italy to a railway car that threatened to uncouple from the convoy and stand still on a track that led nowhere. Why?

"This is a stagnation crisis, and the immediate cause of the stagnation is lack of aggregate demand." A Keynesian situation, then, must be tackled with the instruments indicated by Keynes: fiscal and monetary stimulus. But this path was blocked, for it would have led to inflation and balance-of-payments deficits. What, then? "The fundamental and immediate problem to solve now is the excessive unit cost of labor, which is suffocating profits, destroying every incentive to invest, and so preventing the increase of productivity." And I concluded:

Let me be even more brutally frank and explicit: The level of real wages must be reduced. I realize that in Italy today no politician can take the responsibility of arguing such a thesis, and that even many economists who share this view prefer to express it cautiously and indirectly. But for that very reason I think it would be doing Italy a service to formulate the problem in its real terms, without beating about the bush. It seems to me perfectly clear that until the cost of labor is reduced, or at least until it is certain that the cost of labor will be contained as little by little demand expands, it will not be possible to achieve real expansion and thus reabsorb unemployment. A nasty medicine indeed, but there is no other capable of treating the disease. The only alternative is for the stagnation to continue. The system is in equilibrium at a level of underemployment. This equilibrium may go on for some time, but it is a downward equilibrium, not an upward one—destined, that is, to represent a continual, if slow, decline.

The reduction of real wages would be the more transitory "the more rapidly the social security system can be reformed and productivity increased."

This interview had the effect of a bomb. Articles[37] were written depicting me as a dangerous reactionary, or wondering how I could pass for a liberal and make proposals so contrary to the workers' interests! The first severe comment came from Federico Caffè,[38] who criticized me on the grounds that, before requesting wage sacrifices, the parasite system of unearned income and credit should be attacked. The only article really favorable to me was written by Giorgio Bocca in the *Espresso* of January 18, under a title that I shall never forget, and that might serve as a comment on so many other suggestions of mine: "And Silence Fell over Professor Modigliani."

Bocca was right. Everyone spoke of my proposals. But the more they spoke, the less was actually said—in the sense that their contents were gradually submerged in an ocean of chatter. The success of that interview with Micha was really owing to the fact that during those months, secretly at first, then more openly, the coalition government of national unity was in preparation, which was also to involve the communists. Unwittingly, I had thrown a pebble into the pond, and the ripples somewhat complicated things.

I had immediate proof of this from a series of invitations to meetings and conferences in Italy, all of them on the theme of the economic policy of the left and how to solve the economic crisis. I shall never forget the meeting organized by CESPE, the economic research center close to the PCI (Italian Communist Party), because on that occasion it fell to me to hear some unbelievable things. The title of the meeting—held at Rome on March 12, 1976—was "Italy's Economic Crisis and International Conditioning." The objective, or so I was told, was to define a common policy for the left that should take account of the balance-of-payments restriction. The first to speak, as I remember, was Eugenio Peggio, who was the PCI's economic expert and polemicist, a good man, who had been dealing with monetary questions for years. After Peggio, I spoke, thanked the organizers, and began to say: "And on this point I agree with Peggio . . . And on this maybe I agree with Peggio . . ." Well, at a certain point I heard a high voice from the audience pipe: "But like that you're ruining him!" I found out later that it was Giancarlo Pajetta. He was certainly a very witty person, very likable, acute, trenchant. But I remember that at dinner that evening he told us how in the regions governed by the PCI they managed to reserve public housing only to people who voted for them. It struck me as most immoral.

But the encounter that would remain indelibly engraved in my memory was the clash I had with Claudio Napoleoni, which had been arranged by the industrialists' association of Lombardy. I merely reiterated my criticisms of the mechanism of the fixed-point wage indexation, concluding that wage indexation, in its current form, was ruining Italy. Napoleoni's reply was incredible: He said, substantially, that it was exactly what was needed, since by leading the situation to the breaking point through wage claims it would finally be understood that a revolutionary change was necessary. The stronger the wage claims, the more they would become the destructive element that would sweep away the pockets of parasitic rent. Undermining the equilibrium of the system would help toward making a clean sweep. Napoleoni said, in these very words: "The seriousness of the situation makes it imperative to formulate the thing with a certain amount of extremism."[39] I swear I couldn't believe my ears. It seemed an absurd argument, the fruit of a collective madness. Napoleoni went on to say that the structure must be reformed, one must attack unearned incomes, the parasites; if profits were being suffocated it was not by wages but by parasitic incomes. I answered by remarking that his argument was like that of a person saying: "I want to be paid more until you put the state in order once more!"

The day after, March 13, 1976, I read an interview in the daily *Paese Sera* in which Jacques-Léon Rueff, de Gaulle's former monetary adviser, had been summoned to argue against my theses. According to him, the rise in wages was not the cause but the effect of the increase in prices. He was evidently quite ignorant of Italian affairs.

*   *   *

20   *Dinner with President Carter and Italy's Prime Minister Andreotti*

One fine day at the time when the feasibility of a European monetary agreement was being discussed—what was afterward to be the EMS—I received an invitation to an official dinner at the White House on July 26, 1977. The Italian prime minister, Giulio Andreotti, was visiting the United States, and the idea of inviting Serena and me, too, must have been suggested by the American ambassador to Italy, Richard Gardner, professor of law at Columbia University, a very enjoyable man, married to a wife from the Veneto, who had often hosted us at Villa Taverna during our frequent trips to Italy.

Arriving in Washington, Serena and I dressed up and set off for the White House, where we were just in time for the aperitifs. While we were chatting and toasting one another, I glanced at the seating arrangements and realized that Serena had been placed at the right hand of no less a figure than Vice President Walter Mondale, a person we greatly admired, as a man and as a politician. I experienced a moment of mad envy. Then I stomped gloomily toward table number 10 to which I had been assigned. And then, to my sheer amazement, I realized I had been placed next to the presidential couple, on the left of Rosalyn Carter! On her right was the President, and on Carter's right sat Andreotti, with an interpreter behind him. On my left was a delightful Italian-American lady, Ella T. Grasso, who had for many years been governor of Connecticut. When I had accompanied Serena to her table, she lost sight of me, and only when the arc lamps of the television cameras were projected on the President's table at the close of the dinner did she realize I was sitting there. Serena told me afterward that she was sure I had sat down at the President's table by mistake and that no one had had the courage to remove me from the place I had usurped from someone else. Only when the President said something about me in his little speech did she feel relieved that I had taken the place really allotted to me.

Meanwhile, the dinner was served and I began chatting with Rosalyn Carter. She asked me insistently what I thought of Andreotti. I explained that I had a favorable opinion of the then prime minister, for two reasons. First, he was taking the lira into the new Monetary Snake, showing that he intended seriously to fight inflation. Second, with the support of the communists, he put an end to the scandalous system that lacked an effective budget constraint on local government expenditure, with that famous "consolidation" that, in actual fact, saved the Italian state from bankruptcy. At that time there had not yet occurred the shameful attack on the Bank of Italy against Governor Baffi and Mario Sarcinelli, two of the most honest and dedicated Italian public figures, which was to make me radically alter my opinion of him and the political environment that surrounded him.

We continued to chat amiably about Italian matters. I noted that every so often Rosalyn would murmur something in her husband's ear. When dessert was served and bottles of champagne were uncorked for the toasts, Carter stood up and spoke these words: "We are really happy to have here with us the head of government of a friendly and allied nation like Italy, Prime Minister Andreotti, a person who, as an eminent economist sitting tonight at our table, Professor Modigliani of MIT, assures us, is a great politician who has worked very well for his country." I stiffened in my chair: So Rosalyn had told the President what I had said, word for word. Carter went on to say in his toast speech that, during their conversation that morning, Andreotti and he had discovered they had some common acquaintance with Spanish and so, in order to converse directly without the help of interpreters, which always slows things up, they decided to use that language. But when they came to read over the notes their assistants had taken, they found that Andreotti had accepted that more American troops were to be sent to Italy, and he, Carter, had agreed that a few Italian communists would enter his cabinet, and so they decided to go back to English and Italian, with the help of the interpreters! General laughter. Language was not such an impediment to cooperation. However, I recall my surprise on finding that the then minister for foreign affairs, Arnaldo Forlani, who was accompanying Andreotti, spoke not a word of English.

21   Leaden Years

Serena and I went to Italy in 1978 and were swept up in an endless whirlwind of social events, interviews, and discussions. We were very comfortably accommodated at the Hotel de la Ville in Via Sistina. We found ourselves buttonholed by everybody for some idea of how the Americans felt about the communists entering the Italian government. All this while the fear was visibly growing of a decisive terrorist attack at the very heart of the state.

And, indeed, our trip began with a special edition of a news program on TV Channel One, on the evening of January 6, 1978, in which all the leading figures responsible for the economy took part: Carli, president of the Confindustria; trade unionists like Lama, Macario, Storti, and Benvenuto;

and Tina Anselmi, Enzo Scotti, Andreatta, Ruffolo, La Malfa, Cingano, De Rita, Peggio—and myself. I remember how Peggio was concerned only to find arguments for asserting that the financial markets did not fear the inclusion of communists in the government. I attempted, not very successfully, to show that the alternatives were still those of two years before.

The morning after, I decided to walk from the hotel to the Bank of Italy. Serena was terrified by reports of terrorist attacks, and was even more so after my television appearance. She warned me that if I heard someone calling out to me in the street, I must on no account turn around but just keep walking straight on faster and faster, "Otherwise, they'll shoot you." As luck would have it, I was just setting off when I heard a voice calling: "Professor Modigliani!" I pretended not to hear, but again came the call: "Professor Modigliani!" On I went, resolutely. At a certain point, I felt someone take hold of my jacket. Frightened, I turned—only to see a tiny little bald-headed man, of mild demeanor, who told me: "Professor, I'm the cobbler here on the corner. I just wanted to tell you that I saw you on television yesterday evening and you were the only person who said anything comprehensible."

Our social engagements that month, which always had some political connection, we found almost suffocating. Several people sought us out because they thought I had some influence. On the evening of the seventh, however, we went to dinner at the Grand Hotel with Filippo Maria Pandolfi, Bruno Visentini, and Francesco Cingano, and spent a most delightful time with people to whom we were linked by community of ideas and with whom we shared the same preoccupations. Pandolfi made an excellent impression on us. He really seemed to have the best intentions and to identify the genuine problems of the Italian economy.

On January 11, we were once more guests of CESPE and Peggio, and there we met Giorgio Amendola. I was profoundly struck by the charismatic personality of that great politician. Amendola told Serena and me that he was concerned about the government's weakness before the escalation of terrorism. So much so that, the day after, we thought: "Well, if he had been . . . in the government." We made many contacts with the communists. A journalist friend of ours, Antonio Gambino, invited us to dinner at his house on January 16, where among those present were Paolo Sylos, the publisher Vito Laterza, but also Berlinguer's secretary, Tonino Tatò, and, above all, the gray eminence of the Communist Party, Franco Rodano. Rodano made a really awful impression on us. Serena noted in her diary that he appeared "more Jesuit than Catholic." Rodano started by behaving aggressively toward us; he spoke very ill of American foreign policy, saying that the United States ought to revise its opinion and not object to the presence of the PCI in the government. Then, abruptly, he switched to a flattering, honeyed tone. We were left in no doubt that all this was intended to be a message to the American government. To be conveyed by us?! Still, we had the feeling he knew that the following evening we were going to Villa Taverna, the residence of Ambassador Richard Gardner.

And there, indeed, on the seventeenth we went to dinner with my old colleague from Columbia, who seemed to be perfectly at ease in his new role as ambassador. His wife was in bed upstairs, having broken her kneecap skiing. Gardner welcomed us at the front entrance, and we noted how his wife was irritated because she would have preferred us to be received on the first floor, with herself present. We had a very homey evening. Gardner's family was a large and very pleasant one, with the habit of chiming in on political subjects. Especially his mother-in-law, who was very angry and very anticommunist. The topic of the moment was the rumor, current in Christian Democrat and Republican circles, that the Carter administration had dropped its objection to communists entering the Italian government. But it was false. There was no change of stance on the fundamental questions of liberty, civil rights, and the need for a full and unconditional acceptance of the principles of the Western democracies. The rumor had probably arisen from some necessarily diplomatic attitude on Gardner's part—after all, he had to reckon with living in Italy, where the PCI was a solid reality that couldn't be avoided. We talked about it right through the evening, punctuated by the anticommunist sallies of Gardner's mother-in-law—because, among other reasons, I was invited some days later to our embassy for a seminar with the ambassador and leading functionaries.

On the evening before that, January 25, 1978, we had been to dinner at the house of Veniero Ajmone Marsan, where, together with our old acquaintance Eugenio Peggio, there were Renato Zangheri and his wife and Giorgio Napolitano. Both made a highly favorable impression on us. Napolitano struck us as authoritative, brilliant, intelligent, absolutely perfect. At that time, he was busy preparing for his celebrated trip to the United States and was at pains to assure us of the PCI's absolute dedication to democracy. At one point, Serena spoke up to ask Napolitano frankly, "But why aren't you chief of the PCI instead of Berlinguer?" A moment of intense embarrassment ensued.

Previously, we had been the guests of Vittorio Merloni, which really frightened us because he went about with a bodyguard armed to the teeth. Another evening, Giovanni Magnifico had arranged a dinner for us, where we found Guido Carli and Paolo Savona, as well as Ezio Tarantelli. Carli was gloomy, Savona very jittery. Both had received terrorist threats. That evening, for the first time I heard the expression "civil war" used. The kidnapping of Aldo Moro was not far away. At Giorgio La Malfa's we met his father, Ugo, who was the only one in favor of taking the communists into the government. In his opinion, he said, they were authentic democrats and there was no other way to preserve Italy's democracy. On January 23, we had been to the house of Tommaso Padoa Schioppa, where we met the new guard of the Christian Democrat party, Filippo Maria Pandolfi and Romano Prodi. Also present was Umberto Colombo. We went to the theater to see Dario Fo's production of Stravinsky's Histoire du Soldat—a lively performance, but we thought it went a bit too far. Highly charged, grim, violent. Just like Italy at that time.

At the end of the month we had had enough. Serena said to me, "Everybody asks us what we think of Italy, but when we tell them they don't like it." "Just so," I replied, "and that's the signal that we ought to be on our way home."

22   Sarcinelli Is Jailed

I had been back in America only a few months when there occurred the farcical episode of the incrimination of the Bank of Italy's governor, Paolo Baffi, and Mario Sarcinelli, then deputy director general and in charge of bank supervision. By sheer accident, that evening I had agreed to give an interview on a news program on Italian Channel One about the economic situation. The interview was already under way, live, when the phone on my desk rang and Serena told me that Mario Sarcinelli had just been arrested. Sarcinelli had found serious irregularities in the books of the infamous Banca Privata of Michele Sindona, a shady character who enjoyed the support of top figures in the ruling Christian Democratic Party. They tried threats to persuade Sarcinelli not to inspect Sindona's bank, and when he did, they found a servile judge to jail him. Eventually, Banca Privata went bankrupt. Sindona then descended on America and acquired and bankrupted a good-sized bank, the Bank of Long Island. He was jailed in the United States, and then in Italy where he died, mysteriously poisoned. Indignantly I broke off the interview and said, "I refuse to go on, because I have just had news of the arrest of Mario Sarcinelli, one of the best and most upright people in Italy, and it's a disgrace that such shameful things should happen in this country. Therefore, I shall do nothing further in Italy and on behalf of Italy until Sarcinelli is cleared." This caused something of a stir, and I continue to rejoice that I was able to do my bit in unmasking that horrible machination to millions of unsuspecting television viewers. That time, all Italian economists joined in a march against the judges responsible for the jailing, which was politically motivated.

The economists' protest was organized by the president of the Italian Economic Association, Sergio Steve. I sent a telegram from Boston to say I was with them in spirit; and Steve read it aloud in front of the judge's office.

The letter was published on March 25, 1979, in several newspapers and said:

> I feel so indignant that I have lost all interest in the Italian economy. I don't know whether to believe the press leaks concerning the shady motives underlying the growing campaign of intimidation against the Bank of Italy, which is one of the few buttresses of the country's international credibility. But I do know that the arrest of Sarcinelli is undermining the credibility of the judicial system that ordered it, even as it dishonors the government and the entire nation that allows such a thing to happen.

This dreadful affair led to Governor Baffi's resignation. At that point a very tough battle ensued for who was to succeed him; but, in the event, the Italian authorities brought it to a successful conclusion by making the best choice of all: Carlo Azeglio Ciampi, an outstanding banker and human being, now president of Italy. It is amusing to recall that, amid all the confusion of that time, somebody had the incredible idea—maybe as a joke—of proposing me as governor. I remember how Nino Andreatta phoned me one morning to inquire whether I would be willing to take on the job. Leaving aside questions of nationality, I replied: "Certainly, provided the Bank of Italy moves to New Hampshire." Andreatta: "But why New Hampshire, when you live in Massachusetts?" Myself: "Yes, but in New Hampshire there are more trees for making banknotes."

23   Was It Right to Enter the EMS?

My commitment to have nothing further to do with Italy was short-lived. I wrote a few articles in the *Corriere della Sera* about Italy's joining the European Monetary System (EMS), though these were among the last I wrote. After that, I ceased to collaborate on a regular basis.

Between 1978 and 1979 a very intense, somewhat ideological discussion erupted over the question as to whether Italy should take part in the renewal of the Monetary Snake, which was just then being set up in Europe under the prompting of Helmut Schmidt and Valéry Giscard d'Estaing. The funny thing was that I had the distinct impression that, initially, Andreotti, like the Bank of Italy, was against it. The PCI certainly was. Indeed, no one save my friend La Malfa's Republican Party was really in favor. At a certain point, Andreotti realized that to take Italy into that association might be an extraordinary political achievement and might act as an instrument, an "external constraint," for less inflationary wage bargaining than that implied by the wage agreements then in force. He perceived that the EMS would serve as an anchor in building a different type of society than the one the communists desired. Throughout the negotiations the Communist Party remained against it, whereas the government and the other parties in the national solidarity coalition became gradually more willing to join. I surmise that the communists did not realize that Andreotti had already made up his mind to join—with the result that he took all the kudos for it.

It was in that situation that I decided to write an article in the Corriere[40] to say: "Join!" The gist of the article was: If you really intend to stop "accommodating" inflation, the most effective way to persuade people and the financial markets that you mean business is to accept a constraint on exchange. At that time, Tommaso and Fiorella Padoa Schioppa were our guests in Boston, and Tommaso was all in favor of the EMS. A few weeks previously, I had been much more pessimistic and had said so. I felt that a country so beset with problems as Italy could not engage in such a hazardous game. But as the discussion went on, Tommaso infused me with a little optimism. In the midst of our heated debate, the telephone rang. It was the Corriere asking me to comment on the matter. I jumped at the proposal and asked Tommaso: Why don't we write it together? His answer was that an unwritten rule at the Bank of Italy forbade him to do so. The article therefore appeared under my name alone but was written with his cooperation. It was published on December 1, 1978, and I fancy it tipped the scale in favor of the EMS, at least among my friends at the Bank of Italy, who still harbored some doubts.

What essentially settled the question was that all the advantages that might be preserved by not joining the EMS were in reality illusory. The principal one that might be expected from allowing the currency to float in splendid isolation was to be able to use exchange to stabilize the economy. Quite so, were it not for the fact that in a highly indexed economy like Italy's, devaluation is no longer a stabilization device because, through wage indexation, it immediately translates into inflation and consequent revaluation of the real exchange rate and loss of competitiveness. In the presence of a strongly indexed system, devaluation is unable to restore a current balance surplus. This was precisely the conclusion Padoa Schioppa and I reached in studying the behavior of an economy indexed at 100 percent and more.[41] In this way the advantage of belonging to a new community system would be thrown away in favor of an advantage that was entirely illusory. As we wrote in the *Corriere*:

> A devaluation does not tend to produce a lasting improvement in the current account balance so long as employment and unit cost remain constant; nor will it yield a lasting increase in the rate of employment, which is consistent with the external stability. In so far as devaluation may have favorable effects, these are transitory, due entirely to the inflationary process and to the phenomena of monetary illusion deriving from it.[42]

Those opposing entry into the EMS should have realized that to wield the exchange rate as an instrument of economic policy meant abolishing wage indexation. But of course, at that time, such a conclusion must have sounded like blasphemy, even among diehard conservatives:

> The attempt to preserve the exchange maneuver as a device for reconciling mutually inconsistent unit costs and employment levels is justifiable under one of the following two hypotheses. The first is that efficiency be restored to maneuvering the nominal exchange level in order to modify the real rate. This would require important changes to the system—firstly, that the wage indexation, which is currently the main cause of the inefficiency, be abolished or at least considerably attenuated.[44]

In other words, the EMS was to be rejected in order to retain an advantage that did not exist! Had there been a possibility of doing away with indexation, the situation would have been quite different.

There was another argument that was put forward at that time, not without foundation:

> Linkage to the German mark is said to involve also a heavy sacrifice in terms of growth if Germany continues to be willing to hold its growth rate to a minimum, even while maintaining price stability, and it is added that since Italy still has a very low *per capita* income, it cannot afford the luxury of slow growth.[44]

This argument had, and continues to have, some foundation. In practice, however, staying out of the EMS did not offer strong enough pressure to force Germany to higher growth. This, too, was in reality an illusory alternative:

> To be sure, Italy's balance of payments depends on the demand for Italian products by foreign clients, of which Germany is a large one; if the demand is strong, the level of employment will be higher compatibly with the external equilibrium and thus with the stability of prices. If it is weak, the external equilibrium will cause a lower level of production and employment. For this reason, in the immediate present, slow growth by Germany is dangerous for Italy. It is false, however, to affirm that there is an independent exchange policy which would enable this danger to be avoided. One might attempt to persuade Germany to more rapid growth, and this would presumably be easier inside than outside the EMS; but if this failed, staying outside the EMS would certainly not be a remedy.[45]

This argument was, of course, based on the assumption of a wage indexation at 100 percent and over. In such conditions a functional exchange policy aimed at increasing employment by increasing competitiveness was destined to fail, since it had the automatic result of sending up domestic prices, devouring the entire margin of price competitiveness accruing from devaluation.

24   A Slow Recovery

Little by little, people came to realize how the Italian economy was hampered by its eccentric system. Belatedly, the industrialists, too, began to negotiate to reduce the more freakish effects of the wage mechanism.

I recall how I often invited Vittorio Merloni, at that time president of the Confindustria, for long talks during his visits to Boston. Our discussions occasionally touched high comedy. There was a period in which entrepreneurs and workers refused even to meet in person during negotiations and the unfortunate minister of labor, Enzo Scotti, would enter one room, then exit, and enter another. At a certain point in the talks, Merloni was very pleased at managing to reach agreement on a rounding-out mechanism of a unique sort: The wage indexation was to remain as before, but it was said that the decimal point would be rounded down to the lower whole number. Was that possible? It was nowhere stipulated in writing. And I spent a whole evening with Merloni trying to convince him that an interpretation of that kind was meaningless. And in fact, a few hours later, the unions rejected that interpretation, which Scotti had already announced at a press conference.

In those days, I was beginning to abandon any hope that the Italian economy might ever be able to resume the development process. And, I was beginning to worry even about the survival of democracy threatened by the criminal activity of the so-called Red Brigades. It was a radical, violent organization, whose only real purpose was to destroy the existing order through terror and chaos. For years they killed and maimed the flower of Italian "democratic intelligentsia."

And at their height, they carried out a mind-boggling operation of first kidnapping the outgoing prime minister, Mr. Moro, then keeping him prisoner for weeks and ultimately killing him, dumping his body in the middle of the city. They finally struck very close to me by ambushing and murdering Ezio Tarantelli. He had been a student of mine; we had worked together on the econometric model of the Bank of Italy and had published a number of joint papers, including those dealing with the reform of the escalator clause, mentioned earlier. His association with me was widely known, and many of my acquaintances interpreted the assassination as a veiled threat to me, especially since the killers left a document explaining his execution that made explicit reference to Tarantelli's association with that bulwark of reaction, MIT.

I have a lump in my throat every time I reread the last letter he sent me on July 4, 1983, when he had just been appointed to the chair of Political Economy at Rome:

> Dear Franco . . . let me thank you for everything you have done for me, for the things I have learnt from you over these last fifteen years, and that little bit of economics that, maybe, has lodged in my mind. In view of the new government being formed, I am about to relaunch the proposal for predetermined inflation. As you can see from the enclosed cutting from *Repubblica*, I stand firm on the two points that we established together: predetermination and percentage calculation of the points of the wage indexation. As you may imagine, I am under all kinds of strong pressure from within and without the unions to alter this formulation, even in part. For example, the CISL [Italy's leading labor union] abhors the idea of percentage calculation. But I won't swerve from my line. Whatever it costs in my relations with the unions and elsewhere. Here, I hope you will recognize something of what you taught me. I am also persuaded that your solution of an adjustment

shared by both the negotiating parties is by far the best. It's much simpler than what we worked out together in our two articles in *Repubblica* (with the role of the State as ultimate guarantor vis-à-vis unforeseen and unforeseeable events, remember?), but it does ensure the basic results.

Around the time of Ezio's murder, my dearest and closest associates on both sides of the Atlantic made the loving decision to organize a Festschrift, or volume of essays in my honor. The volume was to be presented to me at a ceremony in Rome in the summer of 1985. However, after what happened to Ezio, we all became convinced that there was no point in exposing me and my American colleagues to the danger of reprisal by the still powerful Red Brigades. As a result, the ceremony was rescheduled to September in Martha's Vineyard, where I was spending my summer. It was a deeply gratifying experience, organized by one of my colleagues, Rudy Dornbusch, and two of my outstanding former students and personal friends, Stanley Fischer and John Bossons. It resulted in a volume titled *Macroeconomics and Finance: Essays in Honor of Franco Modigliani,* which still warms my heart.

With the passing of time, studying the mass unemployment ongoing in Europe, I am convinced that today above all, when eradicating inflation has become the main priority of economic policy, concerted planning of wage and price trends represents the most promising way to ensure price stability without the suffering and wholesale waste caused by the current unemployment levels in Europe. Between 1984 and 1985 the communists campaigned for a referendum intended to reinstate the point of wage indexation that had been canceled by a decree by the prime minister at that time, Craxi. Craxi's measure was less radical than it seemed, since it left the perverse mechanism intact. But it did provide a few months' breathing space for a onetime reduction in the rate at which inflation was increasing, and this duly came about.

At that point, the PCI concentrated all its heavy guns on regaining the lost point of wage indexation. The referendum was rejected. I found it wonderful to see how people had understood that voting in favor of the referendum would only make them accomplices in a scheme that promised them money they would never receive in terms of purchasing power, since reinstatement of wage indexation would surely exact its toll from all Italians in the form of inflation and balance-of-payments deficits. In one of those bursts of pride and clear-headedness the Italians sometimes show, the country came to its own rescue. The referendum marked a turning point, for, after that salutary defeat, even the communist unions, however slowly and ponderously, took the path I had already been recommending unsuccessfully since the mid-1970s—in a process that concluded in 1993, when, at last, even the CGIL accepted the principle of nominal wage bargaining, thanks to the work of the new prime minister, Carlo Azeglio Ciampi.

25   The Hard Law of the EMS

After breaking a lance in favor of the EMS, from 1980 onward I wrote a few articles to throw some general light on entry into the exchange agreement. Fixing the exchange rate is consistent with a method of stabilization that has been used by several Latin American countries, under the guidance of Rudi Dornbusch and others, where, in order to curb inflation and the wage pressure that fuels it in a vicious circle, the government opts for a fixed (nominal) rate. With a fixed exchange rate, every wage increase that exceeds productivity must lead to an increase in prices, including those of exported goods, which tends to make the country uncompetitive and has an adverse effect on employment. The guiding hypothesis is that increasing unemployment—or the fear that it will increase—serves to curb the pressure on wages. Actually, as has been seen in very many cases in Latin America, this method does not necessarily yield good results. For, even while reducing the growth of wages and inflation, it does not generally reduce them sufficiently to prevent a rise in prices relative to international ones. The result is a continual appreciation of the real exchange rate that tends increasingly to worsen the balance of payments. Typically, after a sufficiently long lapse of time, the balance of payments enters a critical stage and devaluation becomes necessary—which, initially, adversely affects real wages and improves the trade balance, but soon restarts the price-wage spiral.

This was more or less what happened in Italy, especially between 1987 and 1992. Following Italy's entry into the EMS, inflation slackened but continued at a higher rate than in the other member countries of the monetary system, with the result that the value of the lira tended to appreciate in real terms, thus leading to a gradual worsening of the balance of payments. The crisis was postponed because the international markets were willing to finance the rising deficit, in the belief that it would gradually be eliminated. Thus, Italy handled the situation partly by attracting capital from abroad with high interest rates, and partly by drawing on her reserves.

This favorable attitude suddenly changed with the approval of the Treaty of Maastricht, by which Italy undertook in a fairly short time to join a fixed exchange system, more rigid than that of the EMS. In the face of a commitment like this, the current exchange was clearly too high and the lira would have to be devalued in order to be incorporated in the union. The market became convinced that devaluation was inevitable. When this happens, operators begin to say they may as well sell their lire before it is too late.

26   The Great Currency Crisis of 1992

What is a currency crisis? It's interesting to observe how everyone talks of "capital flight"—the phrase even bounces into the newspaper headlines. And this obviously did also happen during the great crisis of the European Monetary System between September 1992 and July 1993. Few people are aware, however, that analysis shows that precisely when the currency crisis is at its peak, less movement of capital occurs and more movement of prices and interest rates takes place. Let's see why.

It all begins when large investors wish to liquidate their share of a country's public debt and purchase other currencies. What first happens is that the operators sell their bonds, which thus tend to depreciate; this operation causes interest rates to rise—which should make the bonds more attractive and thus reduce the desire to sell them. Second, the operators wish to convert their lire into foreign currency; and this second operation cannot be mechanically performed: To find dollars, the operators must find people from whom to buy them. This leads to a situation in which everyone is trying to sell lire and buy dollars, and so the lira is devalued on the market.

The devaluation can lead to an increase in the dollar supply in two ways: (a) the classic way, where devaluation of the lira increases net exports, but this is a very slow way; (b) the more immediate mechanism whereby the central bank resists devaluation, selling its currency reserves. When the flight is massive, this second mechanism can have only a limited effect. When a currency floats, devaluation has little effect on an effective outflow of reserves. Or, rather, this happens to the extent that the central bank is willing to liquidate its reserves to uphold the exchange rate.

When a currency is devalued, it might be thought, on the one hand, that having already depreciated, it should reach equilibrium. However, when a currency begins to devalue, people think that the trend will continue. The paradoxical result of these interacting behaviors is that the attempt at capital flight is reflected above all in interest rates and the exchange rate, and only to a small extent in an actual outflow of capital or reserves.

27   One Thousand and More

The forced exit of the lira from the EMS was followed by a period of confusion in which the Bank of Italy sought to support the exchange rate by a policy of high rates and tight money. The hope was for a rapid reentry into the monetary system. In November 1992, my friend and fellow economist, Rudi Dornbusch, published an article that provoked outcry and reproach. In essence, and in contrast with prevailing opinion, he argued that Italy, with its floating exchange, had finally shaken off the yoke of the Bundesbank and the high interest rates it imposed, and ought to use this freedom to lower rates and stimulate investment, allowing the German mark to rise even to 1,000 lire and benefiting from an increase in exports. In conditions of cyclical recession and in the presence of the wage agreement, devaluation would not have an important inflationary impact. And that is exactly what happened through 1993, when the foolish idea of reentering the Monetary Snake in a short time was abandoned. Indeed, following heavy devaluation, Italy witnessed a striking improvement in its balance of payments, and, in spite of that, inflation began to fall.

Italy required a devaluation of seemingly huge proportions in order to restore equilibrium to the balance-of-payments current accounts, revive growth, and offset the effects of shrinking demand caused by a reduction of the public deficit by around 3 percent of GDP, following the restrictive maneuver of the Amato government. Dornbusch's scenario took place: The rates on BOT's (Treasury bonds) fell from over 15 percent in the summer of 1992 to 10 percent in 1993, and the devaluation exceeded 30 percent, but in a phase of recession this had scant effect on prices. This is what I would call the "big star of Italy" factor. In this way, an export-led recovery was effected, with a dramatic turn-about in the foreign accounts thanks to increased competitiveness engendered by the real devaluation resulting from nominal devaluation and the block of wages and prices.

*   *   *

28   *1993, the Year of the Great Opportunity*

Through the 1980s, after my article on entry into the EMS, I wrote very seldom in Italy. It was not until 1993 that I really felt that a moment of great hope had come again, such as I had never experienced since the Liberation in 1945. The year 1993 ushered in four exceptionally favorable conditions for a radical and lasting solution to Italy's historic problems.

The first was the formation of the Ciampi government at the end of April. This was a government of a quality without precedent in Italy since the war—with the possible exception of the Amato government, which had replaced the dullness and self-interest that had characterized the majority of the Christian Democrat administrations after De Gasperi. Ciampi's government was served by honest, able members, deeply devoted to their country—people like Sabino Cassese, Luigi Spaventa, Nino Andreatta, Alberto Ronchey, and Umberto Colombo, to name only the principal members. Along with Ciampi, they deserve their country's gratitude, and I believe Italy and history will acknowledge them.

The second condition was, surely, the ongoing investigation into the ever-spreading corruption scandal, popularly known as *Tangentopoli* (Bribe City).

The third favorable condition was the agreement on the cost of labor and the income policy of July 1993. In signing the pact, thanks to Ciampi, the unions showed they had achieved an almost unbelievable degree of maturity. With that contract, the troublesome wage indexation was ended once and for all, as I had been preaching for over fifteen years. Instead of being the principal engine of inflation through irresponsible wage claims, the unions became a bulwark of price and wage stability.

This was why I sought to encourage Ciampi's effort as much as I could, trying to persuade him that the worst thing at that moment would be a premature return to the EMS. I wrote a long article on the "great opportunity," which was printed on the same day, May 5, 1993, in the *Corriere della Sera*, *Sole-24 Ore*, and the *Financial Times*.[46]

In June 1993 I was invited to Italy by Sergio D'Antoni, who asked me to speak at the congress of his union, CISL. I was assigned the precise task of explaining, from an economic point of view, why the agreement on the cost of labor was beneficial in solving the structural problems that had beset Italy since the 1960s and should be renewed. I accepted, though Serena was very skeptical: "You'll see, they'll pelt you with rotten tomatoes. . . ." Instead, I got a very warm reception. Generous applause came from a responsible union that was by now fully aware of the need to bargain the nominal wage, because in that way inflation would be knocked out, the economy would retain its competitive advantage, and employment, after twenty years of stagnation, could rise again. When I spoke to the CISL congress, the negotiations had reached a very difficult point. The day after that, Ciampi was to speak, making a dramatic appeal to the sense of responsibility of the nation as a whole. And, just before I said my piece, I learned that the talks were on the brink of breaking down. I said what I had to say, speaking with all the industrialists I knew, trying to press them to accept the agreement, which was in everyone's interest, theirs first and foremost. And a couple of days later Ciampi privately invited me for a talk with him at Palazzo Chigi (the official residence of the Italian prime minister).

The meeting with Ciampi was of some importance. I found him perturbed that the Confindustria and the CGIL failed to appreciate the "time" factor imposed by the mechanism of the international markets. The industrialists, for inexplicable reasons, would have preferred postponement till September. But the agreement just had to be signed then and there, for the markets had somehow predicted it: They would react by reducing rates, which would free resources for the private sector, lightening it of its burden of debt, and would allow a less deflationary budget than would be necessary in September, with an extra four months of high interest rates. Lower interest rates were clearly Ciampi's central target and his most powerful device for reversing the cycle. He showed me the drafts for the agreement, with the forecasts for wage increases for future years, and I pointed out that, in my view, once the great decision was made to link wages to planned inflation, he ought to be more courageous and set himself a target of lower inflation. I seem to remember that the inflation for 1994 was programmed at 3.5 or even 4 percent. I argued that, with the exchange at less than 1,000 lire against the German mark, plus a generous reduction in interest rates, due inter alia to the international recession, the goal ought to be 2.5 percent, since, according to my model, if wages are lower, then the whole price structure decreases, and prices can be maneuvered through the nominal wage. Given that this is the mechanism, one might as well bring inflation even lower, since this allows lower interest rates and a larger amount of investment. Ciampi struck me as skeptical, but probably I was wrong and he was already reaching his decision, for, some days later, on July 3, when the agreement was finally signed, I saw with pleasure that the target had indeed been lowered to 2.5 percent.

During my visit to Ciampi an amusing little incident occurred. My granddaughter Leah, who was then twenty-five, had accompanied me to Italy, and I had promised to take her shopping at Rinascente (Italy's leading department store) when Ciampi's invitation unexpectedly arrived. I set off alone, telling her, "In an hour's time, take a taxi and say, 'Palazzo Chigi.'" When the taxi driver heard this novel destination, he turned around incredulously to stare at this presumptuous young American, but Leah insisted: "Yes, Palazzo Chigi." Thus, she arrived in time to meet me at the front door, just as I was coming away from my visit to Ciampi.

During the final round of the talks Ciampi managed to perform another miracle that ought to stand as a model for all the other European countries. He succeeded in convincing the CGIL led by Trentin to renounce any mechanism for automatic recovery of lost purchasing power in case real inflation should exceed the programmed one. The agreement stipulates that this differential "will have to be taken into consideration" in subsequent negotiations over the economic content of the contracts, but does not restore any ex post wage indexation, as the model devised by Tarantelli still entailed. In my view, this marks a historic, definitive turning point not yet sufficiently appreciated in Italy.

Aside from this, the data then available demonstrated that even after the agreement of July 1992, wages in the industrial sector had risen by 2.3 percent and had thus lost a mere 1 percent of purchasing power. The increase in productivity was to enable a wage increase that would have no impact on prices.

Were the unions merely to accept, merely to acquiesce in wage moderation? The Ciampi agreement entailed the opposite. But here the union confederations would have to make the proposals, also in the following years, and promote further structural changes capable of keeping prices down: for example, deregulation in the distribution sector. It was the inefficiency and high markups in this sector that hindered workers from enjoying the fruits of increased productivity. The medieval system of trade licenses should have been abolished without delay, but this had to wait till 1997 with Prodi's government.

There remained a fourth element that swiftly transformed these developments, so beneficial for the country, and turned a situation of slow decline into one full of possibilities for recovery and growth. These things were what filled me with great enthusiasm for the future of Italy and led me to write and give interviews on the subject of the "great opportunity."

This fourth element was the presentation of Ciampi's budget. This was destined to put an end to the old trend of continual deterioration of the ratio of deficit to national income, by formulating a structural reduction of this ratio through improved national revenues that should consolidate the shock treatment applied by Amato in the previous year, and with a real reduction in expenditure that perhaps marked the truly revolutionary novelty of Ciampi's budget. Maybe it wouldn't solve the problem once and for all, but it was the most that could be achieved at the height of an extremely serious recession.[47]

In the case of Italy, I have always felt it useful to adjust the requirement for inflation. But it is also important that the adjustment take account of prospective interest rates. For when inflation has been allowed for, the financial requirement depends only on the real interest rate. And here, as soon as I was able to look at the documents on Ciampi's budget and the corrected balance, I saw at once that the real rates had obviously been overestimated. The plan started out from the assumption that the real rate needed to finance the debt would remain at a constant very high level that prevailed throughout 1993, that is, 5.7 percent, though at year's end it was already only a little above 4 percent (8.5 percent nominal minus 4.3 percent inflation). On the contrary, I was certain that there were good grounds for a further small reduction toward 3.5 percent.

At that time, I continued to oppose a hasty return to the EMS. And, in the article of May 5 on the "great opportunity," I had in a way replied in advance to the criticisms recently made of Italy:

> It might be argued that the expansion Italy is enjoying is simply a repeat of the old game of competitive devaluations. But this interpretation is quite wrong. The truth is, in my view, that Italy must be committed to a revolt against the suicidal policy of high rates by the Bundesbank, as a sort of David, wielding the new weapon of the farsighted unions, against the mighty Goliath. Italy would willingly join the battle for lower rates with other countries having similar problems, like Spain, Ireland, Belgium, and of course France. They, too, should free themselves from the fetters of the Bundesbank, allowing the exchange to float (separately or jointly) and pursuing a policy of lower rates and tighter fiscal attitudes.[48]

David against Goliath, then. But if Italy wanted to be David and brandish a little sling, it must put its public accounts in order, and above all reform its public administration.

In this connection, Sabino Cassese must be mentioned. He was perhaps the least known internationally of the Ciampi government, but the most deserving of all, for he undertook radical reorganization of public administration. On the one hand, he insisted that state employees take their work seriously, but, above all, that they be aware that they are "civil servants" at the service of the public and wield no arbitrary powers vis-à-vis that public.

Cassese brought order to the chaos of state employees' working schedules and, last but not least, succeeded in curbing the increase in the cost of the state bureaucracy, which up to then had been one of the main causes of inflation. For the wage increases state employees had managed to obtain were such as to drive the whole structure of industrial relations upward without the employees' being willing to raise their productivity in proportion.

Another little-recognized member of that government was Alberto Ronchey, who instilled the idea that museums exist for the benefit of the public, Italian and foreign, and not for the convenience of their custodians and other staff. I know of Americans who returned from Italy incredulous at not being able to visit more than a few museums, whose contents are studied in all American universities without actually being physically seen. Americans who suffer this experience normally wonder how Italians can fail to see their museums and works of art as a marvelous, unique, inexhaustible economic resource. And, in fact, in recent years there have been clear signs of improvement in this direction.

As can easily be imagined, both Cassese and Ronchey became most unpopular with the bureaucracy and its protectors, old and new, and this subsequently had an appreciable effect on the popular consensus, which emerged with the debacle of the center and the left in the general election of March 27, 1994.

Whatever the case, the ongoing action to improve public accounts in a year of full recession—as is evident from a comparison of the Italian figures with those of other European countries—impressed the financial markets and restored faith in the lira.

As I have said time and again, in order to assess the degree of trust in Italy and in its ability to manage the public debt, it is sufficient to look at the differential between the rates on bonds of financially strong countries like Germany and those of Italy. This fundamental measurement is the best yardstick of faith in the Italian economy and the country itself, and is indicative of the risk premium that market operators demand for taking the risk of investing in a country with an uncertain future, rather than in Germany. During the Ciampi government's time in office, the differential for a ten-year bond fell from 5.5 to 2.7 percent.

Alas, the result of the March elections ushered in a process that was to wipe out my optimism and slowly replace it with a pessimism that reached its peak early in 1995, when I stated and wrote that Italy was in danger of taking the same road as Mexico, without even realizing it.

*   *   *

29   *Modigliani at Modigliana*

It was in that year of the "great opportunity" that something nice happened. The town of Modigliana (about two thousand souls, but historic and prosperous) in the Romagna region, conferred an honorary citizenship on me, presenting me with a magnificent scroll and a splendid porcelain plate that does honor to the hall of my house in Cambridge.

We had first visited that pretty little town in the mid-1950s, to search in the municipal archives for any mention of the Modigliani family. We found no clear reference, except for a certain Livio da Modigliana, in 1500, who at the end of his life was called Livio Modigliani and had painted frescoes in the cathedral of nearby Forlì. But who knows if he was connected with us . . . ? This much we learned from Michele Framonti, a schoolteacher in Modigliana, a man of great culture who became a dear friend. Framonti was convinced that our ancestors, after their expulsion from Spain at the end of the fifteenth century, could have settled in a ghetto of which traces still exist, but which had a short life, as the pope at once sent all the Jews away. We soon made friends with the great Anglicist Giuseppe Ragazzini, author of a well-known dictionary. Both he and Framonti were authoritative members of the Accademia degli Incamminati, into which I myself was inducted shortly thereafter. This was a learned society whose members are the intelligentsia of the region, and it was founded in the eighteenth century after the famous French academies. The name Incamminati is a very suggestive name; it means those who have started walking and so are well on their way.

These two friends had the idea of proposing me as an honorary citizen, which duly took place in a memorable ceremony. As soon as we arrived, we were met with big posters on the walls proclaiming me welcome. In front of the town hall a fine band in blue uniforms struck up in my honor and marched round the square several times. We were charmed; it felt like being in a film by Fellini! Then we entered the town hall, where the mayor rose to propose my honorary citizenship to the town council and all the councillors voted yes. The mayor pointed out that this was among the few occasions when the voting had been unanimous! Plenty of speeches followed, and when my turn came, to give thanks for the honor done to me, I said that at long last I, a Roman, could feel on equal terms with my wife who, though born in Bologna, always boasted of being Romagnola because one of her grandfathers hailed from Lugo (near Ravenna). Modigliana will always be dear to me, especially for the real warmth of its townsfolk. And I cannot forget the Modigliana wine cooperative, which presented me with a generous sample of the delicious Romagnola wines, from red Sangiovese to white Pagadebit, of which I boast to my American friends as the wine of "my lands." When I was awarded the Nobel Prize in 1985, the mayor of Modigliana sent me a most expressive telegram of three words: *"Evviva, evviva, evviva!"*

30   *How to Measure the Economically Relevant Deficit*

Perhaps none of my theories has aroused so many long-drawn-out arguments in Italy as that concerning the so-called "correction" of fiscal outlays—and hence of the deficit—for inflation, which I have upheld in several writings, including newspaper articles with Mario Baldassari. The concept is really a very simple one. The correct impact of the public budget on the economy, through national saving and investment, not the conventional current accounting deficit, or the difference between revenues and current expenditure, the difference between revenues and current expenditure corrected for the state, as debtor, (and the holders of state bonds lose) through the devaluation of its debt, caused by inflation.

The correction that must be applied to the conventional deficit in order to measure the real deficit of a particular year—which we also called "inflation tax" (because it measures a loss suffered by creditors)—is equal to the product of inflation in the course of the year by the amount of the debt at the end of the previous year. In the same way, to obtain the deficit/GDP ratio (the subject of so much talk these last few years in relation to the mythical 3 percent parameter of Maastricht), one must subtract the product of inflation multiplied by the initial debt/GDP from the conventional deficit/GDP ratio. Alternatively, the deficit can be calculated by correcting the "expenditure for interest" item in the budget, replacing the effective expenditure with a corrected one, given by the product of the debt multiplied by the real interest (the effective rate minus inflation). If inflation and the debt/GDP ratio are low, as is the case in all the EMS countries except Italy, the correction is negligible. Take Germany, for instance, where the deficit/ GDP ratio in 1996 was around 4 percent, with inflation at 1.5 percent and a debt/GDP ratio of 0.60: The correction is by 0.9 percent, and the deficit/GDP ratio becomes 3.1 percent instead of 4 percent, a negligible difference from an economic point of view (though the hysterical Germans might be ready to abandon Maastricht for a difference like this!).

But let's look at the case of Italy, which in 1996 had a requirement/GDP ratio above 6.5 percent; over the year inflation averaged 4 percent and the debt/GDP ratio was a gigantic 1.25 percent. In this case the correction for

1996 is 5 percent and the real deficit/GDP ratio is a little over 1 percent, thus well below the 3.1 percent of Germany, which, till recently, boasted of an exemplary public finance as compared with spendthrift Italy! Italy's spectacular financial spring cleaning in 1997—crowned by entry into the euro—resulted, first, from reducing inflation, thus reducing the interest rate and the accounting deficit it had created.

The correction for inflation that I recommended was no harebrained invention of mine. It was indeed well known to those concerned with inflation accounting.

Unfortunately, it was publicly turned down by the guru of Italian finance, Mario Monti, my friend and respected colleague, at that time rector of the Bocconi University. As far as I know, this is the only point of doctrine upon which we have apparently differed. Monti has offered some explanation for his opposition, but I and others remain unconvinced. The explanation is that he agreed, in principle, with the "correction," which he had himself applied on other occasions, but at the time of our discussion the most important thing for the country was to pass extremely rigorous budget measures; and this could be done only if Parliament was convinced that the deficit was serious enough to create an emergency. Accepting our correction, the deficit would have appeared a modest one and Parliament would have taken advantage of this to return to its old spendthrift habits. From this reasoning one might conclude that a "covering up of the truth" is justified for the good of the country. But I cannot accept this argument at all: I feel an economist has the duty to tell "the truth, the whole truth, and nothing but the truth" that emerges from scientific analysis, and to tell it simply. Any other behavior can only bring discredit on the economist's profession.

The inflation induced error also affects behavior. For, when a saver enjoys an annual interest of 10 percent on a state bond, in the presence of 6 percent inflation, 6 percent of that interest rate represents, not a return, but simply the reconstitution of capital that was eroded by inflation. People frequently fail to take account of this difference and, mistakenly thinking they have received a 10 percent return, spend it, fueling consumption—when in reality they have received only 4 percent plus the revaluation or restitution of their capital. This mistake has become more important with the rise in inflation. In a work written with Tullio Jappelli, I have shown that this phenomenon occurs with some frequency: Inflation drives up consumption and thus contributes to the notable fall in saving that has been observed in Italy from the 1970s onward. I also showed how this happens in a number of countries, including China.

Our analysis leads us to the following conclusion: (a) that the national deficit must be corrected for inflation; (b) that in Italy, applying the correction, it remained appreciable though not disastrous; (c) that it is vital for the country to eliminate even that deficit that remains. To be sure, an economist might think it is more effective to conceal the truth, but in that case he must make it clear that he speaks as a politician, not as an economist.

Another argument, of a different sort, against our correction was that our corrected deficit was too optimistic, since it neglected the very serious indebtedness of the pension system, which is not included in the national deficit but would ultimately be a burden on the state. The objection is a thoughtful one, and it does counsel a look at the consolidated deficit of the state plus the pension authorities rather than that of the state alone, but it in no way suggests that the correction should be omitted.

A more convincing criticism could be based on the fact that the Maastricht parameter is defined in terms of the deficit/GDP ratio, and therefore that is the ratio that counts. But from this perspective an economist would have to reply by remarking that the real reference for the Maastricht parameter must necessarily be the deficit/GDP ratio, and thus that the correction is appropriate. It would behoove the economist to move heaven and earth to persuade the countries of the European Union to adopt this measure, universally applying the correction. And if, by some mischance, in Europe they showed themselves so ignorant of economics as to persist pigheadedly with a mistaken concept, then the wise course for Italy would be to reduce its inflation drastically and swiftly, as we suggested in *The Possible Miracle* (see below, section 35) and as Italy did indeed manage to do—to the astonishment of a world that did not understand the distortions induced by inflation.

After the greatest fit of rage of my whole career, provoked by a mistaken and dishonest headline in the daily *Il Messaggero* in an attempt to stir up a quarrel between Monti and myself, I decided to throw down the gauntlet to my fellow economists by saying: If you have any good objections to the "correction," let's see them! I wrote this openly in a column in the *Corriere della Sera* on January 14, 1994: "I offer the challenge to everyone, especially the experts, inviting them to indicate publicly if and where our argument is wrong. And to all those who, by their silence, give assent to our argument, we give a warning never again to confuse conventional and true deficit and to strive for the corrected measurement to be adopted everywhere." The challenge was met with a deafening silence.[49]

As well as the correction for inflation, there is another "correction" to be made that is indicated in the OECD statistics: correction for the cycle. This starts out from the consideration that the conventional net fiscal balance is not always a good indicator of the fiscal situation. For the difference between revenues and expenditure reflects not only the rates of taxation and transfers but also the highs and lows of economic activity. These are what determine what revenues and what expenditure actually materialize at the given rates. Generally speaking, it is well known that economic instability will be minimized if the tax rates are not altered to counter the effect of the fluctuations in economic activity upon revenues, thus allowing the budget to go into deficit (or to close with a smaller surplus) when there is a contraction in economic activity. This kind of fiscal structure, which causes deficits to increase when activity diminishes, has been used ever since the war as an "automatic stabilizer." Accordingly, the best way to assess a country's fiscal stance has proved to be the so-called full employment (or structural surplus) that would be produced by a given structure of taxes, transfers, and expenditure at an income level that roughly corresponds to full employment. In fact, the 1970s, especially after the 1974 oil shock, were a period of fairly high unemployment, which led to conspicuous cyclical deficits. The correction made by replacing the effective deficit with the estimated full-employment deficit involves a substantial differential for the United States, in some years up to 2.5 percentage points. This correction for the cycle should be incorporated in the rules of the Monetary Union, but after the sealing of the so-called "stability pact" it has been recognized only in an arbitrary fashion, inadequate for the stabilization of the euro economies.

31   My Judgment on Berlusconi

Since the early seventies, the Italians have been under the spell of Silvio Berlusconi, a highly successful businessman who, by now, owns most of private television and has a large financial empire. As is traditional for the great families, he has acquired two newspapers, several periodicals, and a major publishing house. He has used this empire (he passes as the richest man in Italy and with his wealth estimated at $12.8 billion, he was placed at number 14 on the *Fortune* Magazine list of the richest persons in the world) to promote himself politically, founding a new party colorfully called *Forza Italia*, the slogan shouted at soccer matches played by the Italian team. He has become the leader of the right-wing coalition, which held power briefly after the election of 1994, and which many think will win the next election. Through the years, I have criticized him, but not as a person or as an entrepreneur. My objection is his glorification as a striking example of the self-made businessman—while the truth is that his initial success was the result of political favors, mostly by the late Bettino Craxi (who was leader of the Socialist Party and prime minister in the 1980s and later fled the country after being indicted for misappropriation of public money), that allowed him to operate in a regime of concessions by the state. In this, Berlusconi is of course not alone in Italy. However, it undoubtedly paved the way for him, with his great entrepreneurial capacities, to develop an empire.

I began to air my misgivings about Berlusconi's suitability for a major political role during interviews that appeared in major newspapers in January and February of 1994, at the start of the campaign for the March elections. Those interviews were frank, but in no way aggressive. Simply, I did not feel Berlusconi to be fit for the job of prime minister, in view of his lack of political experience and competence in the financial, macroeconomic problems of the country.

But by far, my most serious objection to his political ambitions centered on the issue of conflict of interest, one that is readily understood by Americans to be an essential aspect of democratic government. A man with a huge financial empire, who controls private television, and whose only real competitor is the state-run public television network, cannot avoid a most acute problem of conflict of interest. Yet, during the short period that he was prime minister, he made no effort to separate himself from the source of conflict. More recently, the conflict has increased because several of his enterprises have been investigated for violations of fiscal laws, and he himself has been repeatedly indicted. Much of his activity as prime minister and then as head of the opposition has been devoted to fighting with the judiciary system and supporting laws that protect or extend his monopoly over private television. The skirmishes surrounding those issues have made it impossible to pass much needed legislation to reform the electoral system. What is truly amazing to me is that the Italians do not seem to understand or worry about the great dangers created by the conflict of interest, where one has an incentive to use the power entrusted to him for the good of the community to serve, instead, his own personal goals.

My mistrust was increased by his election campaign, which I found highly demagogic, promising a miraculous reduction in taxes and the deficit at one and the same time, which all economists know to be self-contradictory, and to which I later gave the name of "fantasy finance." The pledge to create one million new jobs in short order, in a situation where the whole of Europe was predicting a stalemate or a shrinkage of employment, was "fantasy economics." It merely exploited people's understandable wish to end the string of sacrifices of the previouspast two years, even though those sacrifices had been made necessary by the excessive post-ponement of rigorous policies by the preceding governments of Amato and Ciampi. Jobs could be created only by continuing along Ciampi's path, keeping prices, wages, and profits stable, and bringing down interest rates, so as to stimulate investment.

As I saw it, then, to keep Italian economic recovery alive it was necessary to continue to reduce the interest rates by confirming international trust: In other words, Ciampi's program had to be carried forward, as the political center and, in part, the left had stated they were willing to do.

I must say that, when a few days prior to the election it transpired that a gap of 16 thousand billion lire was looming, as against the predicted figure, I was very astonished, for the first quarter's data showed that Ciampi's budget had succeeded beyond expectations. One thing is certain: The major components of public expenditure went more or less as Ciampi had forecast, and 1994 chalked up a fairly good result in public finance, despite the complete lack of interest displayed by the Berlusconi government at least until the summer, when the interest rates began once more to rise threateningly.

In any event, Berlusconi sufficiently redeemed his pledge to lower taxes. He gave the impression of not being overly worried about the deficit that, in the absence of any intervention by the Dini government that followed, started rising once more. Far from increasing, jobs in 1994 shrank by 300,000, in line with the increase in interest rates and the fall in world demand.

On the other front, the center-left's indication that it intended to nominate Ciampi for prime minister was not a success, for at that time the government labored under the temporary unpopularity typical of a government that has applied fiscal tightening, although it could justifiably claim to have started tidying up the finances and relaunching the real economy. The tax-payers were annoyed by the minimum tax, the hateful health tax (on the family doctor), the ICI (real property tax), and the wage cuts in public employment. In a country with a developed political system, elections are held taking account of the economic cycle. All governments, American and European, apply tough recovery measures and hope their effects will be felt before consulting the electorate. In Italy, oddly, this elementary reasoning is unknown. As it was, the pledge to continue along the path towards economic recovery actually disadvantaged the center and the left in the elections.

A variety of factors, however, were responsible for the defeat of the forces opposing the right. Berlusconi's political skill successfully created a compact block that presented a single candidate in each constituency.

This was achieved by making concessions to Umberto Bossi and his Lega (a separatist party bent on detaching Northern Italy from the existing republic), which were later to create problems for Berlusconi's government and be the main cause of its collapse. The center and the left, on the contrary, were inexplicably divided, and thus threw to the four winds all the advantages they had gained from making common cause in support of the Ciampi government. By insisting on presenting separate candidates in each constituency, they effectively split the vote against the right.

These details in electoral technique need to be recalled to avoid the error of interpreting the election as a sign that Italy was weary of recovery policies and wanted a swing toward the extreme right. It was not the case that the country had suddenly rediscovered fascism and sunk into a fascist know-nothing mood—as in the dark days Serena and I lived through, that had forced us to abandon our native land. Certainly there was a swing of opinion, but the majority of the country was still moderate.

In the months that followed my fears with regard to Berlusconi were verified. I had advised the Berlusconi government that the main thing was to state openly that they intended to pursue the fiscal rigor, to reduce interest rates, and thus to reduce public expenditure and stimulate private investment, thus increasing jobs—in a straightforward fashion without any tricks. During its first months, however, the right-wing government turned its back on the public finances and, instead, managed to arouse further uncertainty with fascist-like attacks against the Bank of Italy; the international financial community was deeply distressed by such attacks on an institution that enjoys worldwide esteem. And as a result of this inconsistent behavior, so difficult to understand outside Italy, the lira began to depreciate, reaching exchange levels that threatened a resurgence of inflation; this, of course, caused interest rates to rise, which was tantamount to an increase in public expenditure and deficit.

32   *A Strike by Fathers Against Sons*

At length, the government decided to regain the trust of the markets by presenting a package of decidedly restrictive measures accompanying the budget. Berlusconi ate his words and proposed a set of fairly sweeping cuts in expenditure, above all in the pension sector. The basic idea of reforming pensions was right, and I gave my support to Berlusconi's proposal during an interview on athe television news program, that found me on Lake Iseo, where we were spending some heavenly vacation days. I explained that in my view the violent reaction of the unions was unjustified and untimely, as was its proposal to call a general strike.

I tried then to explain that the pension reform was not a class problem, workers against employers, but an intergenerational one. Under the old system, far too generous pensions were awarded to some who were allowed to retire young (seniority pensions) receiving larger amounts than they had actually contributed. The difference between real contributions and real benefits for the present generations would inevitably give rise to a situation of future deficits by which the children and grandchildren would find themselves paying more taxes and getting fewer benefits. This, then, was a classic problem of equity among the generations. I called on union members to desist from this strike, which was against their own offspring. This slogan of mine was instantly taken up by Berlusconi.

But it all ended in the worst way, with a classic postponement of the issue Italian-style. This impacted very negatively on the lira and on the Italian republic's bonds in lire. With customary Italian ingenuity, the fiscal package, which I thought inadequate except for the pension cuts, was passed with the exception of the latter, which were "removed." The postponement implied by that awful word "removal" was a serious mistake. The opposition was wrong to treat it all as a great victory over Berlusconi, for when the problem was tackled some months later it was no longer possible to deal with it calmly and with the necessary impartiality toward the future generations. I therefore organized an open letter that I wrote together with four highly regarded economists. We invited others to sign this protest against putting off the problem; the letter was a *j'accuse* directed at all those guilty of such typical Italian irresponsibility. It was published in the *Corriere della Sera* on December 4, 1994:

> With the removal of the pension cuts, agreed between government and unions, the mini-budget was shorn of its only structural and far-sighted maneuver—namely, the measures that aimed at restoring the equity among the generations so long neglected by previous governments. The necessary measures were known to all and had been incorporated, even if hastily, into the government's program. Other steps would have been needed alongside the pension reform to correct the real defect of the law, i.e. it's stacking a great deal of the reduction in expenditure on to the pensioners. Instead, government and unions decided to ditch the reform, in a shortsighted pact against the future generations, who neither vote nor demonstrate. The same or similar applies to the problems of health and education, which have been

shamefully neglected. It is vital that government, unions and the country as a whole should delay these matters no longer but carry to its
rightful conclusion the topic they had wisely embarked on, instead of
resuming the disastrous policy of postponement.

The appeal did not have the hoped-for effect; instead, its signatories
were exposed to public scorn by those who had promoted the "removal"
of the reform as pro-Berlusconi.

33   On the Brink of the Volcano

What happened next is well known. But there is one point that I think
should be recalled, for it belongs in my reflections on the obscure evil
that has threatened the economic foundations of the country where I
was born. Berlusconi was forced to resign when his parliamentary majority crumbled, partly as a result of his errors in economic policy. He
announced his resignation in Parliament, and even on live television. He
resigned of his own free will. But ever since then he has said obsessive-
ly: "I was deposed by a palace conspiracy; therefore, I desire and insist on
an immediate election." It is my profound belief that Italy's later troubles—before the Prodi government took office in 1996—stemmed from
this very obsession, this haste to hold an election. It was a deleterious
request. For the Dini government (which followed Berlusconi's resignation) was weakened from the start by not having an entirely convincing
majority in the Chamber of Deputies. It immediately presented an emergency fiscal package to get the deficit back under control. As prime minister, Dini did, in timely fashion, what he had been unable to do a few
months earlier as minister of the Treasury. But at this point the tragedy
supervened: The right-wing coalition, in the absence of a commitment
for spring elections, refused to vote for the fiscal package, which passed
by a mere three votes. This sparked off a further "capital flight." Currency
and state bonds slumped. Later, the right was to claim that the exchange
rate worsened because of the instability created by Bossi. But this is only
partly true. The tragedy of the exchange rate against the German mark,
which rose to nearly 1,300 lire, was entirely the result of the refusal to
vote for the emergency measures Dini presented. It was thus caused by
the behavior of the right, which was irresponsible and harmful to the
country. With the exchange rate at 1,300 lire, prices soon rose again, and
inflation, which had fallen below 4 percent, began once more to climb,

nearing 6 percent. This threatened to open an age-old wound in the fundamental wage-agreement mechanism. If the pact on the incomes policy broke down, in the space of a mere six months Italy would plunge into crisis, for it would lose the only device it possessed for a policy of stabilization; inflation would rapidly translate into wage pressure and the latter into further devaluation, amplified by the negative reactions of the markets. At that point, Italy risked the same fate as Mexico, in the sense that the collapse of March was underpinned by the mistrust of the international markets, which has nothing to do with the real economy, whether solid or not. I have never tired of explaining to the Italians a result of my studies on corporate finance: The solubility of a firm depends not only on its profits but also on the capital it possesses. But if management is squandering the capital, the creditors may ask to be repaid even if the debtor continues to pay interest. For a sovereign state, the risk is the greater in proportion to the amount of debt refinanced in the short term.

34   How Far Is Italy from Mexico?

In the spring of 1994, Mexico slid into a serious crisis of insolvency resulting from, a rapid loss of confidence by investors, who wanted to be repaid even while the country did not have the needed reserves. The crisis required extreme remedies. Violent speculation ensued, along with inflation, loss of purchasing power of wages, and a deep general malaise.

Following the attack by the right-wing coalition and the capital flight and depreciation of the lira that resulted, I began to worry that the persistence of irresponsible behavior might lead to a Mexican-style crisis. I publicly aired this concern on several occasions. Many of my friends at once countered that Italy, unlike Mexico, had a very small foreign debt and held large currency reserves.

To which I replied as follows:. To be sure, when you have a debt in foreign currency, you may be unable to repay it because you cannot find the foreign currency to pay the installments as they fall due. Typically, the Mexican debt was in dollars, and at a certain point they were unable to attract sufficient dollars to refinance the amounts to be paid.

As I see it, exactly the same problem arises even if the debt is merely internal, that is, if expressed in domestic currency. Suppose that at some point the government happens to be unable to find people willing to purchase issues needed to refinance the maturing portion of the debt. You can turn to the Central Bank who can buy them by creating money. But this is all wrong; it is the source of the ancient, mistaken, pernicious conviction that a sovereign debtor cannot default because it enjoys the power to create money of its own free will. For, when you create money to finance a debt you are unable to sell, this unleashes monetary inflation. An increase in the money supply fuels inflation, which drives up interest rates, and this in turn increases the state deficit, so the state must print more money, in a vicious circle. And thus even a sovereign state, realizing it cannot pay its debt, will default.

This argument holds good for Italy, too. The risk is felt to be a small one, since the debt in foreign currency is minimal and there are enough reserves to cover it. But actually the argument is weak: there is risk also in the sovereign debt, even if it is a mainly internal debt. For if there is difficulty in financing the debt owing to lack of trust on the part of the creditors, the sovereign debtor has to pay the debt as it falls due by creating more money, and this threatens to ruin the country with galloping inflation. While the creditors bear the risk of being paid in devalued money.

From the end of 1994, when the lira passed the threshold of 1,000 against the German mark, Italy entered an area of risk, in the sense that it reached a level of devaluation that, by causing inflation to grow once more, jeopardized the agreement on the cost of labor. At this juncture, therefore, and in contrast to a few months earlier, I counseled a reentry into the EMS, even while harboring all the doubts about Maastricht that I have expounded at length in the second chapter. Re-entry into the EMS would enable the exchange rate to be fixed, improving the outlook for inflation, which, in the meantime, had not yet affected the long-term interest rates.

A further objection made to me was that Italy differs from Mexico in being a member of the European Union and would thus be able to obtain all the necessary loans. This seems to me mistaken, for there was no reason to count on Italy's being bailed out, especially after exiting from the EMS.

All this was why in May 1995 I argued that Italy was on the brink of the same precipice as Mexico. Several people thought it was just a joke, one of my customary outrageous statements. But this time there was nothing to laugh about. That the danger was indeed real was confirmed by the governor of the Bank of Italy, Antonio Fazio, at a meeting of the Senate in honor of Paul Volcker, during which Fazio recounted a conversation he had had at Basle with the Fed chairman, Alan Greenspan[51].

Italy, then, just managed to save itself from the crisis, but the situation remained out of control, as can easily be deduced from the wide oscillations in the exchange rate, which plunged again and again first after the

speech by German minister Theodor Waigel in September 1995, second
when the motion of no-confidence against the Dini government requested
by the right-wing coalition and by Rifondazione Comunista (the main
extreme left party formed during the break-up of the former Italian
Communist Party, which joined the right)—promoted a vote of no confidence which failed by a handful of votes—and again the announcement
of a rather feeble budget. Inflation thus returned to 6 percent and short-
term rates hit 10.5 percent, with a differential with respect to the German
rates that touched an unprecedented peak of 700 basise points, then settled around 500, a level that implied a real interest rate of 4.5 percent,
compared to a German real rate around 2 percent.

35   Let's Aim at Zero Inflation

As I said in section 30, Mario Baldassari and I had for some time been arguing that the Italian deficit was not structural but was instead the result of
erroneous national accounting caused by inflation. When there is inflation,
the official accounting is incapable of calculating the economic (or real)
deficit and records a deficit that does not actually exist. In 1994 we realized
that it was this very mistake that produced the large official deficit that
kept Italy out of Maastricht. But since neither the Italians nor their
European partners were prepared to understand that mistake, we reasoned
that there was only one way to eliminate it; this consisted in putting an
end to inflation! For, when inflation is close to zero, the official deficit corresponds to the economic one, which in the case of Italy was around zero.
In other words, eliminating inflation would bring about a fall in interest
rates such as to reduce the official public expenditure by an amount about
equal to the existing deficit, thus eliminating the deficit. In Italy at that
time inflation was running at around 6 percent. Therefore, reducing the
inflation to zero would diminish it by six6 percentage points. But Fisher's
law says that this reduction will, in turn, reduce the (short-term) market
interest rate and that on the debt (though somewhat gradually) by the
same amount. With a deficit equal to about 1.3 times the income, a reduction in the interest rate by six6 percentage points reduces the expenditure
for interest, and thence the deficit, by 6 percent, which multiplied by 1.3
makes 7.8 percent of the income. Now, at that time, the planned deficit
was 7.4 percent of the income. Hence, reducing it by almost 8 percent
would take it practically to zero (even allowing for some complications,
such as the taxation of state bonds). This obvious solution, whichthat had

occurred to nobody, we called "the egg of Columbus," from an Italian expression for a solution so simple that nobody thought of it.

The idea was tested by simulations (worked out by a clever student of Baldassari's, Fabio Castiglionesi) of a plan to phase out inflation and its effects, which confirmed the possibility of zeroing the deficit through a swift reduction of inflation. We decided to transform our findings into a plan of action to be published in a book to present to the country and the government immediately after the elections that had been set for April 1996. And this was the source of the book Il Miracolo Possibile ("The Possible Miracle"), which we completed in double-quick time and sent to our publisher for distribution in the bookshops by May 10. I came over from America for the presentation of the volume together with the other authors, at a meeting that was attended by Ciampi, Abete (president of the Italian NAM), and D'Antoni, head of a major union, and that was held in an auditorium dedicated to Tarantelli at the University of Rome and open to all the students. The hall was packed and we received generous applause, but, understandably, the warmest was for Fabio Castiglionesi, a student like the majority of the audience!

Our plan hinged on formulating a working plan for promptly and drastically reducing inflation.

Inflation in Italy stems from two main causes: (a) the trend of wages, which controls the inflation of the prices of domestically produced goods and services; (b) the exchange rate, which controls the prices of imported goods. Regarding the elimination of the inflation of domestic prices, the approach was the one formulated by Ezio Tarantelli (with some initial inspiration from myself) of planning wages, prices, and monetary and fiscal policy through the celebrated three-sided negotiation of government, unions, and employers. This method had been very successfully applied in the Amato agreement of 1992 and especially in that of Ciampi of 1993, which had plotted a descending inflation, with a mean increase in wages and prices of 4.5 percent for 1994 and 3.5 percent for 1995. My impression is that this program was actually realized while Ciampi remained in office, and a few months later inflation did indeed fall to 3.5 percent. In 1995, alas, the inflation started rising again through the devaluation of the lira due first to the Berlusconi government and then fromto the right-wing coalition's opposition to the Dini government's adjustment maneuver, aimed at forcing an immediate election—which caused the historic devaluation of nearly 30 percent inof March 1995, by nearly 30 percent.

The fundamental idea underlying our approach was that the workers, like the firms, should be concerned, not with the growth of nominal wages and prices, but instead with the trend in the wage/s-prices ratio, i.e. the trend of the real wage (and thus of the real cost of labor). The negotiation should hinge on this point alone. But, once an agreement on this point has been reached, the increase in the nominal wage should no longer concern either of the negotiating parties (at least in a first approximation). Therefore, the target of the plan can be set as zero inflation, accompanied by a planned wage increase roughly equal to the productivity increase, in such a way that the cost of labor per unit of product remains constant overin time. If a wage increase greater than this were established, its sole effect would be to create a corresponding price inflation, while leaving the real wage unchanged.

At the time we put forward our plan, the unions were trumpeting demands for heavy wage increases (around 10 percent in the public employment segment) for the next two years, justifying them as follows: 4 percent to recoup the loss of real wages in the period of the labor contract now due to expire, and especially in the last year; and a further 6 percent to offset the inflation that the Dini government had planned for—3.5 percent in 1996 and 3 percent in 1997. This element, the programmed target of inflation as a reference point for the contracts, was a great mistake by the government, which, although able to plan a lower inflation, actually planned a higher one. For, the higher the planned inflation, the higher is the inflation actually achieved, given that the wages adjusts to the planned inflation and thus confirms it. But to this must then be added the other component of the union demands, namely, the recovery of the past inflation. In actual fact, this is a pure illusion that reflects a misunderstanding of the way the economic system works. To ask for an increase today in order to recoup a past loss is impossible. It is utterly illusory because the recovery is relative to past inflation, whereas a true recovery must rest on the relation between future wages and future prices, not between future wages and past prices. Now, if wages rise by 4 percent, all things being equal, firms will shift this increase on to the future rise in prices, and so the recovery will evaporate. Therefore, the workers must realize that, as the Americans say, "bygones will be bygones," or, as the Neapolitans say, "Those who have had, have had, have had; those who have given, have given, have given." The past is past and can't be brought back. If you try to recover it, it turns into an illusory recovery that makes prices rise, eliminating the recovery in real terms.

From the point of view, what counts with respect to the cost of production is the increase in wages, whatever the "reason" behind the increase. It may be because of what happened last year or ten years back or during the last ten years. All wage increases are brought to bear on prices except for the increase in productivity or the reduction in the share of profit, which can be negotiated only by simultaneous bargaining of wages and prices.

This means that negotiation must look to the future. Negotiation must therefore start by burying all claims as to previously lost purchasing power (perhaps with some subsequent compensation) and looking ahead. Starting from the date of the agreement, the increase in prices and tariffs should be programmed at zero; and the wage increase of wages at the rate of the increase in productivity, that is, at around 3–4 percent, in the first year. If the nominal wage rises by 4 percent and prices remain more or less stable, the real wage increases by 4 percent, and this represents a substantial improvement as compared to 1995, when the real wage diminished.

Our proposal for zero inflation has often been misunderstood and, wrongly interpreted. By planning the increase in prices and wages according to the increase in productivity of the production system, our intention was to make the inflation of producers' prices fall to zero within one year—and this was duly achieved. Since the retail price index, or cost of living, is notably out of phase with respect to producers' prices, the fall in the cost of living was planned to be more gradual. And precisely to safeguard a certain increase in real wages, that is, purchasing power, in my work with Baldassari and Castiglionesi we proposed an initial wage increase in the first year a little above the productivity: 5 percent, instead of 4 percent, but phased in during the course of the year. This wage adjustment and the above mentioned led us to maintain that in the first year inflation could be reduced to only 3 percent. But, in the second year, inflation fell to 1.5 percent, as against the 3.7 percent forecast by the Confindustria at that time.

For that this ambitious program to reduce inflation and interest rates to succeed, it was essential that the other cause of inflation, the exchange rate of the lira, should not create problems with depreciation, as had occurred in March 1995. But we were confident that the exchange rate would continue to revalue in support of our plan, instead of against it. The reason can be summed up in a well-known expression: the game of the virtuous circle. The initial fall in inflation, rates, and thus the deficit, would enhance the trust of the international markets in the solvancy of the government and in the favorable prospects for the exchange rate, and this would help to reduce the risk premium and hence the interest rates, further diminishing the deficit and having beneficial effects on inflation and real wages, which would make for more trust, and so on—all of which came true as we shall see in the next section.

At the end of the process of stabilization, but not until the end, we outlined two scenarios, both equally possible and equally valid: either the common currency would come into being, and the lira will be part of it; or it would not, in which case the Italian government would have the possibility of beginning to issue bonds denominated in German marks. For each currency differential of interest rates depends on the movement of the exchange rate. We assume that at the end of the stabilization process, with zero inflation, the exchange rate between the lira and the mark can be fixed by unilateral decision. If you maintain the stability with the mark, you pay your creditors the German interest rate, while if you issue dollar bonds you pay the American rate minus the depreciation of the dollar against the mark. If the mark tends to revalue with respect to the other currencies, maintaining stability with the mark may be difficult, since it could signify revaluation of the exchange rate with the dollar, which might penalize exports and favor imports.

Luckily, scenario number one was what actually occurred.

36   The Possible Miracle Comes True

One year after our plan, in the summer of 1997, a quick glance by an impartial observer would have shown that things were going according to the predictions of Tthe Possible Miracle. Zero inflation of producers' prices, upon which the plan was based, had been achieved despite the general skepticism that greeted it. The consumer's price index inflation registered around 1.6–1.8 percent, well below the expected value, which was a pleasant surprise. As we had thought, the fall in inflation was accompanied by a strong revaluation of the exchange rate, which actually fell below 1,000 lire to the mark, as we had suggested would be appropriate for the end of the program. And all this went hand-in-hand with a drop in short-term, and especially long-term, interest rates. As hypothesized in the Possible Miracle, this fall reflected the virtuous circle on which we had relied, once again in the teeth of the ever-growing skepticism of colleagues, opinion leaders, and politicians. In itself, the fall in inflation directly reduced the interest rates and hence the deficit. This strengthened the faith in the lira, revalued the exchange rate, and consolidated trust in the credit-worthiness of the state, which attracted investment and made it increasingly likely that Italy would join the euro and that, therefore, in a relatively short time, the Italian rates (both short- and long-term) would conform to the others in the system, especially the German ones. On May 2, 1988, Italy joined the euro together with ten other countries of the European Union.

But despite this rosy picture, one must not lose sight of the difficult passage from beginning to happy end and the many crises by which it was interrupted it. For several months after the Prodi government took office, there were serious doubts as to whether unions and employers would manage to agree on the wage moderation and rapid deceleration of inflation that were the underpinnings of our plan. In the last round of wage negotiations the unions had started out with very large claims, and for a long time they were encouraged in this by Fausto Bertinotti, who talked of high wage increases without mentioning their effect on inflation and thus, in his siren song, confusing nominal increases with real increases, which were achievable with wage moderation. I think the government did not do as much as it could to press for lower inflation through a three-sided negotiation; nevertheless, it stood up to Bertinotti. The governor of the Bank of Italy, on his side, pursued a restrictive monetary policy, with high short-term rates, despite the capital inflow, making it clear that he would not assist job creation until there was evidence of moderation in wages and profits.

So, in the end and after much toil, fairly reasonable wage contracts were achieved, even if they were a little more generous than what was desirable, partly owing to the excessive concessions already made by the Dini government with an eye to the election. This line was also favored by a series of severe fiscal maneuvers linked to the ever-firmer intention of reducing the deficit to the 3 percent entailed by Maastricht since 1997.

The first maneuver was operated immediately after the Prodi government took office and was followed by the presentation of the Economic-Financial Programming Document of 1996, which, contrary to our plan, continued to speak of a 4.5 deficit for 1997, but allowed for the possibility of setting "a more ambitious target than 4.5 percent." Subsequently, in September 1996, the Prodi government decided to aim as hard as possible at immediate entry into the euro. This became a central commitment by the government, on both the domestic and foreign fronts, to the point of making its very survival depended on it.

The result was the big reduction of the budget deficit totaling 70 thousand billion lire. At first, I was critical of it, for on the one hand it looked excessive, on the other full of accounting artifices. I found it excessive, partly because it was not necessary, with inflation already under control, and also because I feared its negative repercussions. But my viewed changed after studying it and talking it over in a frank and instructive exchange with my dear old friend Nino Andreatta, at a meeting organized at Modigliana by the Accademia degli Incamminati.

In an article I wrote with Mario Baldassarri in the *Corriere della Sera*, we concluded that this was in reality an extremely skillful mini-budget, for its "false" and purely transitory measures reduced its size to a level we approved and that did not do excessive harm to the economy. They were moreover justified by the fact that similar, or worse, artifices had been introduced into the budgets of France, Spain, and ultimately Germany. For that matter, the idea of a "tax for Europe," stated as transitory like some other provisions, was justifiable through the mnechanism of the virtuous cycle described in our program, which was to bring about a considerable fall in interest rates and thus reduce the need for financing the deficit. Trust in Italy oscillated between high and low, as did exchange and interest rates, in connection with the discussions on the likelihood of the country's joining the euro and the statements of certain financial circles in Germany bent on using the markets to obstruct Italy's participation in the first round of Maastricht. As against that, a beneficial effect was produced by Italy's re-entry into the exchange agreements of the European Monetary System, at a central parity of 990 lire against the German mark, slightly below the 1,000 lire recommended by us.

At long last the miracle was performed. Pessimists can still be heard saying that Italy's recovery has been too rapid to be "sustainable." This shows a failure to appreciate the most original contribution in our book: the miracle was no miracle, but an egg of Columbus. The patient got well again because the illness, that is, the huge deficit, was in great part only fictitious, being due to faulty accounting.

37   Social Security

I   OVERVIEW OF THE PROBLEM AND PROPOSED SOLUTION

A mandated public pension system can be said to aim at helping those covered by it to follow behavior as the rational saver postulated in the Life Cycle Hypothesis of saving (LCH). Those enrolled pay to the pension system a part of their earnings in the working period (the period of the "fat cows"), and subsequently receive a pension in the years after they cease to earn (the period of the "lean cows"). In concept, the pension is assured and paid at a constant (real) level until death.

In the United States, there is such a public pension system known as "Social Security." It has worked quite well for nearly seventy years, but as everybody knows, it is now running into serious problems. The problem is due to population aging: If nothing is done to change the system, receipts from participants' contributions will not be sufficient to cover the pensions that have been promised. Deficits are expected to begin in the next decade and to grow gradually larger. Initially, they can be covered by reserves accumulated earlier, and with government contributions made possible by the anticipated fiscal surplus. However, by the middle of the next decade, it is expected that in order to keep the system solvent, it will require an increase in contribution from the present 12.5 percent to some 20 percent, or by 50 percent, or else a reduction of benefits by one third. This, in essence, is what is referred to as the "Social Security Crisis," and it affects not only the United States but also most of developed countries.

The problem, although easy to understand, is not easy to solve. To be sure, many solutions have been proposed. But all the solutions offered so far require a combination of the following: (i) a prospective rise in contributions; (ii) a cut in benefits; and (iii) an increase in investment risk to be borne by participants. However, a recent paper co-authored with two former students and close collaborators, Marialuisa Ceprini and Arun Muralidhar, shows that currently the United States has a unique opportunity to adopt a solution that would ensure the indefinite maintenance of the existing, popular SS benefits, and in addition, would make it possible to reduce, gradually, SS payroll taxes by a large amount.[52]

The solution relies on the gradual replacement of the existing pay-as-you-go (Paygo) method of financing SS benefits with a fully funded system invested in a common portfolio. A painless transition is made possible by: (i) the (transitory) current and prospective SS surplus, (ii) the budget surplus, already pledged to SS, and (iii) an imaginative investment policy for the Trust Funds (TF), which aims for the highest return consistent with long-run stability and with proper concern for minimizing the role of government in financial markets.

To understand the difference between these two ways of financing pensions (pay-as-you-go versus funded), we have to go back a bit in history. Before the creation of national compulsory pension systems, there were private systems based on voluntary initiatives usually offered by employers, as part of the remuneration, for example by the state, for its employees. The contributions of employee and employer were accumulated in a fund that ensured the employees an annuity on retirement—hence the name of "funded "system."

Lately, funded pension schemes came into being whereby the employee and employer paid so much per year to an insurance company and the amount accumulated through the annual payment and the interest accruing was then converted into an annuity, but the amount of accumulation and the annuity was not specified, but left to be determined ("defined contributions").

In the 1930s, at the time of Roosevelt's New Deal, a highly ambitious national pension scheme was introduced that took its cue from a Bismarck model—known as Social Security. It was a national compulsory scheme in which everybody contributed in proportion to income, and at retirement each would get a pension based on his contribution. The essential, innovative difference between this system and the traditional funded system consisted of the manner in which the pensions were financed. In the traditional approach, they were financed through the accumulation and later liquidation of earning assets. In the new system they were instead financed through so-called "pay-as-you-go" (Paygo), that is, from the current contributions of those working. Why was this method chosen over the traditional one? The answer is simple. Under a funded scheme, pensions are based on the accumulated reserves. This means that when a new system is started none of the retired people is initially entitled to a pensions, and older people will receive only small pensions. But having founded a national pension system, it was thought fair to pay pensions to all retired people, whether they had had an opportunity to contribute or not. There was only one way of doing that, namely, the Paygo system. It resulted, of course, in a large gift to the retired and older people, who received a pension for which they had contributed nothing or very little. Scant attention was paid to the fact that against that initial advantage the Paygo system is seriously inferior to a funded system in many respects:

1. For a given set of benefits, the fully funded system generally requires smaller contributions, and the difference can be very substantial. This is because under Paygo the current contributions are needed to pay the current pensions, whereas with funding they are entirely invested in income-earning assets, and accumulate at compound interest for the benefit of the participants. The earnings from these assets make it possible to reduce the required cash contribution. The size of possible saving depends on the relation between the rate of return on the accumulated assets relative to the "implicit" interest that can be offered by Paygo, which (as is well-known) is the rate of growth of (real) payrolls. Our proposal envisages that the mandated pension saving should be given the opportunity to earn a return commensurate with the overall return on capital. At present and in the foreseeable future, this rate substantially exceeds the possible growth of payrolls, implying lower contributions with a funded system. Using the latest projections of payroll growth provided by the Social Security Administration (SSA) under the "intermediate cost case," and a conservative estimate of the return to capital (with risk adjustment) of around 5 percent, we find that by the

middle of the century the required OASDI (Old Age, Survivors and Disability Insurance) contribution with our funded system is around 6.2 percent. This is approximately one third of the required Paygo contribution, which by 2075 is expected to approach 19.5 percent. (The above reduction measures the gain to be expected at the end of the "transition," when the funded system has reached full funding. During the transition, the reduction will occur gradually.

2. An even more serious shortcoming of the Paygo system is that the contribution required to secure given retirement benefits is very sensitive to the rate of growth of labor income (adjusted for inflation). The reason is that your pension is paid by a fraction of the current payrolls; therefore, the ratio of what you can get to what you paid depends on the ratio of current payrolls to payrolls at the time you were contributing, which is the rate of growth. Whether the payroll growth declines because of a decline in population or in productivity growth, there will be fewer young workers' earnings contributing to, relative to the number of older retired people collecting from, Social Security. Receipts will fall short of the benefits promised. The current so-called Social Security crisis affecting the United States and many other countries on a Paygo system stems precisely from the fact that the pensions the system is committed to pay at present (and for a long time in the future) were based on projections of payroll growth that were much too optimistic, as they did not allow for the dramatic decline in growth, especially population growth, in all developed countries. For the United States, as indicated earlier, if we retain the Paygo, the decreasing growth between the present and the middle of the century would require an increase in contribution of 50 percent. It can be shown that with funding, the required contribution is not only smaller, but also much less sensitive to possible unanticipated changes in relevant "exogenous" variables, such as the rate of growth of population and productivity, or life expectancy.

   First, in a funded system, the required contribution is basically unaffected by growth-related changes in the "demographic structure," because the pension is not paid by the contributions of the younger workers, but by the capital accumulated by the pensioner. Second, changes in productivity growth (or life expectancy)[51] do require some changes in contributions, but only to a minor degree compared with those required under a Paygo system. The main determinant of the required contribution is the (long-run average) return on the Trust investment. But, we demonstrate that even variations in this variable, within historically realistic limits, would not require drastic changes in the contribution rate. We conclude, therefore, that the funded system is far less exposed to the threat of insolvency that plagues the Paygo systems.

3 The funded system (in contrast to Paygo) results in a large accumu-lation of assets and thus makes a valuable contribution to national saving, during the funding process and thereafter (at least as long as income is rising) to the stock of productive capital and national income. This rise in saving is especially valuable at a time like the present, when private saving is unusually low, creating worrisome problems about the level of foreign indebtedness. It is interesting that this effect on saving was not given attention at the start of the Paygo system; one is tempted to explain this by recalling that the system was started in the depth of the depression, when many were concerned with over-saving, rather than under-saving.

4. Finally, one should expect that the much lower contributions required by a funded scheme would reduce the labor market distor-tions created by the current system, encouraging greater participa-tion in the labor force and less evasion of SS contributions. There is some evidence that the enormous Social Security payroll taxes levied in Europe (frequently three times as large as in the United States) bear some responsibility for the huge unemployment rate.

II   ALTERNATIVE WAYS OF ACHIEVING FUNDING

Many of the "experts" agree by now on the superiority of a funded system (at least partial) over Paygo once the steady state has been reached. But one can identify two major areas of disagreement that we will examine in turn. The first relates to the best way to achieve funding, while the second relates to the cost of transition (or non-transition) from Paygo to funding—and whether those costs are worth incurring.

With respect to the first issue, there are two major proposals: one that is very popular at present under the misnomer of privatization of Social Security would require (or at least allow) participants to redirect all or part of their present, mandated contributions from SS to personal accounts, individually managed, with wide discretion. It would result in replacing the present system of "defined benefits" with one of "defined contributions." The other proposal, which we firmly advocate, is to keep the present system of contributions and benefits and to direct all the accumulation into a common Trust Fund. We will elaborate on our proposal first, and then show why it is widely superior to "privatization."

III   A Bird's-Eye View of Our Proposal

III.1   Funding with a Current Portfolio

The first essential and distinctive aspect of our proposal is to make it possible to maintain intact the present structure of Social Security defined benefits. No other funding proposal ensures this highly desirable result. The essential feature of the present structure is that the benefits are predictably based on a participant's life contributions, and guaranteed by the State. The participant is entitled to retire at some standard age (65 at present and gradually increasing over time) with a real pension, which, on the average, represents a replacement rate of roughly 50 percent of her "average life income" (the average wage of her best thirty-five years). But the average replacement rate hides the "progressive" nature of the SS program. In fact, the marginal replacement rate declines notably as the life income of the recipient rises.

To make operational a promise to maintain defined (real) benefits, a pension system must be able to count on a fixed (real) rate of return that is the same for all participants (excluding adjustments for redistribution). We achieve this goal through two devices. The first is by investing participants' contributions in one common highly diversified portfolio consisting of a share of the total United States market portfolio. Such a portfolio is known to have efficiency properties, can be inexpensive to manage, and leaves no portfolio management discretion to politicians or bureaucrats. Note that the recommended portfolio would include stocks and bonds in the market proportions, which is currently around two thirds in stocks and one third in bonds.

In order to ensure that the common real return be fixed, we make use of a recently developed financial contract, namely a swap, between SS and the Treasury. Under this contract, the pension system would exchange the (uncertain) return derived from its market portfolio for a payment by the Treasury of a fixed real return, on the order of 5 percent, safely below the expected (before tax) real market return.

This approach clearly shifts to the government the risk that the market return deviates from that guaranteed to SS. But we contend that the

United States government can afford to and should absorb this risk because of its size and indefinite life. It can spread the risk of a single portfolio over a whole cohort, and that of a single cohort of workers over a large number of cohorts. More important, it should be prepared to undertake the role of insurer of last resort in consideration of the externality that would come from guaranteeing to older Americans the peace of mind that they deserve.

IV   PRIVATIZATION

This approach was first introduced in Chile (aiming at total funding), followed by several South American and other developing countries (World Bank 1994, James and Vittas 1995). In the United States, the best-known formulations of privatization aim at a mixed system with only partial funding, and possibly an "opt-out" provision (e.g., President Bush, Congressmen Archer and Shaw, Professor Feldstein).

We maintain that "privatization" is substantially inferior to our proposal in at least five dimensions:

1. It would eliminate the existing defined and progressive benefits and replace them with "defined contributions"—where in exchange for lifetime mandated contributions, participants do not get a predictable guaranteed pension, but one proportional to the uncertain, erratic performance of one's personal portfolio—that is, in essence, a "lottery ticket." Participants' retirement income will depend on their luck in choosing their portfolio and the date of retirement— whether at the height of a bull or bear market. To require or even encourage people to gamble their retirement nest egg is irreconcilable with the spirit of the current system, which aims at ensuring a minimum retirement income. Indeed, on close reflection, one must conclude that, since the amount and timing of contributions continue to be mandated by the State, the only important thing that privatization "'privatizes"' is individual risk—that is, precisely what a well-designed system would want to share.

2. Privatization has the highly undesirable effect of fostering manmade inequalities in the distribution of retirement income. Under the individual portfolio approach, the average of the returns of all portfolios must be close to the average return of the entire market, which is precisely the return on our common portfolio. But while the average return is essentially the same—except for the much

higher management cost of individual portfolios—in our scheme everybody secures that average, whereas with individual portfolios the individual returns will exhibit wide dispersion even with identical contributions. Some will end up above average and be offset by those who do worse, and among them there will be many whose income is too low to bear such downside risk. The inequalities generated by privatization are especially repellent because they are artificial and serve no useful (e.g., incentive) functions.

3. Individual portfolios will tend to increase the gap between the rich and the poor in two ways: (a) the rich will be in a position to gain more from the option, as they have more investment experience, access to better advice and tools, lower management costs, and because they can better afford the risks inherent in equities and other more remunerative but riskier investments; they will end up with a higher return on their retirement saving; (b) basing the pension on the individual account would eliminate the re-distributional aspect of the present system in which a fraction of the accumulation of the rich is used to subsidize the pensions of the poor. Put differently, the rich are credited with a somewhat lower return than the poor are. This provides a further inducement for the rich to "opt out," if the option is offered, and invest in their own portfolio. As they do so, the subsidy is taken away from the poor and returned to the rich. In the end, the poor will receive smaller pensions or will have to contribute more, while the pensions of the rich will be enhanced.

4. Managing individual portfolios can be very costly, especially for small portfolios. This is confirmed by the South American experience (Guerrard 1998). Managing the fully indexed large portfolio of the SS will cost a small fraction of 1 percent.

5. Some of the privatization advocates understand the dangers posed by downside risk at least for the poor, and have suggested amendments that would ensure some minimum outcome (Feldstein 1996). But these remedies are highly unsatisfactory, for they would encourage excessive risk-taking, since the participants would retain any favorable outcome while unloading unfavorable ones onto SS. This free option is not only economically inefficient, but also may be expected to increase very substantially the contribution that must be charged to keep the system solvent (Muralidhar and van der Wouden 1998).

We conclude that, in general, privatization is a highly irrational approach to funding as compared with our "common fund," unless it is limited to a very small fraction of pension financing or is justified by special circumstances. We have found that much of the opposition to our proposal comes from people who erroneously identify funding with individually managed portfolios, thus failing to understand the essence of our plan: funding with a common portfolio and defined benefits.

V   THE TRANSITION

How do we move from Paygo to a fully funded system? This is the so-called "transition problem" that has been regarded as the major obstacle to moving to a capitalized system. This basically requires funding the unfunded liabilities of the existing Paygo system. It is widely believed that this would impose an intolerably heavy burden on the transition generation, which would be required to pay a double contribution: one to build the new capitalized system and the other to SS to pay the current promised pensions. Drawing on the basics of pension finance and with the help of a number of simulations, we demonstrate that this view generally exaggerates the transition cost. In particular, we show that the United States is in the lucky position of being able to secure all of the additional resources needed to fund the system, without ever raising payroll contributions. The sources of funds to bear this transition cost are: (i) the reserves accumulating in the SS Trust Fund from past surpluses; (ii) the further surpluses accumulating until the middle of the decade; (iii) a portion of the expected budget surplus (which had already been promised to SS by President Clinton); and (iv) an investment policy thatwhich einsures a high and yet safe return.

These four sources, when accumulated and bolstered by a reasonable rate of return, commensurate with the economy wide return on capital, can be shown to be sufficient to carry out the transition to full funding, without ever raising the required contributions, though at the cost of a rather slow transition. The time that is required to complete the transition is long, but it cannot be measured precisely. This is because we can demonstrate that there are multiple possible transition paths to full funding that involve a trade-off between the time at which one begins to cut contributions and the length of time to final equilibrium.

On the basis of the intermediate cost assumption of the Social Security, we find that the shortest time needed to reach full funding can be estimated at about sixty years. But this is not a realistic program, for it would mean that up to 2060 the contributions would stay at the present level of

12.5 percent and then decline abruptly to 6.2 percent. This clearly would result in all the advantage of the reform going to younger cohorts, and none to those retiring in 2060, creating a serious problem of intergenerational inequity. But our approach permits alternative transition paths, in which the cuts begin earlier, to the advantage of older cohorts but at the expense of the younger cohorts that will have to make higher contributions and for a longer time.

The attached graph shows one possible such path for which contributions begin to be cut in 2035, by 1.5 percent and after the middle of the century by half a point every five years, until the funding is completed and the contribution remains fixed at 6.2 percent. But this particular path is not very attractive because it would result in all the advantage of the reform going to younger cohorts and none to those retiring in 2060 or earlier, even though the earlier generation had contributed to the funding process; it would create an unacceptable intergenerational equity problem. But our approach permits alternative transition paths, in which the cuts begin earlier, to the advantage of older cohorts and disadvantage of the younger cohorts that will have to make higher contributions and for a longer time. The graph also shows the estimated behavior of the so-called cost ratio— the ratio of pensions paid to total payroll; it is frequently referred to as the "equilibrium" contribution ratio because, under Paygo, it measures the contribution rate needed to balance the Social Security budget. The rise in the cost ratio from 10.5 to nearly 20 percent reflects the decline in the growth of payrolls and is the cause of the "Social Security crisis."

If Social Security were on a strict Paygo regime, the U.S. contribution rate would have to follow the path of the cost ratio. But in fact we abandoned strict Paygo quite a while ago with the Greenspan reform, which, foreseeing dangers of future insolvency, raised contributions to produce a surplus. That surplus has already resulted in a contingency reserve (the Trust Fund) and is expected to continue until the middle of the next decade. The Clinton Administration plan is also shown in Figure A, by the curve so labeled. Its essential feature is the endeavor to maintain, as long as possible, the current contribution rate of 12.5 percent, making use of the three surpluses (Trust Funds, Social Security, and budget) to fill the increasing gap between the Cost Ratio and the constant contribution rate. Unfortunately, according to the present forecast of the Social Security Administration, by the early 2050s all the reserve will have been exhausted at a time when the currency deficit is at a maximum and is expected to grow further. Hence, to keep the system solvent, it would be necessary to raise the Paygo contribution to the level of the Cost Ratio, which by then is about 18 percent, while our contribution rate is down to 11 percent; and is expected to rise further to some 20 percent, while we are moving down to just over 6 percent!

Figure A is helpful in countering certain criticisms that have been raised against the implementation of our approach. Specifically it has been objected that, even granting that our program is capable of ensuring a transition to a fully funded system, there is no valid reason to jettison the existing Paygo system and undertake the rather extensive reforms that we are proposing. The justification for this view is that there is no real short-term crisis in sight if we keep the current structure. After all, with the help of the intended government subsidy, and the small investment of the TF in equities, contemplated by the Administration, we can go past the middle of the next century without raising contributions or cutting benefits. Are we not making a big fuss about what might happen after most of the people now alive will be dead?

This argument is really untenable. It is true that we normally do not take current measures for things that might occur in the distant future; but this is because typically there is great uncertainty about the implications of the occurrence and about the effectiveness of measures taken far in advance. But in the present instance, because of the predictable nature of demographic development and the sluggishness of productivity growth, we can be pretty sure that if we irresponsibly retain the current Paygo system, by the middle of the next century pension payments well in excess of the current contribution will have exhausted accumulated reserves and will plunge the SS into a financial quandary. This will only be resolved by a huge rise in contributions and/or a cut in benefits. Furthermore, as our simulations show, the measures needed to avoid that trauma must be started a long time earlier, such as right now. Failure to do so would be irresponsible. It has been said that SS is a time bomb with a very long fuse; we answer that the fuse of the remedies is even longer.

VI   PEERING INTO THE FUTURE

I am convinced that our reform, or one along those lines (perhaps involving some mixture of funding and a small share of Paygo), offers a satisfactory solution and the best presently on the table. Does this mean that I am optimistic about the chances of its being implemented? Well, my life experience suggests that the answer is no! Of the handful of good policy suggestions that I have advocated in my life, few have been adopted, some too late, and mostly without acknowledgment. But I promise that I will promote our reform energetically—and for the rest, time (whatever remains) will tell.

38   Epilogue

Some of my best students who have become fellow economists are Italians. Italy is distinguished by an incredible ferment of intelligence, passion, the will to do and understand. And yet, each time Serena and I go to Italy something or other happens to annoy us. What is this something-or-other? On one famous occasion Serena went to the post office to buy five airmail stamps for the U.S. But the clerk told her he did not have them and, besides, if he had them he could only sell her a minimum of 100. Serena could not believe her ears. So she went home and looked in the telephone directory and called a number for "complaints." She told the man who answered that she was an American and she could not believe what the Postal clerk had told her. This polite gentleman asked her details about which post office had given her such a ridiculous answer and added, "Signora, please go back tomorrow and you will be given your five stamps. I am sorry you were given such an answer." And this was absolutely true: The same clerk, with a very sour face, gave her what he had clearly been ordered to do! The attitudes of people such as the postal clerk are slowly changing, especially when it becomes possible to fire employees who are too lazy to serve the public.

Another fault of the Italians is the belief that enforcement of the law is optional. On untold occasions we have discussed with friends, cultured liberal people, who claimed that it was understandable to evade taxes because, "in any case, the state squanders the money it collects . . ." More recently I have heard it said that not paying taxes is OK because, "politicians pocket our money in bribes." It has always seemed incredible that people fail to see how this mentality creates the psychological basis for corruption. By the same token, I have always found it surprising that Italians in general don't realize that tax evasion makes the burdern heavier for everybody. For years, Italy's rates of taxation have been downright theft. If paid up to the last penny, they would have reduced the taxpayer to sheer poverty. So the system assumed that taxes would be evaded and actually sanctioned this. I recall how in 1972 there was talk of the fiscal reform with which Luigi Preti was to introduce the IRPEF (income tax) and the tax substitute., a measure that led half the Italians (the defendant workers) to pay taxes, while the other half were left free to dodge them. Bue the situation that existed previously was absolutely unbelievable, one of illegality and immorality instituted by law. This was why, at the time, I was extremely sceptical as to the feasibility of reform, as I explained in an interview with *Il Mondo*:

It is essential that taxpayers fulfill their duty toward the tax authority, but also that the authority enable them to perform this duty. As, against that, Italy's current system is, in practice, based on the principle that not all pay as much as they should in due amount. On the other hand, those who paid what they owe could not survive. The tax authority mistrusts the taxpayers, and right; but even if they latter told the truth they would be disbelieved just the same. We have, then, an overmighty authority with a total disbelief in the honesty of citizens, while the latter, on the side, have the inveterate habit of not telling the truth. I feel that any reform of the tax system ought first and foremost to aim at setting reasonable rates, making it possible for an honest person to pay the taxes and continue to live decently.[52]

The roots of this aberration lay in an anthropological vision of unbelievable pessimism, which in turn provided the basis for an immoral judicial system:

The tax return should be considered genuine until it is proved false. The principle force in Italy, that provides for negotiation between tax inspectors and taxpayers, is the most obnoxious of all systems: the citizen tells lies, then does a deal. But if a person tells the truth, there's nothing to negotiate. If he lies he must be punished for fraud. In short, the whole principle behind the transaction must be abolished.

The situation was improved by the 1973 reform. But the distorted principle is found everywhere in Italian history and society. Ultimately, what are the official remissions and amnesties, periodically proclaimed, if not the old distorted system of deals between authority and citizens rearing its ugly head once more?

Even more unbelieveable is that in Italy, from time to time, the profound immorality of the civil society and the administration is put forward as an advantage, a "model." For many years, from the end of the 1970s through the 1980s, I attended the seminars of the Studio Ambrosetti at Villa d'Este, Cernobbio. The first occasion was in 1979. A horrible year. The year of the cowardly attack on the Bank of Italy. The year Paolo Baffi and Mario Sarcinelli were made to suffer. But it was also the year when Professor De Rita devised the idea of the "underground" economy for interpreting Italian society. The problem was a real one, a reading of the official economic statistics suggested that Italy should have been sailing in stormy waters for some time, but here was Italy going along quite nicely, all things considered. Why? Well, that glorification of the "underground" economy made me mad. And I said so openly.

> The flourishing of the underground system in Italy is based largely on disobeying laws and regulations currently in force, and therefore relies on exploiting that part of the economy that cannot avoid observing those laws and regulations. In consequence, no one can tell to what extent this underground economy is effectively flourishing and healthy, ie, in equal conditions to compete with the "regular" part of the economy. Secondly, the underground economy generates instability. For, basing itself on exploitation of the open economy, it undermines the roots of its development, as a parasite kills the tree to which it attaches itself. Moreover, in so far as it is successful, it attracts into the underground ever new portions of activity thus increasing the opportunities for judicial uncertainty and tax evasion. I therefore have serious doubts as to whether the illegality of the submerged economy and the protection of the law can be reconciled, as is claimed by those who argue in support of adaptation. If the illegality is allowed very little room it may even be true that the phenomenon is a vital one, economically speaking. But the situation is certainly destructive where the economic operators feel entitled to obey the law only when it suits them or where they fail to find somebody to bribe. In a state of law a principle of this kind cannot be justified by any model of growth based on the capacity for adaptation. The state, however limited its power, is necessary for the good of all, without the state, no economic system can survive.

These feelings were summed up in an interview I had with Gian Antonio Stella in the *Corriere della Sera* on April 20, 1998 titled, "Modigliani: Italians, don't try to be crafty." I quote: "The capital sin of the Italians, their worst vice, their most unforgivable fault is craftiness. Not to pay your taxes or to cheat INPS is normal. You do it if you care. Oh, dear me! The only thing I find consoling is at least that now they have learned not to cheat as exporters because clients abroad would not forgive them . . . But long ago we were in Vietri and we bought and paid for a pottery service for eight, which was supposed to be sent to the U.S. It never arrived . . . What a great country Italy would be if there was less cheating."

After the interview was published, something happened that we found very touching: We were at home when the phone rang, Serena answered and I was puzzled by her end of the conversation. It was the mayor of Vietri apologizing on behalf of his town for the loss of our service! He wanted to send us another and Serena kept reassuring him that this was long ago, it was not his fault, and in 1955 we were young, now we were 80 years old, and we had bought m any other services, maybe too many. We were grateful for his call, but we didn't need a thing.

This episode showed us that Italy is changing and hopefully dignity and honesty are taking over.

TWILIGHT

Here we are in 2001 and I've reached the age of 82. Ten years ago I attained the age limit and officially retired (becoming Institute Professor Emeritus), but in actual fact I continue to work as before: I pursue the various problems dealt with in this book and every now and then I hold a special course devoted to critical examination of my main academic contributions. MIT has done me the honor of creating a chair in my name (the Franco Modigliani Chair of Financial Economics), collecting a sum of $2 million dollars, subscribed by several firms and financial institutions and by ex-students, half of them American, half Italian.

When I look back on my life, I must say how lucky I have been. I have always enjoyed myself, doing what I did., I've worked hard, but always with satisfaction and joy. I was lucky to escape the holocaust, lucky to become American, lucky in my marriage and in my two sons, André, a professor of sociology, and Sergio, an architect. Lucky, too, in my grandchildren: Leah, the eldest, a financial economist employed at Morgan Stanley; Julia, an intelligent scholar of early childhood and deeply committed teacher; David, a young poet who at 21 years of age is a senior at Harvard; and Amelia, the youngest, studying at Milton Academy and getting ready to enter college. All of them healthy, good, bright, affectionate, and intelligent into the bargain. And now, sugar on the cake, a great-granddaughter, Micaela, the one year old daughter of Julia, is our joy.

In 1996 I had the great satisfaction of publishing some research done with Leah on a classical topic: calculating the return on a portfolio corrected for the amount of risk inherent in the investment. This measurement, now becoming quite popular through inter alia subsequent writings by Leah, is known today as M^2 (M-squared) because it's the product of two Modiglianis.

But my greatest pleasure of all is when someone from Wall Street asks me if I'm related to Leah Modigliani, or when the parents of one of Julia's pupils compliment her to her granddad for her outstanding teaching ability and the love she inspires in her pupils.

NOTES

Chapter I

[1] For example, let us suppose that in a country the currency unit is called the "buck," that the domestic income is 1,000 bucks per year, and the stock of money held is 250 bucks. In this case k is 0.25, that is, the stock of money demanded represents one quarter of GNP per year. k represents characteristics of the economy such as payment habits and technology, and can therefore be different for different countries or at different times, but does not depend on Y or M.

[2] Thus, in the above example, since a stock of 250 bucks finances an annual income—final sales—of 1,000 bucks, the velocity of circulation of each unit of currency is, on average, 4 times a year.

[3] In our example, if the price of a basket of goods is 2 bucks per basket and the nominal quantity of money is 250 bucks, then the *real* stock for money demanded is 250 bucks/2 (bucks per basket) = 125 baskets. In other words, in that economy people want to keep in cash a nominal value whose purchasing power is equivalent to 125 baskets.

[4] In 1942 Lord Beveridge presented his famous report, *Social Insurance and Allied Services*, the result of work by an interministerial commission, chaired by him, which laid the basis for the welfare state. Later, on his own initiative, he produced a second report titled *Full Employment in a Free Society* (London, 1944).

[5] J. S. Duesenberry, *Income, Saving and the Theory of Consumer Behavior* (Harvard University Press, Cambridge, MA, 1949).

[6] S. Kuznets, *National Income: A Summary of Findings* (New York: National Bureau of Economic Research, 1946).

[7] D. Brady and R. D. Friedman, "Saving and the Income Distribution," in *Studies on Income and Wealth*, Vol. X (New York: National Bureau of Economic Research, 1947).

[8] I can personally claim vast experience in this field as, a little before Italy entered World War I in 1915, my parents bought a house in Trastevere with my mother's marriage dowry. Soon after Italy's entry into the war, the rents were frozen (and remained so for decades). In 1973, however, after sixty years of frozen rents, I unfortunately sold the house, because in the meantime it had become very decrepit. If I remember rightly, the rents at around $10 a month were insufficient for maintenance work, and one's only hope was that the awful state of the apartments and the fabric would persuade the tenants to leave. Thus, I refused to go on being the landlord of a hovel, which goes against my conscience. With the proceeds of the sale I bought first a farm in the clean atmosphere of New Hampshire, and then part of a house by the sea, which we continue to enjoy with a clear conscience.

[9] F. Modigliani, *"The Life Cycle Hypothesis of Saving, the Demand for Wealth and the Supply of Capital,"* published in Social Research, No. 3 (Summer 1966), pp. 160–217, and reprinted in *The Collected Papers of Franco Modigliani*, Vol. 2, *The Life Cycle Hypothesis of Saving*, ed. A. Abel (Cambridge, MA: MIT University Press, 1980), p. 323: The figure is on p. 328.

[10] *Ibid.*, Vol. 2, p. 128. The two tables are on p. 139 and p. 141, respectively.

[11] F. Modigliani and R. Brumberg, *"Utility Analysis and the Consumption Function: An Interpretation of Cross Section Data,"* in K. Kurihara (ed.), *Post Keynesian Economics* (New Brunswick, NJ: Rutgers University Press, 1954), pp. 388–436, afterward reprinted in *The Collected Papers of Franco Modigliani*, Vol. 2, op. cit.

[12] The second article I published much later, in 1979, under the title *"Utility Analysis and Aggregate Consumption Functions: An Attempt at Integration,"* in *The Collected Papers of Franco Modigliani*, Vol. 2, op. cit.

[13] I. Fisher, *The Theory of Interest* (New York: Macmillan, 1930).

[14] U. Ricci, "L'offerta di risparmio," *Giornale degli Economisti e Annali di Economia*, 67 (February 1926), pp. 73–101, and March 1926, pp. 117–147; "Ancora sull'offerta di risparmio," ibid., 68 (September 1926), pp. 481–504.

[15] See especially *"The Permanent Income and the Life Cycle Hypothesis of Saving Behavior: Comparison and Tests,"* with A. Ando, in *The Collected Papers of Franco Modigliani*, Vol. 2, op cit., pp. 229–274.

[16] This result is reported in the classic article by Bardy and Friedman, "Saving and the Income Distribution," *Studies on Income and Wealth*, Vol. X, op cit., pp. 247–265.

[17] This hypothesis was originally put forward by Sir Roy Harrod in *Toward a Dynamic Economics* (London: Macmillan, 1948), with the name of *Hump Saving*. Actually, the hump is in the wealth, not necessarily in the saving.

[18] *International Comparison of Personal Saving*, ed. J. Poterba (Chicago: The University of Chicago Press, 1994).

[19] *Introduction Growth and Trade. Essays in Honour of Sir Roy Harrod*, ed. W. A. Eltis, M. F. Scott, and J. M. Wolfe (Oxford: Clarendon Press, 1970), pp. 197–225.

[20] "Perché è diminuito il saggio di risparmio in Italia," *Istituzioni e mercato nello sviluppo economico. Saggi in onore di Paolo Sylos Labini* (Rome-Bari: Laterza, 1990).

[21] *The Chinese Saving Puzzle*, in publication.

[22] "Recenti diminuzioni dei saggi di risparmio," *Risparmio, accumulazione, sviluppo*, ed. M; Baldassari, L. Paganetto and E. S. Phelps (Rome: SIPI, Rome, 1991).

[23] M. Feldstein, "Social Security and Saving: the Extended Life Cycle Theory," *American Economic Review*, 66, 1976.

[24] P. Munnell, *The Effect of Social Security on Personal Saving* (Cambridge, MA, 1974).

[25] F. Modigliani and A. Sterling, "Determinants of Private Saving with Special Reference to the Role of Social Security," *The Determinants of National Saving and Wealth*, ed. F. Modigliani and R. Hemming (London: Macmillan Press, 1983).

[26] C. C. Holt, F. Modigliani, J. F. Muth, and H. A. Simon, *Planning Production, Inventories and Work Force* (Englewood Cliffs, NJ: Prentice Hall, 1960).

[27] *Journal of Political Economy*, 82, No. 6 (1974), pp. 1095–1117.

[28] An overview of econometric models for the layman used at that time in "Osservatorio," a regular feature in the *Corriere della Sera*, January 10, 1973. That year was to witness the boom in the American economy.

[29] "Long Run Implications of Alternative Fiscal Policies and the Burden of the National Debt," *The Economic Journal*, 71 (1961), pp. 728–755. Reprinted in J. M. Ferguson, *Public Dent and Future Generations* (Chapel Hill, NC: University of North Carolina Press, 1964). Also reprinted in *The Collected Papers of Franco Modigliani*, Vol. 2, op cit.

[30] See F. Modigliani and A. Modigliani, "The Growth of the Federal Deficit and the Role of Public Attitudes," *Public Opinion Quarterly*, 51 (1987), pp. 459–480.

[31] J. M. Buchanan, *Liberty, Market and State* (New York: New York University Press, 1985).

[32] I made a full analysis of the theories, promises, and effects of Ronald Reagan's economic policy in the article "Reagan's Economic Policies: A Critique," *Oxford Economic Papers*, 40 (1988), pp. 397–462, reprinted in *The Collected Papers of Franco Modigliani*, Vol. 4, *Monetary Theory and Stabilization Policies*, ed. S. Johnson (Cambridge, MA: MIT University Press, 1989), pp. 326–355.

[33] In *Il caso Italia. Seminari dello Studio Ambrosetti a Villa d'Este 1979–1986* (Milan: Edizioni di Communità, 1986), p. 72.

Chapter II

[1] F. Modigliani and P. Kenen, "Una proposta per risolvere il problema della liquidità internazionale," *Moneta e Credito*, 19, no. 3 (March 1966), pp. 3–18.

[2] The paragraph devoted to proposals for international liquidity in the concluding remarks of the *Annual Report of the Council of Economic Advisors* of 1966 incorporates the doubts, but these have a positive tone, as they recommend that in every case it is essential that the negotiations (for establishing new agreements on international liquidity (1) produce fair and effective norms for the creation, distribution, and use of new reserve instruments, (2) facilitate integration of the new instruments in the existing structures, and (3) ensure an appropriate amount of expansion of the global volume of international liquidity to foster healthy development of the world economy.

[3] Modigliani and Kenen, op cit., p. 7: "For practical purposes we assume that the normal field of variation is around a value of more or less 50 percent, which implies that the excess or total balance of payments deficit of a country be not more than 50 percent of T (target)."

[4] F. Modigliani and P. Sylos Labini, "Il dollaro in castigo," *L'Espresso*, January 14, 1968.

[5] Ibid.

[6] Ibid.

[7] E. Despres, C. Kindleberger, and W. S. Salant, "The Dollar and World Liquidity. A Minority View," *The Economist*, February 5, 1966.

[8] F. Modigliani and C. Zappulli, "Processo al dollaro," *Corriere della Sera*, October 5, 1971: "For a long time one liked to think that the position of the dollar, in its triple function as monetary unit, means of exchange, and reserve currency, was extremely convenient and advantageous. Not so. Ultimately, it was subject to the permanent blackmail of the other currencies, playing a purely passive role on the exchange markets. All could maneuver on the dollar, except the dollar itself. In order to reestablish the symmetry of the monetary mechanism, the United States cannot be denied the possibility to intervene in the formation of the exchange rates. The relation of the dollar to the rest of the world's currencies has largely been governed by other countries, which have been able to manipulate it to serve their own particular interests. The result was that the vicissitudes of American imports and exports were at the mercy of non-American wishes. As against that—and here is the other irrationality—the price trend in the United States ended by conditioning the value of the (dollar) reserves of the other countries, but the latter had no power to exact from the United States either price stability or compensation for the damage caused by the instability."

[9] F. Modigliani and P. Sylos Labini, *Il dollaro in castigo*, op. cit.

[10] F. Modigliani and H. Askari, "The Reform of the International Payments System," *Essays in International Finance*, 89 (September 1971), pp. 3–28, International Finance Section, Department of Economics, Princeton University; reprinted in *The Collected Papers of Franco Modigliani*, Vol. 3, *The Theory of Finance and Other Essays* (Cambridge, MA: MIT University Press, 1980).

[11] Modigliani and Zappulli, *Processo al dollaro*, op. cit.

[12] Ibid.

[13] F. Modigliani, "Le complesse trattative per la riforma monetaria," *Corriere della Sera*, December 20, 1972.

[14] Ibid.

[15] F. Modigliani, "Speculazione monetaria ancora in agguato," *Corriere della Sera*, February 21, 1973, and F. Modigliani, "Gli speculatori della crisi monetaria," *Corriere della Sera*, March 9, 1973.

[16] Modigliani, "Speculazione monetaria ancora in agguato," op. cit.

[17] Ibid.

[18] Ibid.

[19] Modigliani, "Gli speculatori della crisi monetaria," op. cit.

[20] F. Modigliani, "In alto mare la riforma del sistema monetario," *Corriere della Sera*, October 25, 1973.

[21] Ibid.

[22] Ibid.

[23] F. Modigliani, " 'Miopia' francese," *Corriere della Sera*, January 24, 1974.

[24] Ibid.

[25] F. Modigliani, "Riformare il 'serpente,'" *Corriere della Sera*, January 26, 1974.

[26] In confirmation of my fury at the selfish, arrogant attitude of the French, I recall how that article ended: "Along with several Italian experts I share the opinion that the Werner plan and the EMS, as initially projected on the insistence of the French, had no real life in it. Before fixing the unchangeable parities, it is necessary to unify the institutions: taxation, discipline of financial markets and intermediaries, labor union policy, etc." After which, I advised Italy to take everyone by surprise and reenter the Snake just as France was leaving it: "This would serve as concrete proof, and not merely in words, which of the two countries really cares about the future of the European Community. Simultaneously with this reentry, wouldn't it be a good idea to suspend France from the EEC, until such time as the wiser, more far-sighted elements that we all know to exist in French politics return to office?"

[27] All the arguments put forward from this paragraph on are reworked and summarized from two studies presented at Frankfurt-am-Main in December 1994 and December 1995. The first version of the paper was published in Italian in *Rivista di politica Economica* (85, series III, fasc. VI, June 1995), titled *"La crisi della disoccupazione in Europa: un approccio monetarista-keynesiano e le sue implicazioni."* The second, more advanced version (not yet published) was presented on December 1, 1995, to the European Monetary Conference at Frankfurt, titled "The Shameful Rate of Unemployment in the EMS: Causes and Cures."

[28]   J. Drèze, *Pour l'emploi; la croissance et l'Europe* (Brussels: De Boeck Université, 1995); and in J. Drèze and E. Malinvaud, "Growth and Employment: The Scope for a European Initiative," *European Economy, Reports and Studies*, 1 (1994), pp. 75–106.

[29] Graph 1 *(Employment and real wages in the United States and the European Community 1970–93)*. Table 1 *(Growth of income, productivity, employment and real wages 1960–90)*.

[30]   See, for example, "Unemployment: Choices for Europe," in *Center for Economic Policy Research (CEPR)*, April 1, 1995; and "Why Is It So Difficult to Reduce Unemployment in Europe?" Ibid., April 5, 1995.

[31]   E. Tarantelli, *L'utopia dei deboli è la paura dei forti* (Milan: Franco Angeli, 1988), pp. 556–561. See also Tarantelli, *La forza delle idee. Scritti di economia e politica* (Rome-Bari: Laterza, 1995).

Chapter III

[1] "L'organizzazione e la direzione della produzione in un' economia socialista," *Giornale degli Economisti e Annali di Economia,* September-October 1947, pp. 441–514.

[2] In *Giornale degli Economisti e Annali di Economia,* 1908, reprinted in *Opere economiche,* Vol. I (Bologna: Zanichelli, 1936), pp. 231–297.

[3] This article was published in the regular "Osservatorio" feature, which I shared with Nino Andreatta and Bruno Visentini, on Wednesday June 13, 1973, under the title, "Il ruolo degli economisti nella Svezia del benessere. Equilibrio perfetto tra socialismo e imprese private."

[4] G. La Malfa and F. Modigliani, "Su alcuni aspetti della congiuntura e della politica monetaria italiana nell' ultimo quinquennio," *Moneta e Credito,* 19, No. 75 (September 1966), pp. 211–57.

[5] The transcripts are available in an edition edited by G. M. Rey and P. Peluffo, titled *Dialogo tra un professore e la Banca d'Italia* (Florence: Vallecchi, 1995).

[6] Rey and Peluffo, *Dialogo tra un professore e la Banca d'Italia,* op. cit., p. 192.

[7] Ibid., p. 191.

[8] Ibid., p. 181.

[9] Ibid., p. 81.

[10] Ibid., p. 82.

[11] Ibid., p. 83.

[12] Ibid., pp. 181–183.

[13] "Tassazione giusta e pieno impiego, le vie della prosperità americana," *Corriere della Sera,* November 20, 1972.

[14] I felt the need to justify this decision in the article "La Spagna rassomiglia a l'Italia del 'boom,'" published in the "Osservatorio" feature in *Corriere della Sera,* April 4, 1973.

[15] Ibid.

[16] Ibid.

[17] Ibid.

[18] Ibid.

[19] "La qualità della vita secondo l'Inghilterra," *Corriere della Sera,* May 16, 1973, "Osservatorio."

[20] The reference is to the telephone tapping scandal that was revealed at the beginning of February 1973. On March 7, Walter Beneforti, who had former-ly headed the secret section when Tambroni was minister for Home Affairs, was arrested. Among the telephones being illegally tapped were those of the prime minister, Andreotti, and the Communist Party secretary, Berlinguer.

[21] *La qualità della vita secondo l'Inghilterra,* op. cit.

[22] Ibid.

[23] Ibid.

[24] *Il ruolo degli economisti nella Svezia del benessere,* op. cit.

[25] "Bisogna ridare fiducia per combattere l'inflazione," in *Corriere della Sera,* July 11, 1973, "Osservatorio."

[26] Ibid.

[27] Ibid.

[28] "Una lezione dall'America sul controllo dei prezzi," *Corriere della Sera,* September 12, 1973, "Osservatorio."

[29] Ibid.

[30] In this connection, see F. Modigliani and T. Padoa Schioppa, "La politica economica in un' economia con salari indicizzati al 100 o più," *Moneta e Credito,* 3   0
No. 117 (March 1977), pp. 3–53.

[31] Carlo De Benedetti has recalled this episode in an interview volume edited by Riccardo Chiaberge, *Un eretico in Confindustria* (Milan: ETAS Libri, 1980): "I recollect that at that time, as president of the Turin industrialists' union, I argued, in absolute good faith, that the agreement was a positive one, and politically I remain convinced that it was so. I also remember that the econo-mist Modigliani wrote an article harshly criticizing Agnelli in the *Corriere della Sera* and Agnelli phoned me, as usual at seven o'clock in the morning, and said: 'Modigliani understands nothing about the Italian situation.' It can now be admitted that, from the economic point of view, Modigliani was right, and the agreement was a mistake."

[32] *Corriere della Sera,* February 3, 1975.

[33] Ibid.

34 La Malfa's reply is summarized in *Corriere della Sera*, March 9, 1975, in an account titled "L'accordo sulla contingenza: nuovo intervento di La Malfa." Here, too, the polemic appears somewhat toned down by the prestige of the newspaper: *Ribadita la posizione critica, ma non pessimista*.

35 "Se un operaio guadagnasse mezzo milione al mese," *Corriere della Sera*, March 9, 1975.

36 Modigliani and Padoa Schioppa, "La politica economica in un' economia con salari indicizzati al 100 o più," op. cit.

37 This provoked a large number of articles, and Serena patiently cut them out and kept them in her books of press clippings. Severe criticism came from *l'Unità* in the article "Una ricetta dagli USA," January 4, 1976. "La diagnosi di Modigliani ha un lato politico," in *Paese Sera*, January 7, 1976. "Modigliani e il menefreghismo," a comment appearing in the *Messaggero* of January 7, which showed more understanding of my arguments. Napoleone Colajanni, then a leading figure of the Communist Party and spokesman on economic policy, attacked me in *Corriere della Sera* of January 14 in his comment: "Perché non sono d'accordo con Modigliani." In addition to his article mentioned in note[39], Federico Caffè continued to criticize me also in *Messaggero* of February 4, in "La non politica per la disoccupazione." I answered these criticisms in two interviews: the first again with Ugo Stille, in *Corriere della Sera*, February 1, "Primo, la disoccupazione"; then in a conversation with Epoca, February 4, "Vi aspettano sudore e tasse." Some cautious willingness to discuss my position came, surprisingly, from CGIL leader, Luciano Lama, in an interview with *Corriere della Sera*, February 12, 1976, "Lama: Siamo pronti a sacrifici, ma solo con un governo di unità nazionale."

38 "La verità del professore," *Il Manifesto*, January 4, 1976.

39 The shorthand transcript of the meeting was published in *Mondo Economico*, March 20, 1976, whose cover is devoted to the meeting.

40 "I pro e contro per l'Italia," *Corriere della Sera*, December 1, 1978. It is amusing to note that the newspaper account, alongside my article on the front page, reported: "It was announced in Bonn yesterday that Germany will not accept to underwrite an agreement stipulating obligatory and automatic intervention on the exchange market in order to prevent currencies from overstepping the permitted boundaries of fluctuation. Italy had requested that the central banks intervene promptly at any sign of tension within the new 'snake.'" Thinking back to the arguments over "unlimited" intervention during the 1992 exchange crisis, one is tempted to say, Nothing new under the sun!

41 Modigliani and Padoa Schioppa, "La politica economica in un' economia con salari indicizzati al 100 o più," op. cit.

42 "I pro e contro per l'Italia," op. cit.

43 Ibid.

44 Ibid.

45 Ibid.

46 "Ciampi, occhio allo SME," *Corriere della Sera*, May 5, 1993. The editor responsible for the subtitles provided the following gloss: "All the conditions are favorable: devaluation that helps exports, wage freeze, falling interest rates. The big star of Italy can help the former Governor. Provided he doesn't wish too soon for the return of fixed exchange rates."

47 I worked on analyzing Ciampi's budget with my friend and colleague Mario Baldassare, in an article where we once again spelled out the difference between current requirement and deficit, explaining why the correction for inflation was necessary: "Il deficit? Non è così grande," in *Corriere della Sera*, January 14, 1994.

48 "Ciampi, occhio allo SME," op. cit.

49 The argument arose out of an article by Mario Baldassare in *Il Sole-24 Ore*, November 24, 1993, which was followed up by the article with the false headline in *Il Messaggero* (January 13, 1994). Baldassari and I then countered with "Il deficit? Non è così grande" (cited in note 48 above) on January 14, and with a second article, again in *Corriere della Sera*, January 31, 1994, "Cari colleghi, ecco il vero deficit."

50 The conversation was published in 1995 by the Senate of the Italian Republic, in the series of papers titled, *Gli incontri di studio a palazzo Giustiniani. Nuove prospettive nella regolamentazione dei mercati finanziari*, with an introduction by the president of the Senate, Carlo Scognamiglio Pasini, and with a contribution by Paul Volcker. Here is the passage where Fazio speaks of the Italian exchange crisis in March 1995: "In one of our discussions at Basle (which has nothing secret about it), right after the Mexican crisis erupted—in February or March of this year—I told Alan Greenspan that we had the same situation in Italy: a inflow of investment of around 60 billion dollars in one year, 1993, and in 1994 an outflow of about 30 billion dollars. Alan Greenspan was really concerned and said to me: 'I have never witnessed a capital flow like that in the United States. Where does it come from?' And I told him: 'I think you supplied in a certain sense what we call the basis; the majority of this capital probably originated from London, or somewhere else, in what we call the eurodollar market; then began this buying up of bonds, taking advantage of the variations, the high interest rates, and the expectations.' With this system the smaller countries found themselves in utter confusion. To complete my remark about short-term capital, I must point out that we continue to call it capital, but it is no such thing: merely monetary flows. In the 1960s one spoke of *hot money*; now *hot money* assumes this form. This is the old system of the eurodollar. We have no precise statistical idea of what is happening in these markets regarding this multiplication of funds, funds that multiply and then vanish. They may have a severe impact on the exchange rates, but also on the rates of interest. I therefore think we are really in a situation where the national economy resembles that of a century ago, when banks and financial institutes began to emerge and it took the experience of serious financial crises to help us understand" (p. 36).

51 Changes to these variables will impact the transition as discussed later.

52 "A Better Solution to the Social Security Crisis: Funding with a Common Portfolio," MIT Sloan School of Management Working Paper, #4060, January, 2001.

INDEX

About TEXERE

TEXERE seeks to become the most progressive and authoritative voice in business publishing by cultivating and enhancing ideas that will illuminate the global business landscape. Our name defines the spirit of our vision: TEXERE is the ancient Latin verb "to weave." In an increasingly global business community, we seek to create an intersection where authors and readers can share the best thinking and the latest ideas. We want to leverage the expertise and insights of leading thinkers by weaving them with TEXERE's capability to deliver them to the marketplace.

To learn more and become a part of our community visit us at:
www.etexere.com
and
www.etexere.co.uk

About the Typeface

This book was set in Meridien Roman.